Why JOHN Is DIFFERENT

UNIQUE INSIGHTS IN THE GOSPEL
AND WRITINGS OF ST. JOHN

Copyright © 2014 by Juan Chapa

The total or partial reproduction of this book is not permitted, nor its informatic treatment, or the transmission of any form or by any means, either electronic, mechanic, photocopy or other methods, without the prior written permission of the owners of the copyright.

Scripture texts from the New and Old Testaments are taken from The Holy Bible Revised Standard Catholic Edition © 1965 and 1966 by the Division of Christian Education of the National Council of the Churches of Christ in the United States. All rights reserved. All copyrighted material is used by permission of the copyright owner. No part of it may be reproduced without permission in writing from the copyright owner.

All references to the *Catechism of the Catholic Church* are written as *CCC*.

Copyright © 2013 Scepter Publishers, Inc.
P.O. Box 1391
New Rochelle, NY 10802
www.scepterpublishers.org

Cover and text design by Rose Design

Printed in the United States of America

ISBN: 978-1-59417-173-4

Why JOHN Is DIFFERENT

Unique Insights in the Gospel and Writings of St. John

Juan Chapa

Scepter

Contents

Preface xi

Introduction / The Work of St. John in Context 1

1. The Situation of Christianity at the End
   of the First Century 3
   Judaism in the First Century AD / *3*
   The Early Expansion of Christianity / *6*
   The Jewish Revolt and Its Consequences / *9*

2. Historical Circumstances in the Background
   of the Books Attributed to St. John 10
   Conflicts with Judaism / *11*
   Gnosticized Religiosity / *13*
   Anti-Baptist Conflicts / *15*
   A Hostile Environment / *16*

3. The Johannine Community 17

PART I / THE FOURTH GOSPEL

Chapter 1 / The Gospel of John as Apostolic Testimony 25

1. Witness to the Apostolic Preaching 25
2. The Beloved Disciple at the Origin of the Testimony ... 28
3. Identification of the Beloved Disciple 30
   The Data of Tradition / *31*
   Other Suggestions / *33*
   Recapitulation / *34*
4. Time and Place of Composition 35
   The Place / *36*
   The Date / *36*
5. Transmission of the Text 37
6. Reception of the Fourth Gospel 39

Chapter 2 / The Testimony of John about Jesus 46

1. The Johannine Question 47
2. Relation to the Synoptics: Common
   and Proper Material 49
   Similarities between the Gospel of John and the Synoptics / 49
   Differences between the Synoptics and the Fourth Gospel / 50
   - *In relation to the structure of the account / 51*
   - *In relation to the narrative contents / 52*
   - *In relation to his teachings / 53*
   - *In relation to the person of Jesus / 54*
   - *Attempts at explanation / 55*
3. The Selective Character of John 57
4. The Composition of the Gospel 59
   The Two Endings / 59
   Differences of Style / 60
   Gaps in the Narrative / 61
   Duplications and Repetitions / 61
   Proposed Solutions / 62

Chapter 3 / Content and Structure 66

1. The Content of the Gospel 66
2. Proposals for Structuring 70
3. Structural Elements 74
4. Structure 78
5. The Prologue and Chapter 21 79

Chapter 4 / Jesus' Signs 83

1. Significance of Signs in the Old Testament 84
2. The Signs Found in the Fourth Gospel 85
3. The Panorama of Signs 88
   Signs of a New Order / 88
   Signs of the Word that Gives Life / 92
   The Sign of the Bread of Life / 93
   The Sign of Light / 96
   The Sign of Victory over Death / 98

Chapter 5 / The Dialogues and Discourses of Jesus 102

1. The Dialogue with Nicodemus and with the Samaritan Woman 103
2. In Jerusalem, a Discussion on the Authority of Jesus . 107
3. Jesus, the Bread of Life 109
4. Christ, the Light of the World 111
5. Jesus, the Good Shepherd, One with the Father 113
6. The Glorification of Christ through His Death 115
7. The Departure of Jesus 116

Chapter 6 / The Glorification of Jesus 122

1. The Death of Jesus in the First Part of the Gospel 122
   The Hour of Jesus / *123*
   "To Be Raised/Exalted" / *125*
   "Giving His Life,"/"Dying for" / *128*
   "The Lamb of God" / *131*
   Two Prophetic Signs / *133*
2. The Supper with His Disciples 133
3. The Account of the Passion 135
4. His Apparitions 141

Chapter 7 / Theological Questions 146

1. Jesus Christ and the Father 148
   The Revealer / *150*
   He Who Was Sent / *152*
   The Son / *152*
   The Pre-existent One / *154*
   "I AM" / *155*
   The Son of Man / *157*
2. The Holy Spirit 159
3. Eschatology 161
4. Faith as a Response to the Signs 163
5. The World 165

6. The Church and the Sacraments 167
   The Church / 167
   The Sacraments / 169
7. Mary, the Mother of Jesus 171

PART II / THE LETTERS

Chapter 8 / The Letters of John 175

I / THE FIRST LETTER OF JOHN 176
1. Witnesses of Tradition 176
2. Transmission 176
3. Content and Structure 177
4. Relation to the Fourth Gospel 181
   Similarities / 181
   Differences / 184
5. The Author 185
6. The Occasion for the Letter 186
7. Date 189
8. Teaching 190

II / THE SECOND AND THIRD LETTERS OF JOHN 191
1. The Author 192
2. Content and Circumstances 193
3. Date of Composition 196

PART III / REVELATION

Chapter 9 / The Revelation of John 199
1. The Last Book of the Bible 199
2. Its Canonicity 200
3. Apocalyptic Literature 201

4. The Formal and Doctrinal Features
   of Apocalyptic Literature 205
5. The Uniqueness of John's Apocalypse 207
6. The Language and Style of Revelation 211
7. Date and Place of Composition 212
8. Audience and Purpose 212
9. The Author 214

Chapter 10 / The Message of Revelation 217

1. Content 217
2. Structure 224
3. God the Father, Jesus Christ, and the Church ... 229
   God the Father / 229
   The Lamb / 230
   The Church / 232
4. The Last Times and the Struggle against Evil ... 234
5. The Johannine Character of the Book 238

Bibliography 243

Index 249

Preface

THE BOOK OF EZEKIEL OPENS WITH A VISION of "the chariot of the Lord" in which the prophet contemplates a majestic manifestation of the glory of God. It includes four beings of human appearance with four faces and four wings. "Each had the face of a man in front; the four had the face of a lion on the right side, the four had the face of an ox on the left side, and the four had the face of an eagle at the back" (1:10). These four beings represent all living creatures—angels, men, and animals—through whom and through whose activity the glory of God might be manifested in all its splendor.

At the end of the first Christian century, the visionary of the Book of Revelation, contemplating God on the throne of his glory, also speaks of these four celestial beings as giving glory to the Sovereign of the universe: "The first living creature [is] like a lion, the second living creature like an ox, the third living creature [has] the face of a man, and the fourth living creature [is] like a flying eagle" (Rv 4:7). As far back as St. Irenaeus, Christian tradition took these four beings to represent the four evangelists as "images of the activity of the son of God" (*Adversus Haereses* 3, 11, 8). Also from very early times, the Fathers of the Church saw the John the Evangelist symbolized in the fourth face, which, as St. Jerome says, "assumed the wings of an eagle and flying swiftly to the heights, reasoned about the Word of God" (*Praef. In Matthaeum*). St. Gregory the Great, for his part, said: "John deserves to be the eagle . . . because when he directs his gaze at the very essence of the divinity he does the same as the eagle who fixes his eyes on the sun" (*Homiliae in Ezechielem prophetam* 1,4,1). This is to say that the image of the eagle, who rises to the heights where he looks directly at the sun, expresses the high theological level of the fourth Gospel that justifies John's being called "the theologian."

It is hardly necessary to recall how important and enlightening it is to know the work of St. John better. The fourth Gospel, as part of Sacred Scripture, is the ever timely Word of God. To explore this document in depth is no less than to listen more attentively to what God himself wants to tell us about the mystery of his Son, Jesus Christ. But if the Gospels are "the heart of all of Scripture as the principal testimony of the life and teaching of the Word made flesh, our Savior" (*CCC*, 125; see *Dei Verbum*, 18) and should therefore be the object of special veneration and study, it is not at all farfetched to affirm that the Gospel of St. John merits special attention as the summit of the four to which one ascends through reading the Synoptics. In fact, Pope Benedict XVI, in his Apostolic Exhortation *Verbum Domini,* uses the Prologue of the fourth Gospel precisely as a guide to present and explore the synod's results as "an admirable synthesis of the whole Christian faith" (5).

But a Gospel is not the only writing attributed to St. John. Three letters and a book of a prophetic character, Revelation (or the Apocalypse), have been transmitted to us as having the same authorship. Tradition stretching back to antiquity attests the Johannine authorship of these books; throughout the history of exegesis, these five works, which belong to three distinct genres (historical, epistolary, and prophetic), have often been considered jointly, although their different character suggests that it would be better to study each independently. From a literary point of view, in fact, there are problems in ascribing them to a single author, while some of the ancient testimonies about St. John and his work are not very clear. Thus Pope Benedict XVI, in one of his catecheses dedicated to John, the son of Zebedee, echoes some of these questions and notes that exegetes argue about the identification of the beloved disciple with John the apostle, leaving to them the task of explaining this (General Audience, July 5, 2006). Moreover, the Apocalypse differs notably from the Gospel and the letters, to the point that most exegetes think they must be the works of different authors.

But leaving aside the particular literary characteristics of the five works studied here, the Church's attribution of them to John shows the apostolic character of these books. Beyond the specific details of the composition and subsequent redaction of each, the Johannine corpus is a witness to apostolic preaching. The works that comprise it amount to a testimony of the life, death, and resurrection of Jesus offered with the help of disciples and collaborators under the guidance of the Holy Spirit. This is what it means to call John their author and what justifies dealing with these books jointly in spite of their differences.

The present work aims only to offer an overview of the fourth Gospel, the letters, and the Book of Revelation to a nonspecialized public. Intended to help in the reading of those works, it is best read with a copy of the New Testament at hand. It originated in a summer course for people interested in going more deeply into the fundamentals of Christian faith. It has hardly any footnotes or bibliographic references, and contains the most common ideas of the great classical commentaries of both ancient and modern times. It concludes with a basic bibliography.

The most extensive body of material is dedicated to the fourth Gospel, although in one of the first lessons there is a brief presentation of some of the historical circumstances that constitute a framework for the Johannine corpus. Insofar as Revelation is historical, knowledge of the context of its composition is necessary to understand better what the authors had in mind in writing.

The seven chapters dedicated to the fourth Gospel are intended to serve as an introduction to its reading, so that one can understand it better and better perceive its riches. The point of departure is provided by the data of tradition, which since the second century has transmitted this book as the testimony of the beloved disciple and received it as part of the canon of inspired books, with an authoritative character in reference to the faith and life of Christians (chapter 1). But since the Gospel of John has been transmitted along with three others, it is useful to consider the special features of the testimony of the fourth Gospel in comparison with the other canonical Gospels. For this purpose, a brief description is given of its principal formal features, and the differences and similarities between the fourth Gospel and the Synoptics are pointed out (chaper 2). Then, in order better to understand St. John's purpose in writing his work, a brief synthesis of the Gospel follows and the internal structure of the narrative is examined (chaper 3).

The next four lessons are meant to complement the reading of the text and provide deeper insight into its content. Following the traditional division of the narrative into two main parts, the "book of signs" and the "book of glory," we first briefly consider the signs in the first part of the Gospel as confirmations of the authority of Jesus' words (grounded in the fact that he is the Messiah and in his divinity) and intended to lead to faith in him (chapter 4). Next comes a brief overview of the discourses and dialogues of Jesus accompanying and complementing the signs and revealing his being and mission (chapter 5). As with the Synoptics, the quantitative emphasis of the Gospel narrative is, relatively speaking, upon the Passion of Jesus, which, in the case of the fourth Gospel, points to his glorification and exaltation in his return to the Father: This, anticipated by the others, is Christ's great sign. These ideas are explained in the following lesson (chapter 6) in light of the description John gives of the last hours of Jesus. By way of conclusion, the section dedicated to the fourth Gospel ends with a brief synthesis of some of the Evangelist's more important theological themes (chapter 7).

After the study of the Gospel comes a lesson focusing on the letters of John, which have differences and similarities among themselves and with the fourth Gospel. The letters shed important light on the Johannine community and on the Gospel (chaper 8).

The two last lessons are dedicated to the Apocalypse. The first situates it in the context of apocalyptic literature while explaining the formal features that distinguish the Book of Revelation from the apocalyptic literature of its time (chaper9). The last lesson deals with the book itself, explaining its content and supplying keys for reading it (chapter 10).

The Second Vatican Council says that in the books of the New Testament "according to the wise plan of God, those matters which concern Christ the Lord are confirmed, his true teaching is more and more fully stated, the saving power of the divine work of Christ is preached, the story is told of the beginnings of the Church and its marvelous growth, and its glorious fulfillment is foretold" (*Dei Verbum*, 20). It is my hope that a better knowledge of the five books studied here will contribute to entering more deeply into the mystery of Christ, in line with the diverse aspects emphasized by each. The book responds in some way to the desires of Benedict XVI, who writes in his post-synodal Apostolic Exhortation on the Word of God in the Life and Mission of the Church: "May John, who 'saw and believed' (cf. Jn 20:8) also help us to lean on the breast of Christ (cf. Jn 13:25), the source of the blood and water (cf. Jn 19:34) which are symbols of the Church's sacraments. Following the example of the John and the other inspired authors, may we allow ourselves to be led by the Holy Spirit to *an ever greater love of the word of God*" (*Verbum Domini*, 5).

Introduction

The Work of St. John in Context

THE MURATORIAN CANON, a list of the canonical books of the Roman Church, possibly dating from the second century, states: "The fourth Gospel is by John, one of the disciples. When his co-disciples and bishops encouraged him [to write], John said: 'Fast with me for three days from today and, what is revealed to us, let us tell one another.' That same night it was revealed to Andrew, one of the apostles, that John should write everything in his own name, and that they should edit it. . . . Why be surprised then that John should continue mentioning those features [essential features of the life of our Lord] in his letters also. . . . In addition John in the Apocalypse, although writing to the seven Churches, was addressing everyone."

Eusebius of Caesarea (fourth century), gathering together earlier traditions, wrote: "And what should we say of the one who reclined his head on the breast of Jesus, John, who has left us a Gospel, although he confesses that he could have written so much that the world would not be able to contain it? And he also wrote the Apocalypse, but they ordered him to keep silent and not to write the words of the seven thunders. And he also left us a letter of only a few lines, and perhaps a second and a third" (*Historia Ecclesiastica* 6, 25, 10).

In addition, according to tradition, this disciple lived in Ephesus until the time of Trajan (98–117). Appealing to the

2 Why John Is Different

testimony of Irenaeus, Justin, Clement of Alexandria, Apollonius, and Polycrates, Eusebius says:

> There are witnesses enough to guarantee that John was still living then, for both are worthy of credence and recognized in the orthodoxy of the Church. This refers to Irenaeus and to Clement of Alexandria. The first, in a certain moment of his second book *Against the Heretics*, wrote the following: "And all of the ancients of Asia who maintained contact with John, the disciple of the Lord, give testimony of what John transmitted, for he remained with them until the times of Trajan." Also in the third book of the same work he said the following: "But even the Church of Ephesus since it was founded by Paul and John remained in it until the times of Trajan, is a true testimony of the tradition of the apostles." On the other hand, Clement indicated at the same time . . . "John left the island of Patmos and went to Ephesus. From there he went, when he was asked, to the nearby regions of the Gentiles, sometimes he went to establish a bishop, to direct entire churches or to designate some priest from among those who had been chosen by the Spirit" (*Historia Ecclesiastica* 3, 23, 2ff).

This is the extent of the data of the tradition. Clearly, though, the books attributed to John do not have the same formal features. Rather, the Gospel, the letters, and the Apocalypse belong to distinct literary genera: narrative, epistolary, and prophetic. Instead of being composed in the same way, each was written at a particular time in response to the particular circumstances and needs of those for whom it was intended. But the cultural circumstances to which they have certain common elements of place and concept—namely, the Palestine of the first century and the Jewish and Christian world of the Eastern Mediterranean at the end of the first century—and this corresponds to what tradition tells us about the Johannine works.

1. The Palestinian framework is evident in the history narrated in the Gospel and in the Evangelist's affirmation that he witnessed the events recounted, which is in line with the tradition identifying the author of these works with one of the first disciples of Jesus. To this framework one can also add the conceptual background of the Old Testament, found in the Gospel and in the Apocalypse and calling attention to the Jewish roots of these works.
2. The Hellenistic world and the Jewish Diaspora are also amply reflected in these books (in the geographical setting which is precisely that of Asia Minor and in the language of the Gospel and the letters). This seems consistent with the tradition that John lived in Ephesus and composed his Gospel toward the end of the first century.

Regardless of any problems of authenticity of these works, the Palestinian framework of the Gospel and the Old Testament roots of the body of John's work imply a knowledge of the development of the Christian communities in Palestine of the first century, when the Christians living in the ancient land of Canaan were affected by a certain series of events. Here, too, one finds a familiarity with the Jewish Hellenistic world of the Eastern Mediterranean and the situation of the Christians attempting to live their faith in a hostile environment, dogged by threats of all kinds, mostly external but also sometimes arising from within their own community.

1. The Situation of Christianity at the End of the First Century

Judaism in the First Century AD

The death of Alexander the Great (fourth century BC) is generally considered the beginning of a new era, the Hellenistic period, in the whole of the Eastern Mediterranean and the Middle East.

4 Why John Is Different

The term "Hellenism" generally refers to the impact of various aspects of Greek culture on the non-Greek world after the conquests of Alexander. Greek culture was fused with the oriental cultures in such a way that many aspects of the life of the conquered peoples remained deeply affected by elements of the civilization, art, techniques, language, and philosophy of the Greeks.

The Jewish people also were affected by the new political and cultural situation that Hellenism brought with it. The Jews who had settled in various parts of the Eastern Mediterranean as a result of war and deportation were more exposed to the Greek influence than those who lived in Palestine, yet Hellenism also penetrated into the territory of Israel. Its inhabitants had to preserve their identity against the pressure of Greek influences, accepting or rejecting them to a greater or lesser extent. Although in the first century the greater part of the population lived according to the laws and customs of Israel, there was no lack of groups who imitated the Hellenistic cities of the time and exercised a certain influence among the inhabitants of Palestine.

During the Hellenistic period the Jews of the Diaspora had to adapt themselves to the world in which they lived. They learned Greek, the language spoken in the Eastern Mediterranean until the Arab conquest, and translated their sacred books into this language since many no longer understood the original Hebrew. This gave rise to the Septuagint version, the fundamental document of Hellenistic Judaism, which reflected the meeting of the Hebrew and Greek cultures and served, indirectly, as an instrument of Jewish proselytism in the pagan world. It was also the sacred text used by the early Christians.

Some Jewish cults in the Diaspora entered into dialogue with the Greek world, and the philosopher Philo of Alexandria (20 BC to 45 AD) was an exponent of a Judaism impregnated with Greek humanism. A believing Jew with Platonic ideas and Stoic ethics, Philo proposed a synthesis of Hellenism and Judaism, and for this reason was ignored by rabbinical Judaism. Even so, his influence was notable. The fourth Gospel contains elements in common with some concepts found in the work of the Jewish philosopher. Especially noteworthy is the use of the term "Logos," which appears in the Prologue of the Gospel of John and in the work of Philo. Other points of contact are the value of Scripture, the use of symbolism to designate the divine (light, font of living water, shepherd), the idea of the knowledge of God as eternal life, etc. But the meaning and use of these elements are different in each author. Therefore they are thought to have shared a common cultural and religious background, especially in relation to the biblical wisdom tradition.

As we have said, Palestine also was influenced by Greek culture, although many of its inhabitants were suspicious of it and in fact continued to speak Aramaic. Nevertheless, Judaism was not understood and lived uniformly in the land of Israel. Various schools had arisen since the time of the Maccabees that gave rise to distinct ways of understanding Jewish religiosity. Together with the Pharisaic and Sadducean currents, with which we are more familiar through the canonical Gospels, there were other groups or tendencies that had other understandings of the Law.

Among these were the Essenes. Not much is known of them, but scholars think that, when Jonathan assumed the high priesthood in the second century BC, a group of Essenes, led by the so-called Master of Justice, retired to a place in the desert close to the Dead Sea called Qumran. There they formed a community of a monastic kind that disappeared at the time of the Jewish war (near the end of the seventh decade of the first century AD). Around the middle of the twentieth century numerous manuscripts were found there. Comparing these with the New Testament writing has shown some parallels and, in particular, led to a debate about a possible relationship between the Qumran documents and the fourth Gospel. In fact, John's Gospel does indeed share certain elements with these writings found in the

6 Why John Is Different

desert, and this helps situate the fourth Gospel in the Palestinian world of that era. But aside from some similarities of language and, above all, a dualistic conception of reality (light-darkness, truth-falsehood, spirit-flesh, etc.) positing conflict between two opposed orders of existence with victory going to God, the message of the Qumran manuscripts, with its strongly apocalyptic character, is not comparable to that of the Gospel of John. Moreover, the faith in Jesus Christ that is the basis of the gospel radically distinguishes John's work from the Qumran writings.

The Early Expansion of Christianity

The second half of the first century witnessed the missionary expansion of the Church. Although the New Testament refers to the communities of Jerusalem, Antioch, and Rome and those founded by or related to Paul, Christian communities linked to the Jewish Diaspora also quickly arose in other parts of the Empire (Egypt, Libya, Spain, Mesopotamia, etc.). Wherever there were Jews, the Christians went, announcing Jesus as the Savior Messiah in whom the Scriptures had been fulfilled. In most cases, they preached the gospel in the *lingua franca* of the day, using the Greek translation of the sacred books of the people of Israel. At the same time, they extended their preaching to all of those, Gentiles as well as Jewish proselytes, who wished to hear them.

In the eyes of the imperial authorities, the Christians during the first years of missionary expansion were not a group separate from Judaism. They enjoyed the shelter of the privileges applying to Jews as members of a *religio licita*. Yet for much of the pagan world, the religion of the descendants of Abraham was an object of rejection and even contempt. They did not look kindly on the fact that Jews considered their God the only true one and had such a negative attitude toward those who did not share their beliefs, and to this they joined envy at the special status Jews enjoyed. For historical reasons, however, the Roman authorities not only conceded Israel's existence as a nation and permitted its members to practice their religion but granted various privileges: respect for their Sabbath as a day of rest, exemption from having to worship the emperor and the official gods, and allowing, even requiring, payment of the didrachma, a special tax for the temple of Jerusalem.

Only the persecution by Nero in the year 64 moved the imperial authorities to begin considering the Christians as a destabilizing group, different in some way from the Jews. It is even possible that this perception of the Christian religion was only temporary or peculiar to Rome and its environs. All the same, as the Christian community began to increase in size with non-Jewish converts, it began to lose its former Jewish status and its members were not allowed the exceptions or "privileges" that the Hebrew people enjoyed. Toward the end of the first century, the situation of Christians as a separate group became evident to the authorities as well.

Christians soon became present in various parts of the empire, including the region of Anatolia (Asia Minor), specifically Ephesus, the capital of the Roman province known as Asia. Jews from there may have been in Jerusalem on the day of Pentecost and may have brought the new faith back home with them (see Acts 2:9). What is certain is that when St. Paul arrived at Ephesus around the year 50, he found followers of Christ (see Acts 19:1), although until Paul had spent three years preaching the Gospel, properly constituted Christian communities do not appear to have existed there. In any case, during the second half of the first century, the Church grew throughout that region, and communities linked to the missionary activity of St. Paul and perhaps other apostles emerged. The First Epistle of St. Peter shows the diffusion of Christianity in regions north of Asia Minor (Pontus, Bithynia), which are not known to have been evangelized by the apostle of the Gentiles. Both Christian sources and non-Christian ones (for example, the letter of Pliny the Younger, governor of Bithynia, to the Emperor Trajan around the year 111, in which he explains his treatment of the Christians) confirm that toward the end of the first century and the beginning of the second Christianity had extended throughout the whole of that region.

Throughout this time and especially beginning with the last quarter of the first century, the Church had to respond to problems arising from the political and social circumstances in which the Christians lived. On the one hand, the apostles, the eyewitnesses of Jesus who had headed the Church, were dying out. Consequently it was necessary to find means to prevent Jesus' message and the Gospel accounts of him from being watered down or misinterpreted. The passing of time itself was required closer attention to certain doctrinal points of special importance. For example, the belief held by some that the *Parousia* was imminent made it necessary to insist on Jesus' teaching on the need to remain vigilant inasmuch as no one knew when the event would take place. The denial by others that Christ would come a second time required affirming the certainty of this truth and its basis, together with the fact, emphasized in John's Gospel, that one must experience the salvation of Christ in the present moment.

Furthermore, within the Christian communities there was a diversity of tendencies that threatened their unity. These included ties, greater or lesser as the case might be, to the Law of Moses, the influence of Judeo-Hellenistic wisdom, and, as can be seen from the letters of John, certain Christological errors. It was necessary now to reaffirm the unity that earlier was upheld by the witness of the apostles and confront teachings not in conformity with the original tradition.

Some have called this period the "sub-apostolic era." In this era of transition and discernment, the apostles and their collaborators guided the Church by preaching the Word and through writings that fortified the faith of believers and clarified doctrinal issues. This, then, was the context for the writings of John.

The Jewish Revolt and its Consequences

Political events in Palestine in the second half of the first century had decisive consequences for Jews and Christians. After the death of King Herod Agrippa I in the year 44, Palestine once more became a Roman province. Constant rebellions were succeeded by open warfare, and in the year 66 Nero dispatched Vespasian and his legions. But in the year 68 Nero died and, after him, the emperors Galba, Otho, and Vitellius, with Vespasian finally acceding to the throne and sending his son Titus to continue the Jewish campaign. In the year 70, after several months of siege, Jerusalem was conquered and the temple destroyed.

The destruction of Jerusalem had enormous repercussions for Judaism. Many things had to change. The Sadducees, who were joined to the high priesthood and were collaborators with the Romans, disappeared. Following the destruction of Qumran in the year 68, the Essenes joined themselves to other groups. Some went to Masada, which was destroyed in 73, while of others nothing is known. The Zealots remained active in the desert, encouraging rebellion in later years.

The Pharisees, on the other hand, reorganized themselves in a coastal city on the coast, Yabne (or Yamnia, as it is also called), under the direction of Johanan ben Zakkay. There they concentrated on the study and application of the Law in order to save the heritage of Judaism. The Great Sanhedrin moved to Yamnia, and the city became the religious and national center of the Jews, with a school that in time became authoritative for Judaism. While there are no data confirming the emergence in this city of the so-called "Assembly of Yamnia" in which the Jewish canon was established and Christians were excluded from the synagogues, it does appear that at this time in Yamnia the canonicity of certain books of Scripture was discussed (the books later were excluded from the Jewish canon because they were not written in Hebrew) and doctrinal points were identified crucial to preserving the identity of the people in the new circumstances. The reconstituted Pharisaic line was consolidated in Yamnia, established itself over the others, and gave rise at the end of the first century to rabbinical Judaism.

The persecutions that had already arisen against the Christians in some parts of the empire—for example, Rome—and the destruction of Jerusalem in the year 70 also had important consequences not only for the Jewish community and the Christians of Jerusalem, but also for the Christian communities throughout the empire. According to Eusebius of Caesarea, the Christians of Palestine took refuge in Pella (in Transjordan) before the siege of the city, and, according to Epiphanias, returned after 70 to Jerusalem, where a Jewish rabbi, Eleazar, reopened the synagogue of the Alexandrians. But relations with the Roman authorities (for whom Christians were a Jewish sect) and with the Jews were becoming more tense and therefore required new responses and attitudes.

During the reign of Trajan (98–117) other revolts occurred, mostly outside Palestine. In the year 132, during the reign of Hadrian (117–138), the second great rebellion broke out in Palestine. Led by Simon bar Kochba, it was crushed after bloody fighting in the year 135, leaving the region completely devastated. In place of Jerusalem, the city of Aelia Capitolina was founded. It was inhabited by pagans and prohibited to Jews under pain of death.

2. Historical Circumstances in the Background of the Books attributed to St. John

The events just described provide the context for understanding the writings that tradition links to John. Each work responded to a particular situation, but all of them share more or less in the same set of circumstances.

Conflicts with Judaism

Tensions with Judaism with roots in the destruction of Jerusalem are reflected in various places in the New Testament, for example, the Gospel of Matthew and in the Gospel of St. John. Christians had already broken away from the synagogue by the end of the first century, when the Johannine corpus is thought to have been formed. This rupture to a great extent was a consequence of the defeat of the Jews by the Romans and the destruction of the temple. As we have seen, the Pharisaic line established in Yamnia after the disaster of the year 70 consolidated a vision of Judaism more centered on the defense of Jewish identity. This new current in Judaism spread through the communities dispersed among the cities of the empire, and its leaders expelled from the synagogue those who did not accept their special traditions—including many Jewish Christians—and rejected writings that did not suit their thinking.

In the Gospel of John, "the Jews" often has a strong theological meaning. Its implications are not always negative, nor is it always used in a univocal way; however, it usually refers to the Jewish leaders insofar as they first rejected Jesus and later opposed his disciples and sympathizers and expelled them from synagogue worship. Many authors see this historical framework behind John 9:22: "His parents said this because they feared the Jews, for the Jews had already agreed that if anyone should confess him to be the Christ, he was to be put out of the synagogue."[1]

The expression "excluded from the synagogue" or some variant thereof is found only in John. It seems to reflect not only a threatened rejection of Jesus' followers during the Master's lifetime but also the situation after the reconstitution of Phariseeism

---

1. The same expression appears in John 12:42: "Nevertheless many even of the authorities believed in him, but for fear of the Pharisees they did not confess it, lest they should be put out of the synagogue" and John 16:2: "They will put you out of the synagogues; indeed, the hour is coming when whoever kills you will think he is offering service to God."

in Yamnia, as reflected in a blessing (the twelfth) added to the eighteen blessings of the *Shemoneh Esreh*, a collection of prayers to be prayed at intervals during the day (morning, afternoon, and night) that was second only to the *Shema* in importance. This new blessing—a euphemism for *curse*—says: "There is no hope for the apostates. . . . The Nazarenes and the *minim* ['sectarians' or 'heretics'] will perish in an instant. . . . Blessed are you, Lord, who subject the tyrants to your will."

It is possible that the term "Nazarenos" is a later addition, but in any case this does not exclude an implicit reference to the Christians in the word *minim*, the term the Jewish leaders used to designate apostates and heretics whom they considered dangerous and avoided any contact with. This "blessing" was meant to ensure that heretics could not be readers in the synagogue. Through the influence of Rabbi Gamaliel II, Christians were officially designated *minim* at the end of the first century.

Nevertheless, in the fourth Gospel the expression "the Jews," although usually used to designate those who rejected Jesus, does not have a pejorative character in reference to the Jewish people as a whole. The Evangelist recognizes the role played by the Jewish people as clearly affirmed by Jesus: "You worship what you do not know; we worship what we know, for salvation is from the Jews" (4:22). In John, Christianity is not opposed to Judaism nor, strictly speaking, does it replace it. For the Evangelist, faith in Jesus means bringing to their fullness and realization the promises made to the ancient people of Israel, who themselves reached fulfillment in accepting Jesus as Israel's Messiah. In any case, the intention of John was to show the superiority of Christianity to Judaism, insofar as it had been replaced by the new faith in Christ. The abundant use of the Old Testament by the Evangelist and the way in which he cites it confirm this attitude while at the same time showing the Semitic foundation of the Gospel. John cannot be understood apart from the Old Testament and its interpretation by the exegesis of his time. This can be seen from the Jewish hermeneutical techniques he uses and cites, his ways of speaking, and his use of themes and images of the Old Testament from the historical and prophetic books as well as the wisdom literature.

Nevertheless, tension with Judaism explains the tradition, passed on by St. Jerome, that the Gospel of John was written against the Ebionites, a group of Judeo-Christians who continued faithful to the Law, for whom Jesus was a great prophet but not the Son of God. The information we have about the Ebionites does not, however, permit us to know their doctrine or in just what particular way they might have moved the Evangelist to confront their positions.

The apparent opposition to Judaism and the interest exhibited by the Gospel in Samaria and the Samaritans (see 4:7–28) has led some to suggest that the fourth Gospel was written to support the Christian mission in Samaria. But even though John's interest and attitude toward the Samaritans are positive compared with the Synoptics, this is not the basic reason that motivated the writing of the Gospel. Still, the references to the Samaritan world do show the universal character of the salvation worked by Jesus.

John's letters do not reflect tensions with Judaism but problems within the Christian community itself. In the Apocalypse, however, although the conflict with the synagogue is not dominant, there are references to the fact that, in some churches of Asia Minor, certain Jews tried to sow disorder among the followers of Christ (see Rv 2:9; 3:9).

Gnosticized Religiosity

At the time the Johannine corpus was written, religious eclecticism was a potential threat for the Christians. The influence of oriental religions in the Roman Empire and the currents of thought derived from apocalypticism and Hellenic religiosity constituted a menace and a temptation. Currents of Eastern thought and Jewish traditions had combined with elements of Greek discourse to give rise to an understanding of man and of the world with a markedly spiritual dimension, so that, for example, in this framework Gnosticism began to take shape. While there is no agreement on its origin or definition, the name Gnosticism embraces a variety of movements of a dualistic character that believed in a heavenly redeemer who came to the world to save humanity from enslavement to the material by some form of "divine knowledge" (*gnosis*). These movements of religious salvation had a great influence in the second century, and many Fathers of the Church wrote against them.

The letters of St. John show how errors had infiltrated among the Christians to whom they were addressed and were affecting the life of the community. The Christological error of the schismatics is complex, and agreement is lacking on its exact nature. It has elements of a Docetist character and may have been a precursor of what later appeared in some of Gnostic movements. In any case, there is evidence of a connection between the letters and Gnostic surroundings. Nor can one rule out an intention on the Evangelist's part to help Christians who were being tempted to understand the figure of Jesus as he was later understood by some forms of Gnosticism.

St. Irenaeus (*Adversus Haereses* 3, 11, 7) recalls a tradition according to which John wrote a Gospel against the heresy of Cerintus, which held Christ, a heavenly being, to have been united in baptism to Jesus the son of Joseph, but to have abandoned him before his death. Along the same lines, some think the Evangelist may have intended to oppose Docetism (from the Greek *dokein*, to appear). This error, derived from a negative conception of the flesh and of the entire material world characteristic also of some currents of Gnosticism, interpreted the incarnation of the Word as a mere appearance. According to the Docetists, Christ only appeared human; his body was not a real body, but the *appearance* of a body.

In the face of these errors and polemics about the divinity and humanity of Jesus, the Evangelist sought to go more deeply into the mystery of the incarnation and death of Christ. Faced with the temptation to flee the world as something bad, he exhorts the disciples to fix their faith in Jesus and, united to him, go into the world to give testimony to the truth. This hypothesis is reasonable. The Gospel is clear about the truth of the incarnation denied by the Docetists: "And the Word was made flesh and dwelt among us" (1:14). So, too, the letters of John that denounce and censor the errors of the schismatics who are disturbing the community: "By this you know the Spirit of God: every spirit which confesses that Jesus Christ has come in the flesh is of God, and every spirit which does not confess Jesus is not of God. This is the spirit of antichrist, of which you heard that it was coming, and now it is in the world already" (1 Jn 4:2–3); "For many deceivers have gone out into the world, men who will not confess the coming of Jesus Christ in the flesh; such a one is the deceiver and the antichrist" (2 Jn 1:7).

The religious climate of the era and the language the Evangelist uses led Rudolf Bultmann and other scholars in the last century to consider the fourth Gospel a Gnostic writing. Some theological concepts in Mandean literature (Mandeism is a religious movement, apparently of a Gnostic kind, that still exists in southern Iraq) find an echo in John. As we shall see later, this opinion has not prevailed, but it points to the Hellenistic character reflected in the fourth Gospel and thus to a Christian point of contact with the pagan world in which it developed. But if John used the language of Gnostic writings, it was to destroy them with their own weapons.

Anti-Baptist Conflicts
The Acts of the Apostles record that, in Ephesus, Aquila and Priscilla met an Alexandrian Jew named Apollos, who spoke with fervor about Jesus, although knowing only of the baptism

of John (cf. 18:25). The Acts also tell that Paul met a group of disciples in Ephesus who had only received John's baptism (cf. 19:1–7). The tradition linking the Evangelist with Ephesus, and the way John the Baptist is presented in the fourth Gospel, have led some authors to suppose that the Evangelist wrote his work as a polemic against those who overvalued the mission of Jesus' precursor (see 1:6–8). It has in its favor that, according to the fourth Gospel, Jesus spent part of his public life close to John the Baptist (see 3:22–36) and that Jesus' first disciples were from among the disciples of John the Baptist.

But although the Evangelist takes all this into account, defending the faith against some such sect is hardly what motivated the writing of his Gospel. John has a purpose that goes much further. Still, his presentation of John the Baptist confirms the precursor's importance in the early tradition and catechesis, as the Synoptics and Acts also do, and like other sources they show that some continued to regard John the Baptist superior to Jesus.

A Hostile Environment

Aside from these intellectual tendencies, those for whom John's writings were intended faced other external dangers, such as superstition and pressure to worship the emperor and other pagan divinities. The Acts of the Apostles tell us that, due to the preaching of Paul, large quantities of books of magic were burned at Ephesus (see Acts 19:19). Here is a reminder of how widespread superstitious and esoteric practices were. This also illustrates the influence of the worship in the city of Diana, in whose honor there was a temple considered one of the marvels of the ancient world (see Acts 19:28). And not far from Ephesus and the other churches mentioned in the Book of Revelation, one finds the region of Phrygia, famous as the center of the mystery cults of Cybele and Attis.

While the Gospel and the letters are silent about difficulties with the Roman authorities and problems related to superstition, the Apocalypse reflects the tensions arising from the threat of syncretism and from the empire's hostility toward Christianity. Some of the sins denounced in the Apocalypse may reflect the rites associated with mystery cults (see Rv 2:14, 20ff). Moreover, as the cult of the divinity of the emperors gained strength, Christians began to experience growing difficulties in remaining true to their faith. With the ascent to the throne of the emperor Domitian (81–96), the situation worsened, no doubt leading to strong pressure on the Christians of Asia Minor. Of the seven churches to which the author of the Apocalypse wrote, only Thyatira is not said to be worshiping the emperor.

3. The Johannine Community

The variety of literary forms found in the writings attributed by tradition to John, with their similarities and noticeable differences, naturally raises questions concerning the authorship of these works. While it is not hard to accept the idea that the Gospel and the letters come from the same author or authors, the Apocalypse plainly has many differences from them, leading readers to ask who wrote it. Yet tradition attributes all five works to the same person.

The most logical solution, and therefore the most tempting, is to say that tradition has joined several authors named John to one emblematic figure, the apostle John, son of Zebedee. This assigns authorship—of the Gospel, the letters, and the Apocalypse—to several different persons. But this explanation, while solving some problems, runs into others equally difficult and conflicts with a tradition transmitted with great firmness. Thus it seems better to accept the broad framework of tradition and see how these several writings can fit into it.

For this purpose, it is interesting to observe that, despite the notable differences, the Gospel, the letters, and Apocalypse refer to a common social and cultural context. Those to whom the Gospel and letters are addressed have problems also reflected in some way in the communities to which the author of the Apocalypse addresses himself. On the other hand, certain likenesses of theme and vocabulary—in particular referring to Jesus as the Logos, or the phrase "whom they pierced"—appears only in the Gospel and the Apocalypse, thus linking these two works. The Apocalypse and the fourth Gospel also share a certain liturgical character. Jewish festivals, reinterpreted in the light of faith in Christ, along with the liturgy of the temple, sacramental references, etc., are prominent in the Gospel, while in the Apocalypse the revelations take place on the Lord's Day (Sunday) and are developed in a liturgical setting.

Above all, from the point of view of content, both compositions coincide in their basic message: Jesus is the victor in the combat between the "sons of darkness" and the "sons of light," making those who adhere to the light and believe in him participants in his victory. Many think the testimony of tradition and the shared features point to a particular community, with its own identity, which grew up around the "beloved disciple," the fourth Gospel's source, whom tradition identifies as John the apostle. The Johannine writings would then be a reflection of this community's life. This explains the writings attributed to John as the source and apostolic authority behind these compositions, even though he did not personally write them.

More specifically, there are some (for example, R. Alan Culpepper) who advance the hypothesis of a Johannine school resembling the schools of antiquity. These schools were known in the Hellenistic era (Pythagoras, Plato, Aristotle, Epicurus) and in the Jewish setting (Hillel, Shammai, Philo). A school was constituted around its founder, a person of eminence around whom gathered a group of disciples who guarded his tradition, studying and developing the master's teaching and, at times, his way of life.

Applying that model to the Johannine writings, more than a few authors, both Catholics and Protestants, think this school originates in John, son of Zebedee; the community's experiences notably influenced the Gospel's way of presenting Jesus. This explains the relevance of the beloved disciple and helps one understand how the community could preserve the tradition through the years until the final writing of the fourth Gospel. The school would have supplied impetus to the Johannine community as it spread through the seven churches of the Apocalypse—that is to say, the churches of the great cities of Asia Minor.

Recent decades have seen efforts to explain how this community arose and what its history and development were. But these efforts are based on presuppositions about the history of the Gospel's composition as well as its intellectual and social setting, so that each hypothesis rests on other hypotheses. In view of all this, some common points appear plausible.

1. The community has its roots in Judeo-Christianity.
2. It suffered expulsion from the synagogue, but there is no agreement on when this occurred, how far it went, and what effects it had.
3. The community arrived at a more developed Christology on the basis of a simple vision of the Messiah, though it is not known how this happened.

There is disagreement in regard to Docetist tensions inside and outside the community and in regard to the relations of Christians who had been expelled from the synagogue with others who remained within it and with other churches.

This historical-literary hypothesis makes possible a solution to the problem presented by the similarities and differences among the five Johannine compositions. Likenesses are attributed to their proceeding from the same school and being composed within the same community; the undeniable differences correspond to diverse historical situations and diverse authors.

The radicalism of proposals that tend to see this community as a sect in opposition to other Christian groups should be avoided. The Evangelist and his community were not isolated, and their conception of Jesus is not that of a sectarian group reacting against the surrounding society. The Gospel's Christology has similarities with the Christologies of the churches of both Palestinian and Hellenistic origin. This is evident from the New Testament Christological confessions and hymns not by St. John (see 1 Tm 3:16; Phil 1:6–11; Col 1:15–20; Heb 1:1–3) and from the Prologue to the fourth Gospel, which reflects the general religious background of the New Testament.

The relationship of the Gospel and the Book of Revelation also show that there was no isolation, since the language and certain theological concepts point to a Johannine community linked to the Christian communities of Roman Asia to which Revelation was directed. Equally relevant is the fact that at the end of the first century, with the eclipse of the Church of Jerusalem, Christianity came to be centered in Rome and in Asia Minor, the empire's most Christianized province. In writing to the seven churches, the author of the Apocalypse signifies his desire to address the universal Church. In light of their consciousness of the unity of the Church, together with a sense of universal destiny and vocation, it is difficult to think of the Gospel and letters as products of a small community with an inferiority complex. Here, rather, is the same universality found in the Apocalypse.

Regardless of the particular environment in which the Johannine corpus was written, it should be studied in conjunction with the data of tradition. From the historical point of view, the weight and authority these documents had in the life of the Church could not be explained without their backing by the apostolic tradition. Supported by the testimony of the apostles, the Church transmitted them as true testimony about Jesus, standing apart from what could be found in other books of that period that did not form part of the canon. From the point of view of faith, this is natural, since the works of John reflect the faith of the community in which they were born, having enjoyed a special divine assistance in their composition. Thus their author or authors expressed essential aspects of the faith of the Church—the "us" to which Benedict XVI frequently refers— even as the Holy Spirit guided them in transmitting divine revelation to mankind.

Part I

THE FOURTH GOSPEL

CHAPTER 1

The Gospel of St. John as Apostolic Testimony

1. Witness to the Apostolic Preaching

IN DETERMINING THE AUTHENTIC "memories of the apostles" that, as St. Justin tells us, were read in liturgical celebrations, the Church recognized four Gospels. In common, they constitute a testimony to the life and work of Jesus, and all seek to show that he is the Messiah in whom the Scriptures of Israel were fulfilled. These texts were a product of careful study of what had taken place from the beginning (see Lk 1:1–4) or else testified to the witness of the apostles presented as the "gospel" (Mk 1:1). But they could also give direct testimony of the life of Jesus. That is the case with the fourth Gospel, a testimony guaranteeing the tradition received from the beginning from those who had been witnesses of Jesus' life (see Jn 20:30–31; 21:24).

Like the Synoptics, the Gospel of St. John as a whole, including Jesus' words and miracles ("signs"), belongs to the initial preaching (*kerygma*) of the apostles. This can be deduced from the Gospel itself by comparing it with texts that summarize the initial preaching of the apostles—for example, the synthesis in Acts 10:37–43, a discourse of Peter containing the fundamental elements of the *kerygma* that correspond perfectly with John's Gospel. In broad terms, the basic elements in common are as follows.

a) *Jesus anointed as Messiah at the baptism by John*

   Acts 10:37–38a: "You know the word . . . which was proclaimed throughout all Judea, beginning from Galilee after the baptism which John preached: how God anointed Jesus of Nazareth with the Holy Spirit and with power."

   John 1:31–34: "'I myself did not know him; but for this I came baptizing with water, that he might be revealed to Israel.' And John bore witness, 'I saw the Spirit descend as a dove from heaven, and it remained on him. I myself did not know him; but he who sent me to baptize with water said to me, "He on whom you see the Spirit descend and remain, this is he who baptizes with the Holy Spirit." And I have seen and have borne witness that this is the Son of God."

b) *The manifestation of the messianic character of Jesus by signs and words*

   Acts 10:38b: ". . . and how he went about doing good and healing all that were oppressed by the devil, for God was with him."

   John 1:35–12:50: The first part of the Gospel of John, in which Jesus is presented as the Messiah by means of his signs.

c) *The passion, death, and resurrection of Jesus*

   Acts 10:39–40a: "And we are witnesses to all that he did in the country of the Jews and in Jerusalem. They put him to death by hanging him on a tree; but God raised him on the third day."

   John 13:1–20; 20:1–18: The second part of the Gospel of John, the passion, death, and resurrection of Jesus.

d) *Appearances to qualified witnesses*

   Acts 10:40b–41: ". . . and made him manifest; not to all the people but to us who were chosen by God as witnesses, who ate and drank with him after he rose from the dead."

   John 20:11–21:25: Jesus appears to his disciples.

e) *Gift of the Spirit and mission to the twelve*

Acts 10:42–43: "And he commanded us to preach to the people, and to testify that he is the one ordained by God to be judge of the living and the dead. To him all the prophets bear witness that everyone who believes in him receives forgiveness of sins through his name."

John 20:19–23: Jesus appears to his disciples gathered in a closed place, breathes his Spirit upon them, and confers on them the power of pardoning sins.

Still other passages of the New Testament showing the content of the apostolic preaching can be found in other discourses in the Acts of the Apostles (see 2:14–39; 3:12–26; 4:8–12; 5:29–32; 13:16–41) and in the letters of Paul (see Rom 1:1–4; 1 Cor 15:3–8; 1 Thes 1:10; 2:8). One does not always find in these texts references to the earthly ministry of Jesus, but his death and resurrection, his exaltation at the right hand of God, and his return as judge do appear as essential elements, along with the consequent call to repentance and to faith. This preaching was presented with and confirmed by texts from the Scriptures of Israel, seen as fulfilled in Jesus. As we shall see, John's Gospel includes all these elements. Besides the passion, death, and resurrection, to which we have already referred, it presents the death of Jesus as an exaltation, speaks of his role as judge, who will return at the end of time, and demands that people make a response of faith in Jesus, to whom the Scriptures testify.

The fourth Gospel also includes an apostolic testimony along lines sketched in Acts 1:8: "You shall receive power when the Holy Spirit has come upon you; and you shall be my witnesses in Jerusalem and in all Judea and Samaria and to the ends of the earth." As will be seen, the Gospel's author presents himself as a witness of the events of the Passion (Jn 19:35) and Resurrection (Jn 20:3–10), and he is among the disciples who saw the Resurrected One and received his Spirit from him (see Jn 20:19–23).

Indeed, the fourth Gospel is notable for being a testimony of the Spirit. As Jesus says in the "farewell discourse" of the Last Supper, it is the Spirit who will recall to them what he has told them (see Jn 14:26).

At the same time, however, the fourth Gospel is, in a sense, an anonymous text. Whereas many of the non-canonical Gospels refer to the identity of their authors—James, Thomas, Philip, Matthias, etc.—to provide support for the authority of their ideas, John's aim is not to transmit his personal experience—although, in fact, he *does* transmit it—but rather the faith of the early apostolic community. This, then, is the Gospel "according to" St. John, because it witnesses to the one gospel of Jesus as presented by this apostle, who identifies himself as the disciple loved by Jesus. He is the guarantor of its testimony.

2. The Beloved Disciple at the Origin of the Testimony

As we shall see, the Gospel as it has reached us was not written at one sitting. Instead it is the product of a laborious process. But it refers to a disciple as the source of the written text before us. For example, 21:24: "This is the disciple who is bearing witness to these things, and who has written these things; and we know that his testimony is true." The "disciple" is the one mentioned in 21:20—"the disciple whom Jesus loved, who had lain close to his breast at the supper and had said, 'Lord, who is it that is going to betray you?'" (see 13:23: "One of his disciples, whom Jesus loved, was lying close to the breast of Jesus"). We also are told of this disciple that it was rumored "he was not to die" (21:23).

The same disciple is mentioned as being at the foot of the cross: "Jesus saw his mother, and the disciple whom he loved standing near" (19:26). Apparently feeling it necessary to emphasize that the Evangelist is identified as a witness to this death, he declares: "He who saw it has borne witness—his testimony is true" (19:35). This disciple also went with Peter to the empty tomb (see 20:2–3). He was, therefore, one of the closest, among the seven named at the beginning of the scene of the miraculous catch (Simon Peter, Thomas, called Didymus, Nathaniel, from Cana in Galilee, the sons of Zebedee, and "two others" (21:1); and when the risen Lord appears, we read: "That disciple whom Jesus loved said to Peter. . . ." (21:7ff).[1]

All this points to the conclusion that the Gospel has its origin in the eyewitness testimony of a disciple whom Jesus loved. The Gospel also bears evidence of being the work of someone who knew the Palestine of the first century and was familiar with the traditions, customs, and feasts of Israel.

a) *Familiarity with Palestine and with Jerusalem in particular.* The Evangelist provides concrete details about Palestine that are not mentioned in the Synoptics: the well of Jacob close to Sichar (4:5–6), the pool of Bethzatha (5:2), the pool of Siloam (9:7), the portico of Solomon in the temple (10:23), the distance between Bethany and Jerusalem (11:18), the garden on the other side of the Kidron valley (18:1), and the Lithostrotos (19:13). Some of these sites have been confirmed by archaeological discoveries or other sources, while others, such as Bethany beyond the Jordan (1:28) and Ainon near Salim (3:23), have not yet been identified. In any case, the author is someone well acquainted with the place in which the history he narrates took place.

---

1. He is often thought to be one of the disciples of John the Baptist who follow Jesus at the beginning of the Gospel (see 1:35ff). Some also identify him with the disciple who introduces Peter into the house of the high priest during the passion of Jesus: (see 18:15). Although this latter passage is sometimes used to deny that John of Zebedee, a fisherman from Galilee, was the one who wrote the Gospel, since he could not have been a relative or acquaintance of the high priest, the text does not exclude his being an acquaintance of a member of the high priest's household, nor does it rule out the possibility that the priestly families of Jerusalem had links to Galilee.

b) *Knowledge of the Jewish world.* One can deduce from the text that the one writing is a Hebrew, who knows the Old Testament very well and bases his interpretation of the life of Jesus on it. At the same time, he seems familiar with rabbinic methods of disputations (for example, 10:34–36). He is also knowledgeable about Jewish traditions and interested in Jewish feasts. He mentions the feasts of Passover (2:13, 23; 6:4; 11:55; 12:1; 13:1), Tabernacles (7:2), and the Dedication (10:22), as well as the Sabbath (5:9; 7:22; 9:14), and shows a knowledge of the rules and theological principles pertaining to them (for example, the meaning of the Sabbath, the importance of water and light in the feast of Tabernacles, etc.). He also makes specific references to certain Jewish practices (the large earthen jars of water for purification in 2:6; not entering the Praetorium so as to avoid contamination and be able to eat the Passover in 18:28; the custom of going up to Jerusalem for feasts in 2:13 and 7:8; the allusion to the paschal lamb when making the point that Scripture was fulfilled in 19:36 ("not a bone of him shall be broken"); and, perhaps, of the seamless tunic of 19:23, taken as a reference to the tunic worn by the high priest).

3. Identification of the Beloved Disciple

Identifying this disciple who gives witness and is at the same time beloved by Jesus is both simple and very complex. It is simple from the point of view of the data of tradition testifying from the time of St. Irenaeus that the beloved disciple was John the apostle, the son of Zebedee, but it is complex in reference to the few data on the Gospel's authorship from its composition until the time of the Bishop of Lyons. The references at the end of the first century and the first half of the second century are scarce and not always easy to interpret. In fact, different scholars draw diverse conclusions from the same sources. Evidently, then, we are operating here in the light of hypothesis. Thus we shall take the data of tradition as our principal source, while briefly mentioning other theories about the identity of this mysterious disciple without entering into more detail.

The Data of Tradition

The earliest and most important witness is that of St. Irenaeus, Bishop of Lyons. He was born around the year 130 in Smyrna (today's Izmir) in Asia Minor. He identifies the beloved disciple with John the son of Zebedee: "John, the disciple of the Lord, the same who reposed upon his breast, wrote a gospel during his stay in Ephesus" (*Adversus Haereses* 3, 1, 1). His testimony has special weight because Irenaeus knew Polycarp, who had known St. John. (According to Tertullian and St. Jerome, St. Polycarp was made bishop of Smyrna by St. John himself.)

Before these testimonies, there are only indirect references, which are difficult to interpret. The data usually cited to confirm Iranaeus's identification are based on the Synoptics.

1. *The special role of some disciples.* The Synoptics transmit the information that Jesus designated twelve of his disciples his closest followers in Mark 14:17–18: "And when it was evening, he came with the twelve. And as they were at table eating, Jesus said . . ."; this also is reported by John (see 13:1ff). The Synoptics further affirm that three disciples occupied a special place within the twelve: Peter, James, and John, the latter two who were sons of Zebedee (Andrew also appears on one occasion with these three: Mark 13:3). Jesus chose them to accompany him at the raising of the daughter of Jairus (Mk 5:37ff), they were witnesses of the transfiguration on Mount Tabor (Mt 17:1–2), and they prayed with him in Gethsemane (Mk 14:33).

According to the fourth Gospel, the disciple whom Jesus loved was present at the supper before his passion. If he was one of the "preferred" ones, the beloved disciple must have been John. He could not have been Peter, since we see Peter and the beloved disciple together on various occasions (see 20:2ff; 21:7, 20); James the Greater is very improbable, since nothing in tradition suggests this. Moreover, James was martyred about the year 44 (see Acts 12:2), and this seems to rule him out as an author of the Gospel, which presumably was written toward the end of the first century.

2. *The anonymity of the sons of Zebedee.* The Gospel never speaks of John, the son of Zebedee. It mentions the sons of Zebedee only in chapter 21, an appendix probably written by a disciple of the Evangelist: "Simon Peter, Thomas called the Twin, Nathaniel of Cana in Galilee, the sons of Zebedee, and two others of his disciples were together" (21:1). Some, pointing out that the Evangelist calls John the Baptist simply "John," argue that this confirms the fact that John, son of Zebedee, is the Gospel's author: i.e., suppressing the name of John the apostle is a device to avoid confusing the two persons. The Synoptics, on the other hand, call the precursor "John the Baptist," perhaps to avoid confusion with the apostle John. In any case, the fact that neither John nor James is mentioned by name in the Gospel is not without significance.

3. *Joint references to Peter and John.* In the fourth Gospel, the beloved disciple always appears with Peter, except at the death of Jesus on the cross. The identification with John is supported by the fact that the Gospel of St. Luke says that Jesus sent Peter and John to prepare the paschal meal in Jerusalem (see Lk 22:8), and the Acts of the Apostles notes that John accompanied Peter in the early days of the Church in Jerusalem (see Acts 3:1–11; 4:13–19; 8:14). Paul also refers to him as among the "pillars" of the Church (see Gal 2:9).

These, then, are the traditional data.

Other Suggestions

A good number of modern critics find these arguments unconvincing. The Synoptics, they say, cannot always be used as historical sources. Moreover, the arguments cited and others that might be advanced are not conclusive and leave many mysteries. For example, if the Evangelist is John the apostle, why doesn't he say anything about the transfiguration or the prayer in the Garden of Gethsemane? In addition, they see obscurities in the most ancient ecclesiastical tradition.

Given these difficulties, both internal and of tradition, critics have proposed others than John, son of Zebedee as the author.

a) The beloved disciple is not a historical person but only a symbol representing the model of the perfect disciple of Jesus (e.g., Alfred Loisy). For those who hold this opinion, the fact that he is never given a name and appears with Peter in scenes in which the Synoptics make no mention of him support his symbolic character. (For example, Mark in his accounts of the Passion and Resurrection does not speak of someone being with Peter.) However, as Raymond Brown rightly points out, this objection is not conclusive. In the Gospel of John, the mother of Jesus, an historical person, also has a symbolic role (as mother of disciples and therefore of the Church) and appears in passages with no parallel in the Synoptics (see 2:3–12; 19:25–27). Peter, too, has a strong symbolic character in the Gospel yet is a historical person; so also with Lazarus and Mary Magdalene. On the other hand, the Gospel speaks of the death of the beloved disciple, as it would hardly do if he were fictitious (symbolic people do not die).

b) The beloved disciple could be one of the known disciples of the New Testament distinct from John the apostle. Those proposed include Lazarus (Joseph N. Sanders, Ben Witherington), John Mark (Pierson Parker), Thomas (James H. Charlesworth), Mary Magdalene (Esther DeBoer). But although elements in the Gospel may support an identification with some of these persons, the arguments are weak and there is no testimony in the tradition to support it. Such identifications also present more problems than solutions.

c) The beloved disciple could have been a disciple of the apostles, not part of the group of the twelve during the ministry of Jesus and too unimportant to be recalled in the Synoptic tradition, who later became a notable person in the Johannine community and embodied the evangelical ideal of love for Jesus. Supporting this view in one way or another are numerous modern authors (Martin Hengel, R. Alan Culpepper, Raymond Brown, Rudolf Schnackenburg, etc.). Some suggest John the Priest, of whom Papias speaks. He might have been born in the priestly circles of Jerusalem and could have been identified as the beloved disciple by the effort of his own disciples and linked to the figure of John the apostle. The proposal seeks to respond to the difficulties presented by the identification of the beloved disciple with John the apostle, but its weak point is its failure to give a satisfactory explanation to the tradition of St. Irenaeus, which is so solid. It would take more proof than they offer to conclude that the Bishop of Lyons was wrong. True, there are obscure points, but that would also be the case with the hypotheses that propose other solutions.

Recapitulation

Elements in the fourth Gospel could make it difficult to identify John, the son of Zebedee, with the beloved disciple who is the author of the Gospel. New proposals eliminate some of the difficulties, but they create others of equal or greater weight. There is no definitive, clear solution. Thus the Gospel's silence regarding the sons of Zebedee remains the strongest argument in favor of the identity of the beloved disciple as transmitted by tradition. It is explained by the fact that one of the two brothers, specifically John, was the apostolic figure who is the source of the Gospel and who humbly hides himself in anonymity.

In any case, this identification does not exclude the possibility that a disciple of the beloved disciple was the actual Evangelist, the one, that is to say, who put the beloved disciple's testimony into writing, nor that there might also have been one or more final writers, who completed the narrative (for example, adding chapter 21). The origin of the testimony is one thing, while its writing is something else. Pope Benedict XVI suggests that Papias's mention of the priest John and some other indications suggest that in Ephesus there was "something like a Johannine school, which traced its origins to Jesus' favorite disciple himself, but in which a certain 'Presbyter John' presided as the ultimate authority. . . . There seem to be grounds for ascribing to 'Presbyter John' an essential role in the definitive shaping of the Gospel, although he must always have regarded himself as the trustee of the tradition he had received from the son of Zebedee."[2]

In conclusion, there are no conclusive objections to taking the beloved disciple as a historical person to whom the testimony of the Gospel can be attributed. The most ancient tradition identifies this disciple with John the apostle, and the Fathers attribute the fourth Gospel to no one else. Undoubtedly, the Gospel itself and the Synoptics contain data that seem difficult to reconcile with this identification, but they do not contradict it. Other proposals regarding the identity of the beloved disciple also present insoluble problems without making matters any more clear than the traditional view does.

4. Time and Place of Composition

Efforts to establish the date and place of composition of the fourth Gospel seek to situate it within spatial-temporal coordinates that help one better understand the text. Some proposals made in this connection respond to the authenticity.

---

2. Joseph Ratzinger/Benedict XVI, *Jesus of Nazareth*, vol. 1, p. 226.

The Place

The ancient tradition of the Church affirms that, after his role as a leader in the Church of Jerusalem, John moved to Ephesus, where he lived until reaching old age in the times of Trajan (the years 98 to 117). With the conflicts the synagogue found in the Gospel, it's possible that anti-Docetist intentions, the presence in Ephesus of groups of baptized persons, and points of contact with the Apocalypse favor this as the place of the Gospel's composition, although this does not exclude the possibility that some parts, or an intermediate edition of the Gospel, might have been written elsewhere.

Besides Ephesus, Alexandria, Syria, Samaria, and Judea have also been proposed. Those presenting these hypotheses make more or less reasonable points, but it is difficult to square such suggestions with the data of the Gospel while testimonies of tradition in favor of such proposals are lacking.

The Date

Dates proposed for the composition of the Gospel range from before the year 70 to the middle of the second century. Defenders of an early date point to features of the Gospel better suited to the period before 70 and the destruction of Jerusalem. So, for instance, terms like "rabbi" and "messiah," John's knowledge of the temple (implying that the sanctuary of Jerusalem was still standing), Jesus' superiority to John the Baptist (corresponding to an early stage of Christianity), and likenesses of the Gospel's language to that of Qumran (a community which disappeared in the year 70), fit better with an early dating.

Those who argue for the second century base their case on the presence of a theology that, in their judgment, is too sophisticated to be explained by anything except a slow evolution in the Church's development. They also adduce the delay in the appearance of the first testimonies about the Gospel, placed by these writers in approximately 160–170 AD, since they reject the idea that writers like Ignatius or Justinian, between the years 100 and 150, could have been acquainted with it.

Nevertheless, the papyruses with fragments of the fourth Gospel found in Egypt show the great authority which it enjoyed and mark out a time before which its writing must have taken place. The most ancient fragment, P^{52}, has been dated at the middle or first half of the second century; however, for a book to have spread to upper Egypt and come to have been recognized as authoritative by about 150, it would have had to have been written earlier than that, probably toward the end of the first century or very near the beginning of the second.

In addition, features like the possible allusion to Peter's death (see 21:18–19), the fall of Jerusalem (see 11:48), or to expulsion of the Christians from the synagogue (see 9:22; 12:42; 16:2), which did not occur until after the Judean war and probably was not fully accomplished until the decade of the '80s, suggest a date after 70, perhaps between the beginning of the '90s and the end of the century.

In short, there seems to be no serious objections to maintaining that the fourth Gospel was written at the end of the first century.

5. Transmission of the Text

John's text has been transmitted with great fidelity. In addition the papyruses P^{52} and P^{90}, which are noted for their antiquity, P^{66}, which preserves the greater part of the Gospel, and P^{75}, which gives witness to part of the Gospels of Luke and of John, are very important.

These last two are from the end of the second century or the beginning of the third. They reflect a text very close to the original, since among them there are very few variations deserving of mention.

The exception is the passage about the adulterous woman (see 7:53—8:11), which is lacking in the papyruses P[66] and P[75] and in some parchment manuscripts, including two very important ones, the Sinaitic and the Vatican (fourth century). It is also lacking among the Greek Fathers until the eleventh century and in some of the ancient versions. The style and vocabulary also differ somewhat from the rest of the Gospel, and the passage seems to be an addition between verses 7:52–53 and 8:12. Some manuscripts place it in the Gospel of St. Luke, after 21:38 ("And early in the morning all the people came to him in the temple to hear him"), where it fits well as a continuation of the questions asked of Jesus before he was taken prisoner (see Lk 20:20–40). Others include it as a fragment at the end of the Gospel.

Several hypotheses have been advanced to explain the inclusion of this passage. Some think that it was part of an oral tradition, transmitted especially by Christians in the West and existing at least since the middle of the second century, which was later incorporated in the Gospel. Others consider it to be drawn from independent narratives that seemed verified in the testimony of ecclesiastical authors (the pardon of a sinful woman that, according to Eusebius, was mentioned by Papias, the intervention of Jesus in an execution that, according to Didymus the Blind, refers to the apocryphal Gospel of the Hebrews). Others think the passage was eliminated in some areas due to rigoristic thinking about the forgiveness of an adulteress but included when this rigorism was overcome. In any case, the text has been received in the tradition of the Church as part of the apostolic testimony.

Another manuscript variation is found in chapter 5. As the second part of verse 3 and the whole of verse 4, the Sixtine-Clementine version of the Vulgate includes the words "waiting for the moving of the water; for an angel of the Lord went down at certain seasons into the pool, and troubled the water; whoever stepped in first after the troubling of the water was healed of whatever disease he had." The Neovulgate, in contrast, omits this, consigning it to a footnote. The omission is based on the fact that the words are not found in important codices and Greek papyruses, nor in many ancient versions.

A variant that aroused the interest of some Fathers and ecclesiastical writers (for example, Irenaeus and Tertullian) was the use of the singular in 1:13: "who was born not of blood nor of the will of the flesh nor of the will of man, but of God," in place of "who were born . . ." This reading may have been introduced to emphasize the virginal character of the birth of Jesus, perhaps through the influence of the singular *autou* ("his") immediately preceding it in verse 1:12. In any case, the principal manuscripts support the plural reading.

6. The Reception of the Fourth Gospel

The prompt acceptance of the fourth Gospel as normative is evidence of the authority assigned to it from early times. As noted, written testimonies show its very wider diffusion within a few decades of its composition. The papyruses mentioned, discovered in Egypt and dated to the middle of the second century, indicate rapid propagation. These discoveries show it to have been well known in Egypt around the year 200.

The Gospel's authority also is confirmed by the use made of it by some Fathers and ecclesiastical writers of the second century, as well as by Gnostic authors. Although they do not cite the Gospel directly, St. Ignatius of Antioch (who died about 110) and St. Polycarp (who died about 150) appear to know it. At least two fundamental premises of the fourth Gospel—that Jesus was the Word or Logos of the Father and that the actions of the Holy Spirit are inscrutable—are a commonplace for St. Ignatius. St. Justin (ca. 150) probably echoed this in saying it is necessary to be born again to enter the kingdom of heaven (*I Apol.* 61, 4; see Jn 3:5), or when he writes: "He has shown that he was the only begotten of the Father of the Universe, having been engendered by him in a special way as his Word and Power, and having afterwards been made man through the Virgin, as we have learned from the recollections" (*Dial.* 105, 1).[3] Aristides of Athens (who died about 130) also seems to have known the fourth Gospel. It is certain that Tatian, a disciple of Justine, used it for the Diatessaron around the year 170, situating it along with the three Synoptics. Theophilus of Antioch used the fourth Gospel to support his theory of the Logos, citing John expressly. Equally, a codex on papyrus at the end of the second or beginning of the third century, the P^{75}, which contains the beginning of the Gospel of John immediately after the end of the Gospel of Luke, confirms its transmission with the other Gospels. In short, despite its differences of form in comparison with the Synoptics, John from ancient times was considered a Gospel and transmitted along with the other three.

St. Irenaeus of Lyons, who knew the Churches of the East and the West well, in 180 for the first time established as canonical Gospels the four we have now (*Adversus Haereses* 3, 11). In doing so, he opposed those like, Tatian in Syria or Basilides in Alexandria, who rewrote the existing Gospels as a single text and those who accepted other writings of an evangelical character then in circulation and now known to us as "apocryphal Gospels." These letters either contained doctrines contrary to the living tradition or else lacked apostolic origin.

In fact, Marcion seemed to reject the fourth Gospel. The Valentinians (Gnostics) used it. Heracleon, a disciple of Valentinus, wrote a detailed commentary on the Gospel of John, probably in the second half of the second century. Using an exaggerated allegorical exegesis, he sought to show a rejection of the flesh by Christ, a division between reason and spirit, or an

---

3. One can see also *1 Apol.* 46, 2; see Jn 1, 1:9; *Dial.* 63; see 1:13; *Dial.* 88; see 1, 20, 23; *Apol* 1, 32, see 1, 4.

effort by the soul to find redemption through wisdom. Origen preserved many fragments of that commentary while criticizing it in a great work of thirty-two books that reached only chapter 13 of the Gospel of which we now have less than half. For the Alexandrian, Christ is divine but at the same time man in body, soul, and spirit. The fourth Gospel is also cited by Ptolemy, another disciple of Valentinus, and by the Gospel of Philip, a Gnostic work.

From the beginning of the third century, the fourth Gospel was already universally accepted as one of the four canonical Gospels and was treated as such by the Fathers. The Trinitarian and Christological controversies of the first councils, in which the human and divine nature of Christ were central, to a great extent concerned the interpretation of the relevant texts of St. John. Tertullian (ca. 150–220), who refuted Marcion (*Adversus Marcionem*) and Valentinus (*Adversus Valentinanus*), made use especially of the Gospel of St. John in his *Adversus Praxean* to rout the Monarchian doctrine of Praxeas, who misinterpreted certain passages of John by identifying the Word with the Father.

In the fourth and fifth centuries, the Gospel was used widely in the controversies with Arius, who appealed to the Gospel of John to support his views. From this period we have the great Eastern commentaries such as those of St. Cyril of Alexandria and Teodorus of Mopsuestia and the homilies of St. John Chrysostom who frequently opposed the Arians, emphasizing the two natures of Christ, and showing which expressions in the fourth Gospel refer to each. The last two were exponents of the School of Antioch, which was characterized by a literal interpretation of Scripture; they emphasized on the basis of the fourth Gospel how God made himself present in the humanity of Christ, underlining above all the impassability of the Logos.

In the West, the *Treatises on St. John* of St. Augustine (354–430), an outstanding work of a more pastoral character, has had an enormous influence up to this day. One of the last works by the Bishop of Hippo, it contains 124 sermons preached over two years while he was also writing his great works *On the Trinity* and *The City of God*. In it he considers the Trinitarian and Christological questions of the period, with the aim of giving the faithful a more intimate knowledge of the Word while at the same time exposing the doctrinal errors of the ancient heretics Sabelius, Photinus, Arius, Mani, and Apollinaris.

In short, the interpretation of the Johannine texts in these first centuries was conditioned by the Trinitarian and Christological debates and reflects a considerable effort on the part of the orthodox to affirm Jesus' human and divine aspects without diminishing one in favor of the other. From this time also came the popular practice of using the Gospel to seek divine protection: from at least the beginning of the fourth century until now the custom has existed in some places encircle the necks of newborn infants with the opening words of the Gospel's Prologue.

The Middle Ages used the fourth Gospel to go into greater theological depth in regard to matters affirmed by the Fathers and the councils. Various writers organized and systematized this material without significant variations. Besides the exposition of St. Bede (673–735), other commentaries dedicated specifically to the Gospel of John were those of John Scotus Eriugena and Rupert of Deutz.

That of John Scotus (ninth century) had great success, since it was used extensively in the commentary on the Gospel of John in the *Glossa Ordinaria,* a standard commentary on the Bible compiled from the ninth to fourteenth centuries. It is characterized by an approach to the Gospel that goes beyond its literal meaning, thus opening up broad theological and philosophical speculation. In this time, too, the fourth Gospel served as a source for mystics and contemplatives, as one sees from the writings of the Franciscan Joachim of Flora (1135–1292) and his interpretation of the promise of the Spirit as a prefiguration of a time of consummation when the dominion of the Spirit will replace the law imposed by the Father and the Church inaugurated by the Son. For his part, Rupert of Deutz (1075–1129), wrote a commentary in fourteen volumes characterized by constant mystical references.

Later came the commentaries of St. Thomas Aquinas (ca. 1225–1274): the *lectura* on John and the *reportatio* of the lectures in Paris on the fourth Gospel. In the first of these, St. Thomas produced a compendium of what had been taught by his predecessors, especially by St. Augustine and St. John Chrysostom. He explains in the Prologue that John the Evangelist deals especially with Christ's divinity, without omitting the mysteries of his humanity, in response to the need to complete the Synoptic Gospels and oppose the nascent heresies. He also distinguishes the different focuses of the Synoptics and John: the former record the birth of Christ at a certain time and insist on his humanity and his human life; John, on the other hand, begins by affirming Jesus' divinity and his communion with the Father. Following the tradition of distinguishing texts referring to the humanity and divinity of Jesus, St. Thomas divides the Gospel into two parts, one affirming the divinity of Christ (the Prologue and chapter 1) and the other showing the divinity of Christ through his humanity (the balance of the Gospel).

The theological teachers of the Middle Ages did not do biblical exegesis in the modern sense, but instead sought the Gospel's support for their speculations. Strictly biblical commentaries on the fourth Gospel appeared later, the first important one undoubtedly being the *Postilla* to the Old and New Testaments of Nicholas of Lyra (ca. 1270–1349). It was succeeded in the same line by the work of Juan de Maldonado (1534–1583), notable for his assiduous use of the teaching of the Fathers and the interpretations of the medieval authors, which resulted in a useful compilation of the thoughts of these predecessors. Also deserving of mention is the commentary of the Flemish Jesuit

Cornelius à Lapide (1567–1637), in which he brings together scientific erudition and abundant citations from the Fathers and ecclesiastical writers for the sake of fostering piety.

The unity of biblical interpretation was, in general, not disrupted by the Reformation, except for what has to do with St. Paul. However, the Enlightenment, in extending scientific investigation to all fields of knowledge, provoked a top-to-bottom reconsideration of biblical studies, especially in Protestant settings. Far from being bypassed by this revolution, John's Gospel, precisely because of the difficulty of interpreting it, was one of the books most studied by the critical exegesis of the nineteenth and twentieth centuries. The line initiated by David F. Strauss (1800–1874) in his *Leben Jesu* (1835)— affirming that Jesus was a mere mythical figure and that the fourth Gospel held less interest for a historian than the others—was followed by the School of Tübingen under the aegis of Ferdinand C. Baur (1792–1860). These authors found in the Gospel's elevated theology an echo of Gnostic doctrines or the mystery religions of Hellenism, though more on the basis of their own liberal philosophical presuppositions than a critique of the actual text. Even so, their critical work was adopted by the following generation, which undertook a searching literary investigation of the Gospel's sources. Richard A. Reitzenstein (1861–1931) and his "history of religions" school contributed even more to the investigation of these sources, finding in John influences from Persian religion and the Mandean sect as well as the myth of the Gnostic *anthropos*.

All these streams converged and found their major exponent in the work of Rudolf Bultmann. He held that the Gospel was composed on the basis of Gnostic sources prior to Christianity and interpreted it in light of existential principles, according to which a mature believer in certain moments faced the need to decide between the will of God and the counsels of the flesh.

Catholic exegesis kept its distance from these discussions until the arrival of modernism. Alfred F. Loisy (1857–1940) in 1903 published his commentary on the Gospel of John, echoing, though in a modified form, the positions of liberal Protestantism. Against Loisy, M. J. Lagrange (1855–1938) wrote his celebrated and frequently reprinted commentary which was republished a number of times. Since then, and reflecting magisterial interventions that clarified the role of historical-critical methods, many commentaries by Catholic authors have appeared. The best known are those of Rudolf Schnackenburg, *The Gospel According to St. John*, I–III (1965–1975), and Raymond E. Brown's *The Gospel According to John*, 2 vols. (1966 and 1971). Other noteworthy studies more recently include Francis J. Moloney's *The Gospel of John* (1998) and Rinaldo Fabris', *Giovanni* (Rome 1992). Non-Catholic studies that deserve mention because of their influence are the commentary of Rudolf Bultmann (*The Gospel of John*, 1941) and the works of Charles H. Dodd (*Interpretation of the Fourth Gospel*, 1953 and *Historical Tradition in the Fourth Gospel*, 1963).

Chapter 2

The Testimony of John about Jesus

ALTHOUGH THE GOSPEL OF JOHN has been transmitted with the other three canonical Gospels, reading it after reading the others is something like entering a different world. The Synoptics begin by speaking of the infancy of Jesus (Matthew and Luke) or the beginning of his public life (Mark). From the Prologue on, however, John's Gospel affirms that Jesus is the Logos, eternal Word of the Father, only-begotten Son of God, God himself, who became man to reveal God to humankind. What for the Synoptics is the end of a development appears in John as a point of departure. With good reason, St. John is symbolically represented by an eagle, for this evangelist addresses us from on high, as it were, in order to tell us about Jesus from God's point of view.

Thus we have three very similar Gospels and one very different from the rest. Can it reasonably be said that the Gospel of John is also a Gospel? Does it tell the same story as the others? Does it have the same purpose? We know that the Gospels of Matthew, Mark, and Luke underwent a process of selection, theological reflection, narration, simplification, etc., from oral teaching to written texts that reached their final form in the second half of the first century. They are the written memory of what Jesus said and did. But can the same be said of the Gospel of John?

1. The Johannine Question

From the second century until the eighteenth century, there were no doubts: John, one of the twelve apostles, had written his own memories, which were collected in the Gospel that bears his name. Up to then, too, the fourth Gospel was generally thought to be more reliable than those of Mark or Luke, who had not been eyewitnesses of the events they related, whereas the apostle John, son of Zebedee, had been. The idea universally accepted was that John knew the Synoptics and, after long years of meditation, wanted to complete them with material of his own.

Yet even in the nineteenth century the peculiar features of the Gospel of John gave rise to some doubts about its authority and historicity. In order to call attention to the differences between John and the other Gospels, Karl G. Bretschneider in 1820 wrote his work *Probabilia de evangelii et epistolarum Joannis Apostoli indole et origine* (Leipzig). Influenced by the ideas of Edward Evanson, an English deist of the end of the eighteenth century, Bretschneider argued that John could not have been the author of the Gospel, since the son of Zebedee could not have had the culture visible in the author of this work, and that the author was not an eyewitness of the events he related. The Gospel attributed to John was no more than an apologetical text directed against the followers of John the Baptist, the Docetists, and the Gnostics. Bretschneider's work marks the initiation of the so-called "Johannine question," whose background then and now revolved around the authenticity of John's Gospel and its historical value.

The fourth Gospel's Christology generates the most problems. Confronted with a Christology more developed than that of the Synoptics, some authors attribute to the Gospel a later date and a different context than those traditionally assigned to it. They therefore dispute whether the author could have really been an eyewitness of the events narrated and whether he knew the Synoptic Gospels. Some critics concluded that the Gospel of John could not have been the work of an eyewitness and deny its historical value of all that is not part of the Passion and some isolated details. For this critical perspective, the Gospel is nothing more than a later theological reconstruction belonging to the second or third Christian generation.

The Johannine question remains alive in many sectors of present-day critical exegesis. Those who deny the Gospel's historical character propose other hypotheses concerning the text. For some, it is a kind of poem about the figure of Jesus, composed on the basis of symbolic miracles (although with some basis in historical reality) and imaginary discourses placed by the author on Jesus' lips. Others interpret it as a synagogal reading of the Old Testament according to the teachings of the Master of Nazareth. Still others understand it as a narrative inspired by the Synoptics, from whom the author drew material for the composition of pure narrative fictions. So, for example, the resurrection of Lazarus, brother of Martha and Mary, is an elaboration of the story of Martha and Mary told by Luke (see Lk 10:38–42) and of the parable of the rich man who wanted the poor man Lazarus to return from the dead to warn his brothers (see Lk 16:19–31); the episode of the wedding feast of Cana is said to be a narrative based on Jesus' words about putting new wine in new wineskins of Mark 2:22, etc. Many variations of these proposals are offered, combining ideas like these with others more or less like them.

Although most critics have not adopted extreme positions, the tendency nevertheless exists to make much of the fourth Gospel's theological value while denying that it contributes to our knowledge of Jesus (inasmuch as the Evangelist is not writing history but transmitting a message). Those who think this way find support in the historical-critical methodology applied to the Gospel of John in comparison with the Synoptics.

As a literary work of the end of the first century, John's Gospel certainly can and should be studied from the historical, philological, and literary points of view according to the methodology of these sciences. Their correct use is necessary and helps us better understand the revealed message that the Gospel transmits. But one should determine when a particular methodology is reaching conclusions that question the historical character of the narrative, under the influence of certain prior assumptions, and in this way jeopardize the nature and message of the gospel of Jesus. This question will be considered here, while we show the relationship between the Synoptics and John, the possible process of composition of the fourth Gospel, and the value to be attached to its testimony, so as to demonstrate that the Gospel of John is not essentially different in its composition from the other canonical Gospels but provides a special witness to the words and works of Jesus of Nazareth.

2. Relation to the Synoptics: Common and Proper Material

Similarities between the Gospel of John and the Synoptics

As we have seen, simply reading the fourth Gospel makes one aware of its numerous differences from the Synoptics. Sometimes, though, people exaggerate and say this is a "completely different" Gospel. Before we examine the particular features of John, therefore, it is important to understand that the differences stand out precisely because of the resemblances. John and the Synoptics share the same story, the story of Jesus of Nazareth, based on a common apostolic proclamation. Otherwise, instead of speaking of differences, we would have to speak of heterogeneous realities difficult to compare.

Like the other three Gospels, John's account relates the teachings and works of Christ. Jesus, anointed by the Spirit in baptism, is the promised Messiah who manifests himself by his works and words, and reveals his glory in his passion, death, and resurrection (see chapter 1, section 1: "Testimony of the apostolic preaching"). Specifically, the beginning and the end of the story told by John follow the same sequence found in the other Gospels, beginning with John the Baptist (it speaks of his arrest in 3:24, but does not give other details) and ending with the empty tomb. Jesus preaches in Galilee and Jerusalem, passes through Samaria, is followed by twelve disciples whom he designates to continue his mission. He teaches that God is present in himself and that salvation is given to those who believe in him. He encounters opposition among the authorities that ends with his being handed over to the Romans after celebrating the Pasch with his disciples on the night before he dies. He is condemned to death by Pilate, rises on the day after the Sabbath, and appears to his disciples.[1]

While these are the basic elements common to John and the Synoptics, one could also assemble a list of sentences and an enumeration of historical data, vocabulary, and theological concepts found in all four Gospels. Each of the canonical Gospels clearly refers to the same history and contains a narrative that coincides in its essentials with the others.

Differences between the Synoptics and the Fourth Gospel

But even though the four Gospels tell the same story, the differences between the Synoptics and the Gospel of John are not

---

1. As William Davies points out, this nucleus of the story that John narrates finds its parallel in a schematic way in some of the decisive episodes of the Gospel of Mark, which in turn have parallels in the other two Synoptics: the mission of John the Baptist: 1:14–23 (compare with Mk 1:4–8); the multiplication of the loaves: 6:1–13 (compare with Mk 6:33–44); Jesus walks on the water: 6:16–21 (compare with Mk 6:45–52); the confession of Peter: 6:68–69 (compare with Mk 8:29); his entrance into Jerusalem: 12:12–15 (compare with Mk 11:1–10); the anointing in Bethany: 12:1–8 (compare with Mk 14:3–9); the Last Supper: 13:1–17:26 (compare with Mk 14:17–26); his capture: 18:1–11 (compare with Mk 14:43–52).

small ones. They involve both form and content. Let's look at the principal ones.

In relation to the structure of the account:

1. *The chronological framework.* John differs from the Synoptics in regard to the length of Jesus' ministry and the date of the Passover.

    a) From the Synoptics one might conclude that everything happens in little more than a year: the preaching in Galilee, his going up to Jerusalem, and the ministry in the Holy City, where the events of Passover occur. John, on the other hand, speaks clearly of three Passovers, corresponding to three different years. In the first one (2:13–23), Jesus is in Jerusalem, and there purifies the temple; the second (6:4) takes place a little after the first multiplication of the loaves; the third is that of the Passion and death (11:55; 12:1; 13:1, etc.). Thus the ministry would have extended over two full years, plus the months between Jesus' baptism and the first Passover.

    b) Regarding the Passover, the Synoptics agree that the disciples prepared the Last Supper "on the first day of the Azymes, when, the paschal lamb was celebrated" (Mk 14:12; see Mt 26:17; Lk 22:7). That is to say, Jesus celebrated the Last Supper in the first hours of the fifteenth day of Nisan, the day of the Passover (the day began when the sun set), and died in the last hours of that same day, before the Sabbath began. In contrast, according to the Gospel of John, Jesus ate with his disciples and died on the preparation day for the Passover (see 19:14; 19:31; 18:28), that is to say, on the fourteenth day of Nisan, the day before the Passover.

2. *The geographical framework.* The three first Gospels tell of only one going up to the Holy City during Jesus' public

ministry, that during which he died. John, on the other hand, focuses above all on the activity of Jesus in Judea and in the temple of Jerusalem, where he goes at least three times on the occasion of feasts (see 2:13; 7:10; 12:12); he refers to only a few details of Jesus' activity in Galilee. Also emphasized is his passage through Samaria (see 4:3–42). There are also differences about details of geography and topography, in which John is at times more concrete than the Synoptics: Ainon, near Salim (see 3:23); the pool of the five porticos (see 5:2), etc.

3. *Development of the account.* The Synoptics bring together episodes and sayings of Jesus easily separated from one another. John, in contrast, organizes his narrative very carefully around theological themes that are developed in dialogue or in discourses interwoven with events matter-of-factly narrated.

In relation to the narrative contents:

Some elements and significant episodes found in the Synoptics do not appear in John and vice versa.

1. The Passion aside, John contains only five narratives in common with the Synoptics; the rest are unique to his Gospel. The common narratives are: the expulsion of the merchants from the temple (2:13–16), the multiplication of the loaves (6:1–13); Jesus walking on the water (6:16–21); the anointing in Bethany (12:1–8); and the triumphal entry into Jerusalem (12:12–15). But even in these passages, John's account of events has certain features of its own.

    The fourth evangelist does not directly narrate the baptism of Jesus, the transfiguration, and the institution of the Eucharist, nor does he speak of diabolical possessions and exorcisms. In addition, the Gospel says Jesus baptized with his disciples before beginning his ministry in Galilee (although later this is nuanced). Other episodes, such as the meetings with Nicodemus and with the Samaritan woman, are proper to John.

2. Of the twenty-nine miracles that the Synoptics narrate, John refers to only two, the multiplication of the loaves and Jesus walking on the water (see 6:1–13; 6:16–21); while he speaks of five different miracles, two very significant: the wedding feast of Cana (see 2:1–11) and the resurrection of Lazarus (see 11:33–44). The other three are: the healing of the son of a royal official (see 4:46–54), the healing of the paralytic at the pool of Bethzatha (see 5:1–9); and the healing of the man born blind in Jerusalem (see 9:1–41). The most notable feature of his presentation is that he presents the miracles as "signs, that serve as a basis for John to speak of realities deeper than might at first appear.

3. In the account of Jesus' passion, death, and resurrection, the fourth Gospel coincides with the Synoptics, but it tells of these events from a separate perspective. Jesus' foretelling of his passion in the Synoptics emphasize the appropriateness of the Son of Man's suffering (see Mt 16:21); in contrast, John emphasizes the appropriateness that the Son of Man be exalted (see 3:14–15; 8:28; 12:32). The passion is Christ's glorification. At that moment his "hour" becomes manifest (see 2:4; 7:30; 13:1; 17:1); here is when the Father glorifies the Son, who, in dying, overcomes the devil, sin, and death, and is exalted above all things (cf. 12:32–33).

In relation to his teachings:

1. The content of Jesus' teaching in the fourth Gospel has nuances that distinguish it from the Synoptics. For example, he speaks only once of the kingdom of heaven (see 3:5) while the Synoptics, especially Matthew, mention it often (see Mt 3:2; 4:23; 5:3; 11:12; 13:24). Various matters with moral overtones, such as Jesus' love for sinners and for the poor (so

important in Luke), play a marginal part in John or are presented from other points of view. John does not deal with subjects that come up often in the Synoptics—the Sabbath, Pharisaical legalism, etc.—while, on the other hand, he speaks of life, truth, light, and glory, themes scarcely appearing in those terms in the first three Gospels. As for liturgical feasts of the Jewish calendar, John mentions the Passover, Feast of the Tabernacles, and the Dedication of the Temple, and displays a special interest in their significance, while the Synoptics refer only to the Passover when Jesus died.

2. There are also differences in regard to Jesus' way of teaching. In the Synoptics, Jesus uses images and parables, employing ordinary things and popular customs and speaking in simple and direct language. In John, Jesus' teaching is done through discourses in dialogue form, often polemics with the Jewish authorities. Often the language is metaphorical (for example, using the ideas of light, truth, water, the spirit, testimony of God, etc.). Especially notable are the affirmations "I AM" and other formulas of deep significance ("you in me and I in you," "remain in me," etc.). John, in addition, favors strong antitheses (light–darkness, life–death, to be of here below–to be of there above, truth–lie) and often uses expressions with a double meaning ("to exalt" meaning to be crucified and exalted; "to see, to look," in the material and spiritual sense simultaneously, etc.)

In relation to the person of Jesus:

1. In the fourth Gospel Jesus is conscious of having pre-existed with God before coming to the world: "And now, Father, glorify thou me in thy own presence with the glory which I had with thee before the world was made" (17:5). He is the Father's eternal Son who came into the world to reveal God. John applies more numerous titles to him than the Synoptics do. Besides Messiah, Son of David, Son of Man, Lord, (used

also in the three first Gospels), John also speaks of Jesus as Son, Logos, Prophet, Savior, Lamb of God, King of the Jews, and he who is sent.
2. In the Synoptics, faith in Jesus as Messiah grows until he is recognized as such when his public life is well advanced. In contrast, in the fourth Gospel the disciples recognize Jesus as Messiah and Son of God from the beginning of his ministry.

Attempts at explanation:
The obvious question in light of these resemblances and differences is whether John knew the Synoptics, was influenced by them, and wished to complete them, or whether he took up certain traditions about Jesus independently of the other Gospels.

The answer is much in dispute. In general, one might say that although dependence by John on Matthew, Mark, or Luke is not obvious, there are similarities that sometimes involve very specific details. Brown sums up as follows.

1. *Mark:* The same order of events appears in John 6 and Mark 6:31–54; 8:11–33, as do the concrete details of certain phrases: "genuine nard of great value" (Jn 12:3 and Mk 14:3), "three hundred denari" (Jn 12:5 and Mk 14:5), "two hundred denari" (Jn 6:7 and Mk 6:37).
2. *Luke:* Similarities are more in persons and events than in words: the reference to Martha and Mary, the mention of Annas, the absence of a judgment of Jesus during the night before Caiphas, the triple repetition of Pilate's judgment that Jesus was not guilty, the appearances after the Resurrection in Jerusalem to the disciples; the two disciples running to the tomb, the miraculous catch (see Jn 21:1ff and Lk 5:1ff).
3. *Matthew:* Similarities are fewer here, but one that is clear and important is John 13:16: "Truly, truly, I say to you: a servant is not greater than his master, nor is he who is sent greater than he who sent him" and Matthew 10:24: "A disciple is

not above his teacher, nor a servant above his master;" see also John 15:18–27 and Matthew 10:18–25.

Present day exegetes do not agree on dependence or independence. The most common views reflect four attempts at explanation:

   a) John is completely independent of the Synoptics because he does not know them (for example, P. Gardner-Smith). This explains the differences, but it does not account for the likenesses.
   b) John drew on Mark or one of the other Synoptics (for example, Marie-Émile Boismard, Frans Neirynck). This hypothesis explains the similarities but involves difficulties regarding John's original material.
   c) John did not know the Synoptics, but he did know the pre-Synoptic oral tradition (for example, Charles H. Dodd). This is an intermediate position that explains the points shared in common but not certain concrete questions. Taking this line, some try to be more specific: John and Mark shared the same pre-gospel tradition, oral or written (for example, Bultmann, Brown, Schnackenburg). Although John had not seen the written version of Luke, he was familiar with the traditions Luke incorporated into the third Gospel (for example, Julius Schniewind, John A. Bailey, Anton Dauer).

4. John knew the Synoptic tradition and completed it from his own recollections. This is the traditional position of some of the Fathers of the Church such as Clement, Origen, and St. Augustine.

The dominant view is that there is no direct literary dependence on the Synoptics. But this does not rule out the idea that the Evangelist might in some way have been familiar with the written Synoptics, perhaps as a result of reading material drawn from the Synoptic Gospels for use in liturgical ceremonies. In any case, the tradition reflected in the words and works of Jesus as presented in John should be considered just as ancient as those in the first three Gospels.

It is therefore possible that there was no literal dependence of John on the Synoptics—that is to say, John did not have all or any of the Synoptics before him while writing his Gospel—and it is also possible that John did not consciously try to complete the other three Gospels and give us a portrait of Jesus more elevated than theirs. Even so, the fourth Gospel did complete and go more deeply into the contents of the other three by taking up certain specific subjects for examination from its own point of view.

3. The Selective Character of John

On the supposition that John's Gospel is an apostolic witness and that the Evangelist offered that testimony following a process of selection among abundant materials available to him, we can call John selective. Let us consider an example.

In the first Christian generation, the transcendent character of the revelation of the Son of God in the world caused it to be seen as something like light. The image of light symbolized divine revelation and helped illuminate the mystery of God and man. For Paul, vocation is an interior illumination. The Letter to the Hebrews says of Christians that they are illuminated. Baptism was called *photismos*, illumination. But these expressions are derivative. The true light is Jesus. Referring to the preaching of Jesus, St. Matthew shows this clearly at the beginning of his public life: "The people who sat in darkness have seen a great light, and for those who sat in the region and shadow of death light has dawned" (4:16). St. Luke, in the *nunc dimittis* of Simeon at the presentation of our Lord in the temple, makes the same point: Jesus is the "light for revelation to the Gentiles and for glory to thy people Israel" (2:32). More examples could be given, but these will suffice.

John thought deeply and comprehensively about this reality. What the other evangelists said in passing, he made one of his principal themes. From his Prologue on he speaks of the light that illuminates the world; that light, a traditional image of the presence of revelation, he identifies with the revealer. He presents divine reality as it manifested itself in Christ (1 John illustrates this theme abundantly). He treats extensively this manifestation of Jesus as the light of the world throughout the whole of his Gospel (the term *light* appears twenty-five times). This is how Jesus refers to himself at the Feast of Tabernacles, when great bonfires that illuminated all of Jerusalem were lit at the corners of the temple. And the idea is abundantly explained in the episode of the curing of the man blind from birth.

Jesus is the Light of the World in regard to which one must make a decision. There is a close link between the light, considered as a manifestation of the truth, and the judgment pronounced upon man regarding his attitude toward this true light (see 9:39–41). Jesus has brought the light that judges: "This is the judgment, that the light has come into the world, and men loved darkness rather than light, because their deeds were evil" (3:19).

We could pause to consider each of these aspects mentioned: light, judgment, truth, and many others present in the Gospel. But here I refer only to light, to illustrate the Evangelist's selectiveness in taking elements from the apostolic preaching to show their implications in detail. Another clear example is the Eucharist. Rather than giving an account of its initiation, he speaks of it at length in the discourse on the Bread of Life.

In addition, John is selective not only in relation to certain themes, but in the very focus he gives the Gospel. For example, as Benedict XVI recalls in his book *Jesus of Nazareth*, Jesus' dispute with the Jewish authorities of the temple, taken as a whole, anticipates his future trial before the Sanhedrin, which John, unlike the Synoptics, no longer treats as a trial in the proper sense. Instead, he is concerned to show from the start that Jesus is the Word made flesh whose entire ministry made up the trial that ended with his being condemned to death. That is to say, John sees the whole life of Jesus as his trial before the world, by which the One Judged judges the world.

Examples could be multiplied, but the point is simply that, out of the abundant material at his disposal, the Evangelist chose that which suited his intention in writing.

4. The Composition of the Gospel

The process of the Gospel's composition offers several clues to the special character of John and his difference from the Synoptics. The text as it has come to us shows that the Evangelist composed it in stages. It appears that there was not one writer but several, as the following features suggest.

The Two Endings

The final chapter of John (21:1–25) is an appendix added by someone close to the beloved disciple. This can be deduced from the verses which precede it (20:30–31), where we find a first epilogue or conclusion to the Gospel: "Now Jesus did many other signs in the presence of the disciples, which are not written in this book; but these are written that you may believe that Jesus is the Christ, the Son of God, and that believing you may have life in his name." The text refers to the fact that other material existed that the author of the Gospel could have included but did not.

Following this, the Gospel tells of the miraculous catch of fish in Galilee, the triple confession of St. Peter, his confirmation in the primacy, and Jesus' prophecy about the death of the beloved disciple. It closes with another ending: "This is the disciple who is bearing witness to these things, and who has written these things; and we know that his testimony is true. But there are also many other things which Jesus did; were every one of them to be written, I suppose that the world itself could not contain the books that would be written" (21:24–25).

The words "this is the disciple" refer to the beloved disciple, of whom it is said in the previous verse that some thought he was not going to die (see 21:23) and who gives testimony to the death of Jesus in 19:35: "He who saw it has borne witness—his testimony is true, and he knows that he tells the truth—that you also may believe." But the writer of the final chapter speaks in the first person plural ("we know") and is, therefore, different from the beloved disciple.

These two endings suggest that, rather than conclude the Gospel in its primary form (and probably before it entered into circulation), someone made some additions. This is thought to have been someone other than the one who composed the first edition, since that first writer would have felt free to include the material now contained in chapter 21 before the ending composed for chapter 20. Thus it is commonly supposed that the present chapter 21 was added after the Evangelist had died. The appendix then points to the conclusion that not one person but at least two had a hand in the Gospel as it has come to us: the Evangelist who composed the body of the Gospel and a writer who later made additions—at least chapter 21 and probably some other passages throughout the Gospel.

Differences of Style

Chapter 21 differs from the rest of the Gospel by its language. Certain terms are peculiar to it. The same is true of the Prologue, whose poetic style distinguishes it from the rest of the Gospel and uses some theological concepts that do not recur elsewhere in the book. These differences, too, suggest that more than one hand was involved in the writing.

Gaps in the Narrative

Certain features of the Gospel suggest that it was composed in stages: For instance, several rapid transitions take the reader by surprise.

1. The connection of chapters 14—15. In 14:31, Jesus ends his address with the words: "Rise, let us go hence." This would fit well with the beginning of chapter 18: "When Jesus had spoken these words, he went forth with his disciples across the Kidron valley." Before that, however, we have a prolonged discourse and the priestly prayer (chapters 15—17).
2. The succession of chapters 5—7. Chapter 4 ends in Galilee; chapter 5 describes Jesus in Jerusalem; chapter 6 shows Jesus back in Galilee. Chronologically and geographically considered, chapter 6 seems a logical continuation of 4, which tells of the second trip of Jesus to Galilee, while chapters 5 and 7 take place in Jerusalem.
3. The beginning of chapter 10. The discourse on the Good Shepherd (see 10:1-8) seems to interrupt the thread of what Jesus is saying at the end of chapter 9 about the blindness of the Jews (see 9:40-41), a theme that could continue in 10:19-21, where we find the reaction of "the Jews" to the healing of the blind man.
4. The sequence of chapter 7. The reference in 7:20-24 to having cured a man on the Sabbath would seem to go better with the account of the cure of the paralytic in 5:1-8.

Duplications and Repetitions

At times the Gospel repeats the same thing in a different form and with new theological nuances. For example, 3:31-36 (where it is not clear who is speaking) seems to duplicate things said in 3:7, 11-13, and 15-18 about the descent and ascent of the Son of Man and the need to believe in him; 5:25-29 is like an elaboration of 5:24: "He who hears my word and believes him who sent me, has eternal life; he does not come into judgment, but has passed from death to life;" what is said in 14:1–31, about Jesus' going to the Father and the sending of the Holy Spirit appears again in 16:4–33.

Proposed Solutions

How can one explain these gaps and instances of apparent abruptness? Is this the work of a single author? Did several hands introduce material later? Numerous explanations have been proposed, but none of them satisfies everyone.

It has been said that the gaps in the narrative reflect a displacement after the author's death of the various parts of the book (perhaps accidentally in reorganizing individual pages, or perhaps intentionally at the hands of an editor-disciple seeking to put order in the original that he received). But this hypothesis creates more problems than it resolves.

Some explain the differences of style and content, the gaps in the editing, the duplications, etc., by the Evangelist's use of other documents. The theory of the three sources, proposed by Rudolf Bultmann in the last century, has been an influential hypothesis. According to Bultmann, the sources adopted by the author in composing his work were three: 1) collection of signs (*Semeiaquelle*) consisting of a number of miracles selected from a broader collection; 2) source, originally in a poetical form in Aramaic (*Offenbarungsredenquelle*), containing the discourses of a revealer from heaven, translated into Greek and adapted so as to serve as discourses of the Johannine Jesus; and 3) narrative of the Passion, taken from the Synoptic material.

The most widely held view today is that the hypothetical sources share so many common features as to call their existence into question. The hypothesis of a source of discourses based on parallels dating to a time after the writing of the Gospel and not Christian but Gnostic has been rejected; stylistic consideration provide no sufficient basis for affirming their existence. Still, some authors think that, although there is no source of the discourses, John does draw on the other two sources proposed by the German exegete. So, for example, Robert Fortna has argued that the source of miracle accounts and of the Passion is a "Gospel of Signs."

Some feel the apparent disorder can be explained by the fact that John offers a highly schematic account of Jesus' ministry and is not concerned with the transitions unless they have a theological purpose (for example, the careful sequence of days in chapters 1—2). That schematic character can also be seen in the series of feast days in chapters 2, 5, 6, 7, and 10 that serve as a framework for the ministry of Jesus, where little attention is paid to the long interval that separates them.

Finally, others think the Evangelist wrote his book in stages, adding new material to what he had already written. A variation on this hypothesis holds that, if not the Evangelist himself, then some final editor responsible for the Johannine tradition collected and added ideas or traditions, such as the appearance in Galilee, not included in the written version he had received and not part of the Evangelist's original plan: Not wanting these traditions to be lost, this writer added them to the Gospel. He might also have added other things resembling the text in its primitive form (perhaps because they originated in the same preaching that was the source of that text.)

In any case, the data all point to a Gospel elaborated in different stages in which more than one person must have collaborated. The hypotheses about their composition are many and varied and have not been reconciled. Still, a possible explanation, starting with the Gospel's eyewitness character and its development within a Johannine community, could be as follows.

The work presents the testimony of the beloved disciple, whom tradition identifies with John the apostle. The Gospel's content corresponds to and originates in the testimony of this disciple. What he taught and preached was put into writing in various stages under the assistance of the Holy Spirit until it reached its present form. In the process of compilation within the circle of the disciples of the beloved disciple, the priest (author of the second and third epistles of John) might have intervened as the party responsible for preserving the tradition received from the beloved disciple, playing a key role in the definitive redaction of the Gospel text and of 1 John.

Clearly, this is one among many possible explanations of the complex composition of the Gospel. But more important than any particular attempt at explanation is the fact that the fourth Gospel is an apostolic testimony that, through a special providence of God, allows us truly to know what Jesus of Nazareth did and taught.

In conclusion, one can say that the Gospel of John reflects the same three stages of composition as the Synoptics. First are memories of what Jesus did and said, not always the same as those preserved in the other three canonical Gospels. Second, the recollections preserved by the beloved disciple were influenced by the experiences communities with which he had ties and of the preachers who transmitted those recollections. Finally, the Evangelist gave written form to the tradition as it was transmitted in that second stage.

But this process does not refer only to certain occasional historical circumstances. As Benedict XVI points out, the fourth Gospel "rests upon the remembering of the disciple, which, however, is a co-remembering in the 'we' of the Church. This remembering is an understanding under the guidance of the Holy Spirit; by remembering, the believer enters into the depth of the event and sees what could not be seen on an immediate and merely superficial level. But in so doing he does not move away from the reality; rather, he comes to know it more deeply and thus sees the truth concealed in the outward act. The remembering of the Church is the context where what the Lord prophesied to his followers at the Last Supper actually happens: 'When the Spirit of truth comes, he will guide you into all the truth" (Jn 16:13)."[2]

Thus both the Synoptics and John are witnesses of Jesus—apostolic witnesses preserved in the most ancient tradition—that were an object of theological reflection at the time Jesus' message was adapted to subsequent believers. They were put into writing under the guidance of the Spirit until attaining the form in which they have reached us.

---

2. *Jesus of Nazareth*, vol. 1, p. 233.

Chapter 3

Content and Structure

AS WE HAVE SEEN, the Gospel's sudden transitions, repetitions, differences of style, and so on, have led some authors to see it as a compilation from various sources. But leaving all that aside, it is interesting to consider the Gospel as a unified whole, with an integral meaning as we have received it. The Church has received this text in its final form as an apostolic testimony about Jesus. For this reason, we should try to understand it according to the way in which it has been preserved.

To this end, it is useful to establish the narrative structure of the work. This will help us to discover what the author seeks to tell us, combining what he says with how he says it. For this purpose, we have to analyze the argument, the subject or central idea the author wishes to transmit, his point of view, and the form in which he structures his message. We need to know not only what the author is telling us and the principal message he wishes to transmit, but also how he organizes his message in coherent, related units, marking out the core elements that structure his narrative and the relations among them. Thus one can better understand both the author's intention and the text's meaning.

1. The Content of the Gospel

In order to proceed logically, it is useful before outlining the structure of the Gospel to familiarize oneself with the content of the narrative (although most readers of this book will probably have read the account more than once).

As we have seen, the fourth Gospel and the Synoptics generally follow the same schema the apostles used in their oral preaching: Jesus begins his public ministry by being baptized in the Jordan by John the Baptist, he preaches and performs miracles in Galilee and Jerusalem, and he finishes his life on earth with his passion, death, and glorious resurrection. Following this pattern, the Gospel is developed as follows:

After a poetic Prologue (see 1:1–18), extolling Jesus Christ as the eternal Word of God who existed from the beginning along with the Father and who became man, the narrative begins with the witness of John the Baptist (see 1:19–34) and the calling of the first disciples, summoned by Jesus from among John's disciples and friends of theirs (see 1:35–51).

Next comes the public ministry of Jesus, beginning in Galilee with the account of the "sign" of the changing of water into wine at the marriage feast of Cana and his stay in Capernaum (see 2:1–12). This sign is followed by a first trip by Jesus to Jerusalem at Passover, when he purifies the temple (see 2:13–25) and meets with Nicodemus, a Pharisee who follows the Master secretly. After receiving further testimony from the Baptist (see 3:22–36), Jesus returns to Galilee, passing through Samaria. During this trip, he speaks with a woman at the well of the city of Sichar, where, after their encounter, he remains two days (see 4:1–45). Upon returning to Cana, he affects by his word, despite the distance, the healing of the son of a royal functionary who is sick in Capernaum (see 4:46–54).

Later, during another trip to Jerusalem in connection with a feast, Jesus cures a paralytic at the pool at Bethzatha in Jerusalem (see 5:1–18). This sign provokes a controversy with the temple authorities during which he expressly affirms his divine character (see 5:19–47). Back in Galilee, he performs the sign of the multiplication of the loaves and fishes near the Sea of Tiberias (see

6:1–15). After this miracle, he appears to his disciples walking on the water of the lake (see 6:16–21). Arriving at Capernaum with them, he delivers the discourse on the Bread of Life in the city synagogue (see 6:22–59). His words provoke conflicting reactions among his disciples (see 6:60–71).

After this episode, Jesus goes up to Jerusalem again, this time for the feast of Tabernacles (see 7:1–30), and his teaching gives rise to conflicting opinions about him (see 7:31–53). The episode of Jesus' forgiveness of the adulterous woman (see 8:1–11) is followed by other controversies with the temple authorities in which he presents himself as sent by the Father and the light of the world (see 8:12–20) and reprimands the incredulity of the Jews (see 8:21–59). On a Sabbath, Jesus cures a man born blind (see 9:1–23), and this provokes a new dispute with the Jewish authorities about his authority over the Sabbath. In the debates, Jesus points to the blindness of the rulers of the people (see 9:24–41) and presents himself as the Good Shepherd (see 10:1–21). Later, during the feast of the Dedication, he again affirms his union with the Father (see 10:22–39).

Next Jesus retires to the other side of the Jordan (see 10:40–42). Later he goes to Bethany, near Jerusalem, where he raises Lazarus and presents himself as one with the power to resurrect and to grant eternal life (see 11:1–44). This sign moves the Jewish authorities to decide on his death, and that leads Jesus to retreat to a city called Ephraim, near the desert (see 11:45–57). Six days before the Pasch, he returns to Bethany, where he is anointed by Mary (see 12:1–11). On the following day, he makes a triumphal entrance into Jerusalem, is acclaimed as the messianic king (see 12:12–19), and announces his glorification on the Cross (see 12:20–36). Following this, and as a compendium and epilogue of what has been said so far, the Evangelist offers considerations on the need for faith in Jesus and on his rejection (see 12:37–50). Thus the Evangelist signals the conclusion of his account of Jesus' public ministry.

The next scene shows Jesus dining with the twelve in Jerusalem on the eve of the Passover and delivering his farewell discourse to them. First, though, he washes their feet (see 13:10–20), announces the treachery of Judas (see 13:21–32), and proclaims the new commandment, predicting also that the disciples will abandon him (see 13:33–38). In the midst of his farewell, Jesus reveals the Father (see 14:1–14), promises the Holy Spirit (see 14:15–31; 16:1–15), speaks of his union with them, using the image of the vine and the branches (see 15:1–8), again promulgates the law of love (see 15:9–17), and predicts the world's hatred toward his disciples but also their joy (see 15:18–27; 16:16–33). His discourse ends with the so-called "priestly prayer" of Jesus, expressing his consecration of those he will send into the world and asking for his disciples' unity at all times as a reflection of the unity of Persons in the mystery of God (see 17:1–26). After the supper, we have the passion and death of Jesus: his capture in the garden across the Kidron valley (see 18:1–12), the interrogation by Annas and denials of Peter (see 18:13–27), the trial before Pilate (see 18:28–19:16), Jesus' crucifixion and death (see 19:17–37), and his burial in a garden by Joseph of Arimathea and Nicodemus (see 19:38–42).

The Gospel then tells of the apparitions of the risen Christ to the apostles. Peter and the beloved disciple, whom Mary Magdalene had told of Jesus' empty tomb, come to the sepulcher and find that his body is not there (see 20:1–10). Jesus then appears to Mary, who has returned to the tomb (see 20:11–18). Later, the Evangelist relates Jesus' apparitions in the cenacle in Jerusalem, first to the apostles without Thomas and later with him; he then ends the Gospel with a conclusion explaining his purpose in writing (see 20:19–31). Immediately following, however, he goes on to describe other apparitions of the resurrected Christ (this time in Galilee). Included are a miraculous catch of fish (see 21:1–14) and a dialogue between Jesus and Simon Peter in the presence of the beloved disciple (see 21:15–23). The Gospel ends with a new conclusion (see 21:24–25).

2. Proposals for Structuring

Obviously, there are many ways of structuring this material, and the suggestions for doing so are almost as numerous as their authors.

Some proposals concentrate on thematic-literary devices employed by the Evangelist in determining the nuclei or units that shape the outline of the work (Raymond Brown, Charles Taylor). For example, the Evangelist seems frequently to use the technique of inclusion—i.e., in pointing to the beginning and end of a passage or section by repeating a detail or an allusion or an antithesis. This technique can be discerned by the analysis of more or less extended sections and even by considering the work as a whole. Thus, the Prologue's affirmation that Jesus is the eternal Word of God (1:1) has its correlative at the end of the Gospel with the words of Thomas, "My Lord and my God!" (see 20:28); ideas found in the Prologue (see 1:1-18) are scattered and amplified throughout the whole Gospel and gathered especially in the final summary of the public life as a kind of conclusion of the section (see 12:37-50). The words, "This happened in Bethany, on the other side of the Jordan where John was baptizing" (1:28) have their parallel at the end of chapter 10: "He went away again across the Jordan, to the place where John first baptized, and there he remained" (10:40), and so on.

There also are instances of inclusion delineating briefer sections. For example, "This is the testimony of John, when the Jews sent priests and Levites from Jerusalem to ask him: 'who are you?'" (1:19) is echoed by: "This took place in Bethany, beyond the Jordan, where John was baptizing" (1:28). The Evangelist: "This, the first of his signs, Jesus did at Cana of Galilee, and manifested his glory; and his disciples believed in him" (2:11) has its parallel in "This was now the second sign that Jesus did when he had come from Judea to Galilee" (4:54). See also 9:2-3 ("And his disciples asked him: 'Rabbi, who sinned; this man or his parents that he was born blind?' Jesus answered: 'It was not that this man sinned, or his parents, but that the works of God might be made manifest in him'") and 9:41 ("Jesus said to them: 'If you were blind, you would have no guilt, but now that you say, "We see," your guilt remains'"); and 11:4 ("But when Jesus heard it he said, 'This illness is not unto death; it is for the glory of God, so that the Son of God may be glorified by means of it'") and 11:40 ("Jesus said to her: 'Did I not tell you that if you believed you would see the glory of God?'"). The examples could be multiplied and testify to the Evangelist's careful structuring.

Besides suggestions that focus on literary elements, others give more attention to content or especially significant references in the text. For example, the Gospel's message has been traced by following the line of feasts mentioned (Donatien Mollat). This analysis starts from the fact that the Gospel presents the revelation of God the Father by means of the sending of his Son, the Word Incarnate, who grants eternal life to those who believe in him, but it understands revelation as concretized in the liturgical feasts of Israel that are emphasized in the work. Particular significance is attached to the fact that, although the Synoptics mention only the Sabbath and Passover, the fourth Gospel refers not only to those two feasts but two others: Feast of the Tabernacles (Booths) and the Dedication of the Temple.

Furthermore, and most important, the feasts have, according to this reading, a deeper meaning. Jesus is the new Moses, who replaces the precept of Sabbath rest (see 5:1–47); he is the Bread of Life that replaces the manna, the food the Messiah gives when he reveals himself on the night of the Passover (see 6:1–71); he is the fountain of living water and the light of the world, replacing the ceremonies of water and of life enacted at the feast of Tabernacles that point to messianic times (see 7:1–10:21); he is the one consecrated to God in place of the altar of the temple, whose consecration was celebrated at the feast of the Dedication, and the true Lamb of God, condemned to death at the hour when the lambs for the paschal meal were sacrificed in the temple.

In short, according to this schema, the Evangelist sought to show that Jesus brought to fulfillment the liturgical celebrations and worship of ancient Israel, inaugurating a new and unitary spiritual worship in his own Person, which is that of the Eternal Word of the Father, who became man and "pitched his tent" among humankind. Jesus is the new temple of the Lord, where men can enter into direct contact with God.[1]

Along the same lines, some authors (Aileen Guilding, Michael Goulder) have gone further and proposed a structuring according to which the Gospel is a Christian commentary on the cycle of readings of the Law in Jewish worship—in effect, a Judeo-Christian commentary on the three-year cycle of Old Testament readings in synagogue worship. This hypothesis is very difficult to demonstrate, inasmuch as very little is known about actual Jewish worship in the first century of the Christian era. Still, it is clear that Jesus' revelations about himself in the fourth Gospel are related to aspects of the worship of the people of Israel.

Other proposals focus on matters of symbolism. Some think the Gospel may be structured around the number seven, whose presence is clear in the narrative (Marc Girard, Marie-Émile Boismard). Thus, we find seven signs of Jesus: the changing of water into wine (see 2:1–1), the cure of the son of a royal official in Capernaum (see 4:46–54), the cure of the paralytic at the pool (see 5:1–9), the multiplication of loaves (see 6:1–13), his walking on the water (6:16–21), the cure of the man born blind (see 9:1–7), and the resurrection of Lazarus (see 11:1–44). On seven occasions Jesus says, "I am," followed by a noun as predicate: "I am the bread of life" (6:35), "the light of the world" (8:12), "the door" (10:7), "the good shepherd" (10:1), "the resurrection and the life" (11:25), "the way, and the truth, and the life" (14:6), and "the vine" (15:1). Seven testimonies in favor of Jesus were reported: that of the Baptist (see 1:8), of Jesus himself (see 3:11), of his works (see 5:36), of

---

[1]. This is the same idea that we find in the Letter to the Colossians, which speaks of Christ as the place in which "the whole fullness of deity dwells bodily" (2:9).

the Father (see 5:37), of the Scriptures (see 5:39), of the apostles (see 15:27), and of the Holy Spirit (see 16:8–11). Seven days pass between the initial testimony of John the Baptist and the wedding feast of Cana ("on the following day," repeated three times, 1:29, 35, 43, and later "on the third day," 2:1). Jesus makes seven trips through Palestine (see 1:43; 2:12; 2:13; 4:3, 46; 5:1; 6:1; 7:10). Seven scenes comprise the process before Pilate, and so on.

Still, one should not exaggerate the importance of seven as a structural key, even though its repetition cannot be dismissed as coincidence. In fact, a structural proposal by the Anglican exegete Charles H. Dodd, which in part assumes the symbolic value of seven, has had considerable influence on later studies. Dodd studied the fourth Gospel from the perspective of key ideas—eternal life, the knowledge of God, truth, the Spirit, the Word, light, glory, and judgment—and divided the Gospel into three major parts: prelude (see 1:1–18, Prologue, and 1:19–51, testimonies); the "book of signs" (see chapters 2—12); and the "book of the Passion" (see chapters 13—20, with chapter 21 as an appendix). He also analyzed the "book of signs" in seven episodes (not all, however, with a sign at their center): the new beginning (see 2:1—4:42); the Word that gives life (4:46—5:47); the Bread of Life (see chapter 6); the Light and the Life—manifestation and rejection (see chapters 7—8); the judgment by the Light (see 9:1—10:21, with an appendix in 10:22–39); the victory of life over death (see 11:1–53); life through death—the significance of the Cross (see 12:1–36); and, an epilogue to these seven episodes (see 12:37–50).

For Dodd, the key to understanding the book is found in chapters 2—4, where the inauguration of a new order of life in the Word made flesh is manifested in a succession of symbols expressing this newness: new wine, new worship, new birth, new couple, new water that gives life, new people where before there had been two, new life. And all of it is marked by the two signs in Cana: the transformation of water into wine (see 2:1–11) and the healing of the son of the royal functionary (see 4:46–54).

Consistent with this structure, signs alternate with discourses, transmitting teaching by stages, so that a later episode assumes an earlier one, with frequent allusions to earlier episodes, until we reach the culmination of the Gospel, the death and resurrection of Jesus. This interpretation has been compared to a path that winds upwards around a mountain, each turn uncovering new perspectives, or to the waves rushing one after another toward shore as the tide rises.

These are just some ways of looking at the Gospel, but there are certainly many more. Some interpreters, taking a theological-symbolic perspective, think the Evangelist drew the plan of his work from an Old Testament subject such as creation or the exodus. Others, such as R. Alan Culpepper, view the narrative as a drama centered on the Passion. Some, concentrating on chronological and geographical details, draw the structure of the work from the indications of place and time (i.e., Ernest-Bernard Allo, John Henry Bernard), others from Jesus' journeys (i.e., Mathias Rissi). Although none are conclusive, all have a certain validity and are complementary in a sense since all shed light on important points the Evangelist wished to make.

3. Structural Elements

Without dismissing any of these proposals, then, it may be helpful to focus on certain points made by the Evangelist that are fundamental to understanding the Gospel's development. We find a key in the first conclusion of the Gospel: "Jesus did many other signs in the presence of the disciples, which are not written in this book; but these are written that you may believe that Jesus is the Christ, the Son of God, and that believing you may have life in his name" (see 20:30–31).

This says we have before us a work that collects a number of signs to foster readers' faith in Jesus as Messiah and the Son of God, that they may come to possess a "life" not of the natural order. The fundamental elements thus seem to be signs, faith, and eternal life.

1. *Signs.* We have already seen what these are. The point here is that the Evangelist wished to show their consequences for the people who witnessed them. This is apparent from the discussions of their meaning after Jesus has performed them. The Evangelist emphasizes that although the signs are sufficient to arouse faith in the first disciples, they are not sufficient to sustain belief in him. The disciples who began to believe in Jesus in response to the sign performed in Cana (see 2:11) need to persevere in faith in the face of difficulties. For the signs themselves do not settle matters once and for all, but are rather occasions for determining whether the disciples really believe in him. So, for instance, Jesus' announcement that he will give his body as food, which is closely related to the sign of the multiplication of the loaves and fishes, led some of his disciples to cease following him.

2. *Faith.* The signs therefore relate to the beginnings of faith but do not in themselves suffice for faith. The reason is the newness and radicalism of faith's content, as appears from the words of the conclusion quoted above. To believe that Jesus is the *Son of God* means accepting the novelty of the revelation he brings that continues through his glorification on the Cross.

Although the formula "Son of God" could be accepted by a Jewish contemporary of Jesus, the title's meaning goes much further. At the beginning of the Gospel, the Evangelist shows that John the Baptist and the first disciples recognized Jesus as the Messiah, the Christ or Anointed One of God. John the Baptist affirms that Jesus was anointed by the Holy Spirit at his baptism (see 1:33) and is the Son of God (see 1:34); similar witness is given by the first followers of Jesus, who called him "King" (Messiah) and "Son of God" (see 1:41, 49). Nevertheless, in referring thus to Jesus, they used those titles in the traditional sense given them among the people of Israel. The king of Israel, the anointed of the Lord, was the Son of God, insofar as he represented the people, personifying Israel as the Lord's firstborn, who had been chosen by him. For the first disciples, Jesus was that anticipated Messiah who was to come to save his people. Initially, they could understand what it meant to be Messiah only as it was presented in the Jewish Scriptures. As Benedict XVI says, the disciples "rightly drew upon the Old Testament's words of promise: Christ, the Anointed One, Son of God, Lord. These are the key words on which their confession focused, while still tentatively searching for a way forward. It could arrive at its complete form only when Thomas, touching the wounds of the Risen Lord, cried out, in amazement: 'My Lord and My God' (Jn 20:28)."[2]

What the Evangelist sought to show was precisely how Jesus, by means of signs and words, revealed himself as Son of God properly so called: as God's natural son and eternal Son of the Father. For the Jews of that day, this was something absolutely new and unsuspected, heralded in Jesus' response to the confession of Jewish faith pronounced by Nathaniel: "You are the Son of God! You are the King of Israel!" (1:49). Jesus replied: "You shall see greater things than these. . . . You shall see heaven opened, and the angels of God ascending and descending upon the Son of man" (1:50–51). Thus the Gospel might be said to be an explanation and development of these words of Jesus, a series of "greater things," until the final confession of Thomas: "My Lord and my God" (20:28).

Therefore, proceeding along lines suggested by M. Fabbri, one can structure the Gospel in two stages, corresponding to its traditional division with the "book of signs" and "book of glory," the first leading to the second. At Cana, Jesus manifests his glory to his disciples by working the first of his signs. We are told elsewhere in the Gospel that these signs that glorify Jesus nevertheless do not

---

2. Benedict XVI, *Jesus of Nazareth*, vol. 1, pp. 304–305.

show his full glory, which is only seen later (see 7:39; 11:4–40; 12:16) at his "hour," the hour of his death, when he is raised on the Cross. Then "the heavens are opened" and people will have definitive access to God by faith in him. Then his raising on the Cross will be visible to all as a means of his glorification and will exercise a great attraction on all (see 12:32). That is because his death is followed by his resurrection, the manifestation and guarantee that those who believe in Jesus will have eternal life.

3. *Eternal life*. Faith in the Messiah as the Son of God in the strong sense is not limited to belief in a certain number of truths whose acceptance guarantees salvation. Rather, it is a pathway to eternal life. But what does this eternal life consist in? Again it can be said that the Evangelist gives his answer in stages, in line with the two main parts of the Gospel.

The life Jesus brings is dominant in the "book of signs," while in the "book of glory" the central subject is the eternal and Trinitarian character of that life. Jesus' signs show that he is life and brings life; the readers of the Gospel should participate in that life through faith in Jesus who was crucified and died. Not only will they attain a life that endures after death—they will have "eternal" life here on earth as well.

Eternal life in the fourth Gospel is nothing else than participation by means of the Spirit in the life of Jesus and so in the love of God revealed and made incarnate in him. It is life in its fullness in this world, loving as Jesus loved, and also in the future life, in definitive union with God. "Eternal life is not—as the modern reader might immediately assume—life after death, in contrast to this present life, which is transient and not eternal. 'Eternal life' is life itself, real life. This is the point: to seize 'life' here and now, real life that can no longer be destroyed by anything or anyone."[3]

---

3. Benedict XVI, *Jesus of Nazareth*, II, pp. 82–83.

4. Structure

An approach to sketching the Gospel's structure is then possible in light of what has been said. We begin with the foundation on which the Evangelist bases the "greater things"—things superior to what pious Israelites awaited—by which one sees Jesus in relation to the eternal life that he brings. In the first part of the Gospel, the Evangelist teaches the superiority and newness of Jesus, "the greater things," in reference to Israel. An Israelite who has fulfilled God's will as expressed in the Law, the Torah, now finds true life in Jesus.

John progressively teaches the superiority of Jesus and the life he brings. First he shows the absolute novelty of Jesus and his new way of relating to God. With Jesus, a new spousal covenant is established between God and man. He is superior to the institutions of the people of Israel, including the temple and its ceremonies (see chapters 2—4). He is superior as well to the Torah, the foundation of the very life of the people, since he is the Word that gives life (see chapter 5). In fact, he is the food of life, superior to the food Moses gave them (see chapter 6). He is the life which is light and gives light (see chapters 7—9). And insofar as he is Light, he has the capacity to reveal those who accept or reject that life (see chapters 9—10). It is not to be understood metaphorically; the life Jesus offers is life in its proper sense because he has power over death (see chapter 11) and gave life to others when he died on the Cross (see chapter 12).

In the second part, the Evangelist no longer stresses Jesus' superiority in relation to Israel; rather, in line with Jesus' words to Nathaniel, "You will see the heavens opened," the object of attention here is not only Israel but the whole of humanity. Jesus does not say, "You, Israel, will see greater things," but, "You [all of humankind] will see the heavens opened"—you will see the glory of God. This second part will show and specify the eternal, universal character of that life Jesus is and brings.

The Evangelist does this by linking life to love, as at the beginning of the narrative of the "book of glory": "Now before the feast of the Passover, when Jesus knew that his hour had come to depart out of this world to the Father, having loved his own who were in the world, he loved them to the end" (13:1). The heavens open in the face of Jesus' love. He gives his life for love—the life that was absolutely new and unequaled, the love that was no less than the very love with which God gave his Son: "For God so loved the world that he gave his only Son, that whoever believes in him should not perish but have eternal life" (3:16).

The quality and intensity of that love is shown in the account of the Passion following the Last Supper (see chapter 13), in Jesus' words of farewell (see chapters 14,—16), and in the "Priestly Prayer" that he directs to the Father (see chapter 17). What he expresses and shows at the supper is explained and confirmed in his trial (see chapter 18), death (see chapter 19), and resurrection (see chapter 20): there is no greater love than the love of one who gives his life for those he loves (see 15:13). Jesus' expiation on the Cross is the pouring out of that love (see 19:30: he "gave up his spirit") to all those who believe in him. The Resurrection confirms that God has the power to extend that love, which conquers death and gives a life without end: Jesus' life is eternal because God's love is eternal. This is the new life that enables the new man to live, as God made Adam live, breathing upon him the breath of life (see 20:22: "He breathed on them, and said to them, 'Receive the Holy Spirit'").

5. The Prologue and Chapter 21

In line with what has been said, the conclusion of chapter 20 provides the key elements to establish a possible structure for the Gospel. But something must be said about the so-called Prologue (see 1:1–18) and the final chapter of the Gospel, which seems to be an appendix (see 21:1–31). Both have features of their own and could be additions to an existing body of the work—an introduction and an afterthought, as it were.

Exegetes disagree on whether the Prologue was an already existing poetic piece used by the Evangelist in his account (perhaps a hymn sung in the Church of Ephesus) and more or less adapted to suit the Gospel, or whether he composed it either before or after writing his work. In any case, the Prologue contains in summary form what the rest of the Gospel develops in full. A relationship can be discerned between what it says and the two main parts of the Gospel: First, that Jesus, life and light, came to his own, the people of Israel, and they did not receive him (see 1:11) despite the signs, "the great things" they witnessed; and second, that to those who received him, his disciples, "he gave the power to become children of God" (1:12), making them participants in his divine life, "opening the heavens to them."

The Prologue also gives the reader a key for understanding the Gospel as the Evangelist understood it, even while disappearing, so to speak, in order to give his testimony from God's point of view. Without the Prologue, the text proceeds very much as the Synoptics do, tracing the progressive revelation of Jesus as the Messiah desired by Israel. Jesus' disciples gradually acquire more understanding than the rest of those who hear his words and witness his works, but only in becoming witnesses of his death and resurrection do they acquire a full understanding of what it means for Jesus to be Messiah. This is to say that without the Prologue, the fourth Gospel would have a narrative form closer to that of the Synoptics, placing the reader in the situation of Jesus' companions, until, the words and signs of Christ having taken on their full significance in light of his death and resurrection, they reached the ultimate understanding expressed in the confession of Thomas.

With the inclusion of the Prologue, however, the reader is allowed the advantage of already knowing "the greater things"—knowing more, that is, than those who met Jesus and little by little grew in faith in him. The Prologue says at once that Jesus is the eternal Word of the Father through whom all things were made: he is the Word become man, the only begotten Son of God, who is in the bosom of the Father and is the only one who can reveal the Father's face. The reader thus knows from the beginning what the glorification of Jesus means. And so "the heavens are now opened." With this key, he can understand the often enigmatic words of Jesus found in the Gospel; he will participate also in the faith of the Evangelist, who wishes to avoid any hint of being a protagonist. The protagonist is Jesus, the Son of God, and all the author of the Gospel wants is that his readers believe in Jesus and, believing, have life through the revelation that he brings (see 20:31).

The appendix reaffirms the Evangelist's practice of stepping aside so that Jesus is constantly front and center. Like the Prologue, it too presents a summing up of the whole Gospel. Not, however, in a poetic form, but through a narrative drawing its conclusion from what the rest of the Gospel affirms. The disciples' ignorance about Jesus (whom they do not recognize when they are fishing) gives way to faith in him: from the sign of the fish to communion with the resurrected One. It also explains what Jesus' glorification through dying means in practice. A disciple who believes, as Peter does, and has been freed of his sins should take up the cross of our Lord and follow his Master. Hence the triple reparation for Peter's denial: "You know that I love you" (21:15–17) and the words of the risen Lord: "'Truly, truly, I say to you, when you were young, you girded yourself and walked where you would; but when you are old, you will stretch out your hands, and another will gird you and carry you where you do not wish to go.' (This he said to show by what death he was to glorify God.) And after this he said to him, 'Follow me'" (21:18–19).

The appendix also gives a finishing touch to the Gospel. Like a colophon, the final item of a book, where one frequently finds the name of the printer and the place and date of printing, the words of 21:24 are: "This is the disciple who is bearing witness to these things, and who has written these things; and we know that his testimony is true." Those who have collected the testimony of the beloved disciple (the printers, as it were) are his disciples, who know his testimony is true. Implicitly, they situate the Gospel's place of publication in the universal Church, guided by Peter, and not a marginal community. No date of composition is required, since the Gospel is always timely: what matters is that readers in every age are part of the "we" who give the true testimony found in the Gospel.

Chapter 4

JESUS' SIGNS

WE SAW IN THE PRECEDING CHAPTER that the primary conclusion of the Gospel contains the fundamental elements that enable us to understand its structure: "Now Jesus did many other signs in the presence of the disciples, which are not written in this book; but these are written that you may believe that Jesus is the Christ, the Son of God, and that believing you may have life in his name" (20:30–31).

This follows the confession of Thomas, which ends with Jesus' words: "Have you believed because you have seen me? Blessed are those who have not seen and yet believe" (20:29). The book could have ended here, but following this, and by way of conclusion, the Evangelist states precisely his reason for writing. Henceforth "those who have not seen"—the readers of the Gospel—can believe on the basis of the testimony of Jesus' companions. This testimony has been collected in writing in the fourth Gospel, a communication by those who have seen to those who have not, enabling the latter to believe. Everything is directed at fostering faith in Jesus, so that the reader will believe in him. To that end, the writer makes use of some signs from among the many Jesus performed, and these signs therefore occupy a central place in the Gospel. They are directly related to its content and purpose.

1. Significance of Signs in the Old Testament

In the Old Testament miracles are generally called "prodigies" (*mophetim*), "signs" (*'ôtot*), or "works" (*maaseh*). The terms are translated into Greek, respectively, as *térata*, *sêmeia*, and *erga* (or *dynameis*). They are usually related to extraordinary events, and it is not always easy to grasp the particular purposes they serve.

a) The "prodigies" (*mophetim*) are wonderful or marvelous events, containing an element of strangeness or rarity.

b) The "signs" (*'ôtot*) place more emphasis on the purpose of a powerful or extraordinary action. They do not necessarily connote the miraculous; *'ôt* by itself signifies a pledge or sign between two men, or between God and a man, or at times a sign of things to come, such as a foreshadowing or portent. It is applied especially to the symbolic actions of the prophets.

c) The "works" (*ma'asim*) is a more neutral term that can also be applied to the acts of God.

The two first terms have the most importance in the Old Testament. For example, when God grants to Moses power to change a staff into a serpent and make leprosy appear or disappear on his hand, he adds: "If they will not believe you, or heed the first sign, they may believe the latter sign. If they will not believe even these two signs or heed your voice, you shall take some water from the Nile and pour it upon the dry ground; and the water which you shall take from the Nile will become blood upon the dry ground" (Ex 4:8–9). The Hebrew text calls the act of turning the staff into a serpent, and the appearance and disappearance of the leprosy *'ôt*, "a sign." That is because the actions extend beyond their own significance to the power of God which he has conceded to Moses. Their significance does not stop with the astonishment they might cause but refers to something more—to the power of God.

As has been said, however, there are also actions that, without being prodigious, can be converted into signs. We find examples in the prophets. The Book of Isaiah says God ordered the prophet to walk as though he were a prisoner of war, half naked and barefoot (see 20:1–6). This was to be a sign to his contemporaries that this was how those who entrusted themselves to the protection of Egypt and Ethiopia would be carried off by the Assyrians. In the Book of Jeremiah, the prophet walks at God's order with a yoke on his neck (see 27:1ff). This signifies that Jerusalem should not try to free itself from the Babylonian yoke but should submit to it to save its life; only submission to Nebuchadnezzar would bring peace and well-being. In the Book of Ezekiel, the Lord commands the prophet to construct a model of Jerusalem besieged and then turn it on its left side for 390 days (see 4:1ff). The action meant the Lord had set the dates for the events that would occur in the holy city.

In all of these cases, acts performed by the prophets symbolized realities to which they wished to point. The actions corresponded to something ordained by God to occur in the real world. More than mere illustrations, they were inspired by God and were efficacious actions meant to lead those who witnessed them to convert or change their attitude. The sign helped in the realization of what was signified; the symbol in a sense contained the thing symbolized.

2. The Signs Found in the Fourth Gospel

In referring to the miracles of Jesus, the Synoptics frequently use the word *dynameis*, which means "acts of power." These actions of Jesus have to do above all with the establishment of the kingdom of God and manifest Jesus' special authority over Satan, as the expulsion of demons and the healings make clear. The extraordinary element of Jesus' action is therefore emphasized together with the reaction of the people who praise God after witnessing the miracle. In addition, faith is normally required for Jesus to work a miracle.

In the fourth Gospel, by contrast, John does not use the word *dynameis* to designate a miracle. Instead he employs two terms: *ergon*, "work," and *semeion*, "sign" (which, in the Synoptics, usually refers to signs of the last times or signs that prove something). "Works" refers to all of God's liberating action during the Exodus; "signs" refers to what God worked by means of Moses. Specifically, John uses these two terms to show who God is, the purpose of his activity, his glory, and his relationship with the Father.

The word *ergon*, meaning "work," expresses the divine aspect of something done. Therefore, it was applied by Jesus to his own actions. Hence the fourth Gospel contains frequent references—especially in dialogues with the Jewish authorities—to "works" of his that manifest his divine condition.

The term *sêmeion*, meaning "sign," which appears seventeen times in John, indicates the human perspective, directing attention not so much to the miraculous itself as to what the miracle reveals to those who see beyond it. This is something that truly takes place yet contains a more profound meaning than the literal event. The actions to which the term "sign" is explicitly applied are considered miraculous, although the word does not originally refer to that which is miraculous, nor is it always used to designate miracles. In any case, it can usually be translated as a "miraculous sign."

For example, (2:11); "This, the first of his (miraculous) *signs*, Jesus did at Cana in Galilee, and manifested his glory; and his disciples believed in him"; (2:23); "Now when he was in Jerusalem at the Passover feast, many believed in his name when they saw the (miraculous) signs which he did"; (3:2); "This man came to Jesus by night and said to him, 'Rabbi, we know that you are a teacher come from God; for no one can do these (miraculous) signs that you do, unless God is with him.'"

In addition, John treats other actions of Jesus as signs, in the manner of the signs of the Old Testament prophets. Some of these actions, like the purification of the temple or the washing of feet, are especially revealing.

One should also recall that, in Hellenistic Judaism, the variations of *semeion-semainein* are used with special reference to symbolic signification. Philo, for example, finds in words of the Old Testament an ordinary literal meaning and a symbolic meaning. "Sign" is thus very close to "symbol" and to the action's significant or symbolic meaning. In this sense, the Evangelist wanted all the events narrated in the Gospel to be understood as signifying events—as "symbols"—that at times should be interpreted in light of the discourses that accompany them and at other times according to the methods and conceptions of the Evangelist.

In contrast to the Synoptics, in John the number of "miracles" is rather small. Traditionally, seven miracles are pointed out. They are found especially from chapters 2 through 12. This first part of the Gospel has for this reason been called the "book of signs." These seven signs are the following:

a) The changing of water into wine at the marriage feast in Cana of Galilee (see 2:1–11).
b) The cure of the son of a royal functionary (see 4:46–54).
c) The cure of a paralytic next to the pool of Bethzatha (see 5:1–16).
d) The multiplication of the loaves (see 6:1–13).
e) Jesus walks on the waters of the Sea of Galilee (see 6:16–21).
f) The cure of the man born blind at the pool of Siloam (see 9:1–17).
g) The resurrection of Lazarus (see 11:1–44).

Not all writers agree with this list. Some include among the signs the purification of the temple (see 2:13–22), or do not count Jesus' walking on the waters (see 6:16–21), or add the miraculous catch after the Resurrection (see 21:1–14).

In most cases, these signs are a point of departure for dialogues or discourses in which Jesus transmits his teachings. This is a characteristic feature of the Gospel; everything is interrelated, and each section must be seen in light of all the rest.

The sequence is reversed in the second part of the Gospel, the so-called "book of glory" (see 13:1—20:31). The passion and death of Jesus (see 18:1—20:31) is preceded by his farewell discourse to his disciples in which he teaches what the Church's life should be like when the Christ has been exalted (see 13:1—17:26). At the same time, the whole "book of glory," centered on the passion, death, resurrection, and exaltation of Jesus constitutes the sign par excellence, preceded and explained by a long "discourse"—the whole of the "book of signs" (see 1:19—12:50).

We should not become bogged down in further details, however, nor is there room to discuss each of the signs at length. Next we turn to a brief summary of the signs that appear in the Gospel.

3. The Panorama of Signs

In broad terms, the most relevant signs in the fourth Gospel can be grouped according to the narrative sequence. The meaning of which John speaks at the end of the Gospel is visible in all: the signs are meant to nurture belief in Jesus. Thus each sign evokes either a response of faith by the disciples or rejection by those who do not believe.

Signs of a New Order

The first signs of which the Gospel tells (the wedding feast at Cana and the purification of the temple) show Jesus establishing a new order of grace and salvation. They teach that Jesus brought the religion of Israel to its culmination and made a present reality that the Israelites thought would occur at the end of time. Water became wine and the announcement of a new temple represent what St. Paul expressed in words: "The old has passed away, behold the new has come" (2 Cor 5:17).

Among other things, the events at Cana (see 2:1–11) have symbolic meaning: With the coming of Jesus, the Jewish religion, represented by the water "for the purifications of the Jews" (2:6) is transformed into the religion of the Gospel, represented by the wine. "For the law was given through Moses; grace and truth came through Jesus Christ" (1:17).

In the thinking of those times (for example, in Philo), wine symbolized the divine gifts of grace, joy, virtue, wisdom—in short, the spiritual life. John is pointing to all that Christ brought to the world (on the newness of wine, see Mt 9:17; Mk 2:22; Lk 5:37), which also is the fulfillment of what the prophets had foretold concerning the abundance of wine in messianic times (Am 9:13–14; Hos 14:7; Jer 31:12; see also Gn 49:10–11). The scene complements the multiplication of the loaves, with the two episodes constituting an allusion to the bread and wine of the Eucharist. Jesus' response to his mother shows that the sign was not gained through the bonds of flesh but by faith, of which Mary is the model. The final words: "This, the first of his signs, Jesus did at Cana in Galilee, and manifested his glory" (2:11) recall the words of the Prologue: "And the Word became flesh and dwelt among us . . . ; we have beheld his glory" (1:14). Christ's glory is manifested through a sign showing that with his coming the old plan of salvation is replaced by the new one.

The response of faith before the sign is clear: "And his disciples believed in him" (2:11). From this perspective, the changing of water into wine signifies the effect Jesus can have in people's lives. The whole episode speaks of transformation when Jesus is present. As the One who transforms everything, he comes to give life in its fullness to men (see 10:10); and the transformation takes place when the words of his mother are taken seriously: "Do whatever he tells you" (2:5).

The purification of the temple (see 2:13–22), with its reference to destruction and rebuilding, is an allusion to the death and resurrection of Jesus and confirms the new salvific order inaugurated by Christ. The passage has its parallel in two scenes from the Synoptics: 1) the purification of the temple (see Mk 11:15–19; 27–28), which situates it at the beginning of the week in which Christ died; and 2) the appearance of the false witnesses in Jesus' trial before the Sanhedrin in which they testify that he said he would destroy the temple (see Mk 14:58; Mt 26:61; Acts 6:14). It is as if John combined the scenes, situating them at the beginning of his Gospel, in order to depict Jesus' public ministry as a kind of trial culminating in his being condemned to death.

Against the false witnesses' claim to have heard Jesus say "I will destroy this temple," John points out that he didn't say, "I will destroy," but "Destroy" (2:19). Jesus added that he was not going to substitute another sanctuary, but that the same sanctuary would be rebuilt; and the Evangelist explains that the sanctuary was Jesus' body, "destroyed" by "the Jews" but raised by Jesus. In fact, the temple is brought to perfection by the body of Jesus, the true holy place, where the eternal Word is made flesh and the glory of God dwells. The ancient Israel is brought to completion in the new Israel, in the new order Christ inaugurated, which is the Church. Jesus speaks of the foundation of the Church through his resurrection. The doctrine is thus linked to the teaching of the letter to the Ephesians, where the Church is spoken of as a body.

As in the Cana episode, John shows the response of faith before the sign: "When therefore he was raised from the dead, his disciples remembered that he had said this; and they believed the scripture and the word which Jesus had spoken" (2:22). But the Evangelist also points out that Jesus did not trust in their faith because they fixed upon the marvelous aspect of the sign without understanding its deep significance (see 2:23–25).

The sign at Cana and the sign of the purification of the temple are both allusions to the passion and glorification of Christ. Mentioning that the wedding was celebrated "on the third day" (2:1) also recalls the fact that Christ manifested his glory by rising on the third day. "My hour has not yet come" (2:4) refers to his passion and glorification. It thus reflects that, for the Evangelist, the whole ministry of Jesus, insofar as he is the Word made flesh, contains the glory manifested "on the third day," when he arose from among the dead. In the purification of the temple, Jesus' words about the temple destroyed and rebuilt clearly refer to Christ's death and resurrection. The zeal for God's house that devours Jesus leads him to the death that is to be his glorification.

What these signs teach is confirmed by Jesus' dialogue with Nicodemus (see 3:1–15) and with the Samaritan woman (see 4:5–45). Nicodemus comes to see Jesus and is surprised when Jesus speaks to him of a new birth, pointing to the contrast between what is born of the flesh and what is born of the Spirit. We are told that one only enters into that new world established by Jesus by virtue of the Spirit, the gift that proceeds from God himself; by one's own strength it is not possible. The connection with the Spirit is through a material element, water. The transition is from physical birth to spiritual rebirth, from wind as a physical phenomenon to the Spirit: the visible suggests the invisible.

In the dialogue with the Samaritan woman, this truth is emphasized, and two realities are contrasted: Jacob's well and "living water" (4:10), the grace of the Spirit, which Christ brings; Samaritan and Jewish places of worship (Gerizim and Jerusalem) and the new worship established by Jesus. Jesus is the One in whom God and man meet "in spirit and in truth" and whose time has now come: "The hour is coming, and now is" (4:23), he says to the Samaritan woman.

Signs of the Word that Gives Life

The two signs that follow—the cures of the son of the royal official and of the paralytic at the pool of Bethzatha—reveal Jesus as the giver of life. His word gives life to those nearly dead.

The curing of the official's son (see 4:46–54) is introduced as the second sign to take place in Cana, where he first manifested his glory (see 2:11). As with Jesus' mother in the account of the marriage, the one who makes the request here is apparently rejected; but thanks to his perseverance, Jesus grants what is asked. The lack of faith of those of his own country (see 4:44) contrasts with the faith of the royal official, who believes Jesus' life-giving words: "Your son lives" which the text twice repeats (4:50, 51, 53). The official returns to his home so strengthened that his whole family believes. Jesus appears as the Word made flesh (see 1:14) who restores life by his word, even though spoken at a distance.

The connection between the sign and faith is evident: "Unless you see signs and wonders you will not believe" (4:48). The whole incident is an invitation to believe in that Word, even without being a direct witness of the admirable signs; see the reproach to Thomas at the end of the Gospel: "Have you believed because you have seen me?" (20:29).

In the following sign (see 5:1–16), the paralytic at the pool of Bethzatha also recovers his health at Jesus' word. The context is an unspecified Jewish feast. The day is also a feast, a "Sabbath" (5:10).

The symbolism of water reappears here. Like the water at the wedding feast at Cana and the meeting with the Samaritan woman at Jacob's well, the water of the pool is also efficacious. There is an implied contrast with the Torah, the Law of Moses, which sometimes was likened to water. Unlike this law that does not give life, the Word of God has power to give the will and the strength to live. "Do you want to be cured?" (5:6), Jesus asks the sick man. And again the Prologue's words become reality: "The law was given through Moses; grace and truth came through Jesus Christ" (1:17). Jesus says to the sick man, "Rise" (5:8), using a word that evokes the resurrection. The new creation awaited by the Jews is becoming a reality; with Jesus, the hour has come. God, Jesus' Father, has given his Son power over life and death.

The response of faith before the sign is found in the words of the Master to the man just cured: "See, you are well! Sin no more, that nothing worse befall you" (5:14). The sickness is related to sin. Jesus shows that the real misfortune is not sickness but failure to believe in him. The cure relates not only to the body but also to the heart.

The discourse that follows (see 5:17–47) explains Jesus' power to give life: He has the same power as the Father. "For as the Father raises the dead and gives them life, so also the Son gives life to whom he will. . . . For as the Father has life in himself, so he has granted the Son also to have life in himself" (5:21 and 26).

The same idea appears in John 5:39–40: "You search the scriptures, because you think that in them you have eternal life; and it is they that bear witness to me; yet you refuse to come to me that you may have life." The Father, for love of the Son, has given him power to give the life he himself possesses. In Jesus, God's power is present. And "the Jews" grasp his reasoning: "This was why the Jews sought all the more to kill him, because he not only broke the Sabbath but also called God his Father, making himself equal with God" (5:18).

The Sign of the Bread of Life

The scene changes again from Jerusalem to Galilee, where Jesus performs the sign of the multiplication of the loaves and fishes (6:1–12). The sign continues the theme of life, since it is intended to show that, both as Word and as Eucharist, Jesus is the Bread of Life. The Eucharistic intention is clear from the beginning of the narrative. John notes that this sign occurred when "the Passover, the feast of the Jews, was at hand" (6:4), a reference suggesting that the Eucharistic banquet prefigured in the multiplication of loaves and explained in the discourse in the synagogue was to be the New Pasch instituted by Christ.

As reported by John, the episode shares many details with the two Synoptic accounts of multiplications (the first of them followed by the walking on water). Some elements are more like the first account, others more like the second. Unique to John are: the crossing of the sea (see 6:1), the closeness of Passover (see 6:4), the role of Philip and Andrew (see 6:7–8), the fact that the loaves were made of barley (see 6:9), and Jesus' command that nothing be lost (see 6–12). Also characteristic is John's apparent allusion to the Second Book of Kings (see 4:42–44) which tells how Elisha miraculously provided food to the people in a time of famine.

In the background of the passage, one is aware also of God's feeding of the Israelites in the desert in Moses' time (see 6:31–32), which is suggested by the amazing way in which the multitude is fed and by the fact that, as the Synoptics tell us, the multiplication of loaves occurred in a desert place. John nevertheless notes that there was abundant grass there, as if Jesus' presence transformed a desert into a garden.

All these details link Jesus' ministry to the two most noteworthy periods of miraculous activity in the history of the people of God: the ministry of Moses and that of Elijah and Elisha. Jesus' acts have features in common with the miraculous actions of the great servants of God in Israel's history. In a way, too, they evoke the transfiguration, when Jesus appears with Moses and Elijah speaking of his imminent death.

The description of the sign, recalling that Jesus took the loaves and "gave thanks" (6:11), also has a Eucharistic meaning. This is the same action the other evangelists record in relating the institution of the Eucharist at the Last Supper: Jesus "blessed" (Mt 26:26; Mk 14:22) or "gave thanks" (Mt 26:27; Mk 14:23; Lk 22:17–19) and distributed the bread. "Bless" and "give thanks" both suggest the prayer that was to give its name to the Eucharist: the *beraká*, a prayer of thanksgiving in the form of a blessing directed to God.

Like the Samaritan woman (see 4:19), the multitude recognizes Jesus as the prophet who was to come, at which an attempt follows to make him king. But Jesus rejects that inadequate understanding of himself and instead manifests his real identity to his disciples when he appears to them walking on the water, calming them by telling them, "It is I" (6:20), an allusion to the Hebrew name for God.

After the miracle and the walking on the water, the discourse in the synagogue of Capernaum explains the sign: God gives eternal life through Jesus, not through Moses and not as the multitude expected. The people supposed that Jesus, as a prophet in the style of Moses, had to renew the gift of manna. But Jesus, as a new prophet, brings to fullness the gifts Moses had offered the people. The manna was a sign, but Jesus is the true bread (see 6:26–34)—the bread of life and he who gives life (see 6:35–47)—and he gives that Bread of Life in the Eucharist (see 6:48–59). It is necessary to eat his flesh and blood in order to have eternal life.

As in other places, Jesus' words constitute a decisive act separating those who have faith from those who do not. Many of his disciples did not understand and were scandalized because they did not have faith. Jesus spoke of how the flesh given as food would be the Son of Man returned from heaven—that is to say, a flesh animated by the Holy Spirit: "It is the spirit that gives life, the flesh is of no avail; the words that I have spoken to you are spirit and life" (6:63). These words evoke Calvary, where water and blood will pour from Christ's side, indicating the power of the grace that is to come from him. But to accept this teaching, it was necessary to have the Spirit—to have faith, like that reflected in Peter's confession: "Lord, to whom shall we go? You have the words of eternal life; and we have believed, and have come to know, that you are the Holy One of God" (6:68–69).

The Sign of Light

Next, once more in Jerusalem, the Evangelist prepares in chapters 7 and 8 for the sign of the cure of the blind man (chapter 9). Jesus reveals himself to the world as light by means of seven dialogues showing Christ as life and light, an affirmation provoking both acceptance and rejection. The Evangelist tells us that after life comes light, as the Prologue had said: "The life was the light of men" (1:4).

The context of the sign is the feast of Tabernacles, which Judaism associated with the day of the Lord, the final judgment, when he would establish his definitive kingdom (see Zec 14:16). The feast lasted eight days and included a pilgrimage to Jerusalem. Besides celebrating the harvest that took place in September and October, it included prayers for rain. A daily procession was held, carrying water from the pool of Siloam to the temple. In the "court of the women," huge sanctuary torches were also lit. It was probably after this symbolic ritual took place that Jesus presented himself as water and light: "If any one thirsts, let him come to me and drink. He who believes in me, as the scripture has said, 'Out of his heart shall flow rivers of living water'" (7:37–38); "I am the light of the world; he who follows me will not walk in darkness, but will have the light of life" (8:12). Water and light, terms applied to the Law (the revelation of God for the Jews), are now applied to Jesus. But his words meet with opposition from the authorities. From now on, Jesus' death comes more and more to hover over the Gospel.

The sign of the healing of the man born blind (see 9:1–11) confirms the preceding chapter's revelation of Jesus as light of the world. It presents a contrast with the blindness of the Jews who oppose him. Here is the triumph of light over darkness, its connection with life indicated by the reappearance of the symbol of water.

Like the water of Cana, the water of the well of Jacob, and the water of the pool at Bethesda, the water of the pool of Siloam (which means sent) is not efficacious by itself but illuminates only if the actual "sent one" is the Son sent by the Father. As elsewhere, the man born blind is a type of the encounter of faith with Jesus. After washing himself in the waters of Siloam, he exemplifies the one who is illuminated—that is, baptized—who sees who Jesus really is only after suffering rejection, as Jesus did. Rejection affords him the opportunity of attaining a much more profound faith and is an instance of every Christian's calling to confess Christ before men.

The sign is explained by Jesus' dialogue with the blind man and the Pharisees. Jesus is the judge of those who encounter the light and a sign that brings judgment. The Pharisees are scandalized that Jesus cures on the Sabbath (see 9:16). They also are skeptical because they do not know his place of origin, so, judging him guilty, they condemn Jesus together with the man who was blind, and expel the latter from the synagogue. In the end, however, the tables are turned (see 9:35–41), and the judges are judged—they are the ones who are blind and have been found guilty. But the man who was blind believes and prostrates himself before Jesus (see 9:38). "When all is said and done, Jesus is the one through whom and in whom the blind man is cleansed so that he can gain his sight. The whole chapter turns out to be an interpretation of baptism, which enables us to see. Christ is the giver of light and he opens our eyes through the mediation of the sacrament."[1]

The explanation of the sign continues in the discourse that follows (see 10:1–21). Because of the blindness of the leaders of the people, God has sent the shepherd promised by the prophets, the Messiah: Jesus is the Good Shepherd, sent by God to Israel, who gives his life for his flock. His death is the means of communicating life to his sheep, who now are not only from Israel but the whole world: "I have other sheep . . ." (10:6). Those who reject light and life, preferring darkness, are presented as

---

1. Benedict XVI, *Jesus of Nazareth*, vol. 1, p. 242.

drawing down God's judgment upon themselves. They prepare the death of Christ, by which he is going to give life to the world and which is a judgment on those who reject the light. Before the rejection that provokes his affirmations (see 10:22–39), at the Feast of the Dedication, Jesus openly manifests himself as the Son of God (see 10:36), one with the Father (see 10:30), giver of eternal life.

The Sign of Victory over Death

The scene shifts to outside Jerusalem. The next sign recounted shows Jesus as the resurrection and the life (see 11:1–44).

The dialogue explaining the value of the sign follows the cure in the account of the man born blind (chaper 9) but in this new sign, the dialogue precedes the sign and the sign interprets the dialogue. The account begins by telling of a sick person (see 11:1) and ends with his cure after having died and been buried: "The dead man came out" (11:44). For Jesus, the purpose of the sickness is to reveal his own glory as Son of God; thus he does not go immediately to the sick man's assistance. But when the sick man is dead and his death is certified, he raises him.

The theme of Jesus' death provides the background of this whole episode. We hear of the threats against Jesus' life: "Rabbi, the Jews were but now seeking to stone you, and are you going there again?" Only when there is no possibility of human help does he return to Judea in order to confront death and overcome it. The preceding chapter's words about the Good Shepherd who gives his life for his sheep become a reality (see 10:10–11), and it becomes clear that Jesus' power to give life is related to his own sacrifice, even unto death: plainly, he does not think and act as others do. But the important thing remains being close to him, as Thomas affirms: "Let us also go, that we may die with him" (11:16), an expression equivalent to that in the Synoptics: "If any man would come after me, let him deny himself and take up his cross and follow me" (Mk 8:34).

But death, a physical phenomenon, also points to a spiritual reality. Jesus assures Martha that her brother will return to life. She thinks of the bodily resurrection that will take place at the last day. Jesus, however, is speaking of a present reality. In contrast to her "If you had been here" (11:21), which looks to the past, Jesus affirms that what she awaits in the future (in Judaism, the resurrection was related to the end of time) is already present in his person, because he has the power to give life: "I am the resurrection and the life" (11:25).

As with the other signs, in this one, too, the need for faith is shown. Believing in Jesus here and now means overcoming death and entering into the true life already present in him. Life, whether as a present reality or as a future gift at the end of time, is possessed by Jesus. Whatever good one might imagine is in him. The measure of all living is Jesus Christ because he is the true life—the life that gives life and conquers death.

The resurrection of Lazarus is followed by the Sanhedrin's decision condemn Jesus to death. Here is the assault of darkness upon light. Jesus went to Judea to give life to Lazarus, and his life-giving act provokes his condemnation to death. But his death is a free offering of his life in sacrifice. Moreover, the Good Shepherd not only gives his life for his sheep but attracts others of a different flock. In effect, the prophecy of Caiaphas—"It is expedient for you that one man should die for the people, and that the whole nation should not perish"—is explained by the Evangelist when he says Jesus was to die "for the nation, and not for the nation only, but to gather into one the children of God who are scattered abroad" (11:51–52). Jesus is the Good Shepherd who brings the "other sheep: so that there be only one flock, just as there is only one shepherd" (10:11–16).

After the resurrection of Lazarus and the authorities' decision to kill the One who had given life, the Evangelist relates actions of Jesus more similar to the symbolic acts of the prophets mentioned earlier: the anointing at Bethany and the entrance into Jerusalem. These confirm that Jesus gives life through death and has the power of restoring life.

The significance of the anointing by Mary at Bethany (see 12:1–8) is found in 12:7: "Let her alone, let her keep it for the day of my burial." Jesus is anointed as one anoints a dead body. This introduces the idea of dying and being buried to which Jesus refers a little later: "Unless a grain of wheat falls into the earth and dies [that is, if it does not die and is not buried], it remains alone" (12:24). The action is a sign that Jesus was to be buried.

The triumphal entry into Jerusalem (12:12–15) does not differ substantially from the account in the Synoptics (see Mk 11:1–10; Mt 21:1–9; Lk 19:28–40). As in the episode of the purification of the temple, where it is said that only in light of the Resurrection did the disciples understand that the announcement referred to Christ's death and resurrection, the Evangelist indicates here that the disciples did not understand the meaning of the triumphal entry until he was glorified—that is, until he died in order to resurrect: "His disciples did not understand this at first; but when Jesus was glorified, then they remembered that this had been written of him and had been done to him" (12:16).

The idea of Christ's royalty is extremely important for John, and the entry into Jerusalem is a sign that Jesus exalted on the Cross would one day be universally recognized by all mankind. The Evangelist uses the words of the Jewish authorities to express this: "The world has gone after him" (12:19). That "world" is the whole human race that God loves (see 3:16) and Christ came to save (see 3:17; 4:42). Universality is confirmed when Jesus is visited by some Hellenists (see 12:20–22), proselytes of the Jews who for John represent the world in general. The meeting is the occasion for a discourse on the universal implications of Jesus' death (see 12:23–33) by which he defeated death itself. Like the seed that in dying produces much fruit (see 12:24), Jesus' death created a universal community, the Church.

Jesus' uneasiness when his death is imminent (see 12:27) corresponds to the Gethsemane of the Synoptics. John shows the hour of shame to be the hour of his glory. Through his death, a force is generated that in time will draw all things toward God in a movement of reconciliation. This is how one understands the glory of God, manifested in the very first of his signs that led his disciples to believe in him (see 2:11). It is the opposite of what men understand. The hour of his death is the hour in which his glory is manifested and the world is judged. Death is the glorifying action of God.

To sum up then: there are many fewer signs in the fourth Gospel than there are miracles in the Synoptics. There are no summaries of Jesus' miraculous actions and no exorcisms. Rather than concentrating on the miraculous, John emphasizes the controversy aroused by the signs by means of the dialogues that follow. The signs of Jesus are acts of power with a symbolic character that reveal his origin and manifest his glory and his mission as the Son of God. They are closely linked to faith, while those in the Synoptics are related above all to the inauguration of the kingdom of God. The people—at least some of them—come to believe as a result of seeing the signs Jesus performed. Although the signs are intended to arouse faith in him, we also see here rejection and failure to admit that they are works of God. Thus the signs alone are insufficient for faith. Yet they are a path leading to recognition of the greatest sign of Jesus, his glorification through his death on the cross.

Chapter 5

THE DIALOGUES AND DISCOURSES OF JESUS

AS WE SAW IN THE LAST CHAPTER, accounts of Jesus' signs are accompanied by discourses meant to show their significance. The signs cannot be separated from the narratives explaining them. Taken together, both help us understand how John organizes the picture of Jesus that he presents.

This chapter concentrates on Jesus' words, collected by John in the form of discourses—often extensive and marked by dense, profound language. Jesus speaks here in a solemn, majestic, sometimes even poetic manner. The style resembles that attributed by the Old Testament to God when he speaks through the prophets or the personified divine Wisdom of the wisdom books. It is a style befitting the divine condition of Jesus, the pre-existing Word who reveals the Father.

The discourses often alternate with signs and other episodes and on occasion take the form of dialogue. The principal ones are these:

The water changed to wine and the purification of the temple (see 2:1–22)	The dialogue with Nicodemus and with the Samaritan woman: the new birth and the new worship (see 3:1–21; 4:1–42)*
The cure of the paralytic at the pool of Bethzatha (see 5:1–16)	Discourse on the authority of Jesus (see 5:17–47)

The multiplication of the loaves (see 6:1–13)	Discourse on the Bread of Life (see 6:26–59)
Jesus at the Feast of Tabernacles (see 7:1–16)	Dialogue and discourse about Christ, the Light of the world (see 7:14–52; 8:12–59)
Cure of the man born blind (see 9:1–7)	Discourse about Jesus, judge, good shepherd, one with the Father (see 9:8—10:39)
Some Greeks ask to see Jesus (see 12:20–22)	Discourse on the glorification of Christ through his death (see 12:23–36)
Passion and death of Jesus (see 18:1–20:31)	Preceded by discourses of farewell about the life of the Church (see 13:1—17:26)

* Between the two dialogues we find the episode in which John the Baptist is questioned about Jesus in Aennon, near Salim (see 3:22–26). This is also accompanied by a discourse: John has to decrease and Jesus to increase (see 3:27–36).

The pattern is not rigid or exceptionless. For example, the sign of Cana (see 2:1–11) seems isolated, without any discourse; after the purification of the temple (see 2:13–16) there is only a brief dialogue; in chapter 10, the connection of the discourse on the Good Shepherd with the sign preceding it is not all that evident; the sign of the raising of Lazarus is accompanied by a dialogue concerning Jesus as the resurrection and the life, etc. Here we will briefly deal with the discourses and dialogues identified above.

1. The Dialogue with Nicodemus and with the Samaritan Woman

There are two dialogues of Jesus that are connected with the sign of the conversion of water into wine and the prophetic sign of the purification of the temple: those that he held with Nicodemus and with the Samaritan woman.

In the dialogue-discourse with Nicodemus (see 3:1–21), the Evangelist presents a clear revelation of who Jesus is, the salvation he brings to mankind, and the precondition to attain it: the faith which is received in baptism through the action of the Holy Spirit.

Nicodemus was a Pharisee and a member of the Sanhedrin. He comes to Jesus "at night" (3:2; see also 19:39); that is, he does not yet belong to the light (darkness implies ignorance—see 9:4; 12:35), and he recognizes him only as a teacher who is motivated by God (see 3:2) but who had not truly come from God. Like the Samaritan woman or the man born blind, Nicodemus represents a faith that is not yet full, as is evident by his inability to understand Jesus' words. He misunderstands the need to be "born anew" (3:3).

By using the double meanings of various words (*anothen* in Greek means "again" and also "from above"; *pneuma* means "wind" and "spirit"), Jesus explains to him that, in order to enter the kingdom of heaven, one must be born from above, born of the Spirit. Being born of the Spirit evokes the "born of God" of the Prologue (1:13). When one receives the Word made flesh, one becomes a child of God. Nicodemus is thinking of the natural birth from a Jewish mother which makes one a member of the chosen people, a people that the Old Testament considered children of God (see Ex 4:22; Dt 32:6; Hos 11:1). But Jesus tells him that the only thing that the flesh can engender is flesh (see 3:6). Jesus is making a radical change here in what constitutes being a child of God. The new birth takes place in baptism, when someone is baptized in water and receives the Spirit of God.

The "irony" typical of John appears in 3:9–11. Before Nicodemus, who comes saying "we know" (3:2) but cannot understand, Jesus tells him on the contrary: "We speak of what we know and give witness of what we have seen" (3:11). Jesus speaks for those who believe and can understand the need to be born of God, because he himself came from God. After the dialogue, in

3:11 there begins a monologue, in which he once again evokes the ideas of the Prologue. Jesus speaks of the only begotten, bringer of life and light who descended from heaven, became flesh, and reveals the Father. He will return to heaven, making it possible for those who believe in him—for those who receive him—to receive eternal life and be born anew. This rebirth in the Spirit is only made possible by his incarnation as a man and his death on the Cross. Like the serpent of bronze that Moses raised in the wilderness, Christ is the cause of salvation for those who look at him with faith. He is the Son of God who has come to the world bringing the life of God himself, the supreme love of God for mankind, so that all who believe in him will have eternal life. By this the world is already judged.

In 3:19 the text moves from the idea of life to light: the new birth to eternal life is also the coming of light, in whose illumination judgment is passed on men's response to Christ. Jesus came to give life, not to judge, but those who prefer darkness to light condemn themselves.

The testimony of John the Baptist (see 3:23–36) continues some of the ideas of the dialogue and serves to unite the ideas of water and Spirit through the baptism of Jesus, which is conferred in the Church (as opposed to the baptism of John). The new birth is accomplished through baptism "in the Spirit," given by Christ inasmuch as he both possesses and baptizes in the Spirit and so communicates eternal life to the believer.

Traveling from Judea to Galilee, Jesus stops in Samaria beside the well of Jacob in Sichem or Sichar. Here he has a long conversation with a woman (see 4:1–42), who represents a particular kind of faith encounter with Jesus in which faith comes despite obstacles.

The subject of 4:7–15 is the "living water." The expression has a double meaning. It could mean "running water" (as might be the case with the water of Jacob's well), but in the sense Jesus gives it, it is the "water that gives eternal life." In the rabbinical tradition, water is a symbol of the Law, the Torah, God's "gift" to his people. The Torah purifies, satisfies thirst, nurtures life. As with the water of Cana intended for the purifications of the Jews, however, this "water" (the Torah) was insufficient. In contrast, Jesus gives water by which men are born into the kingdom of the Spirit. "Water once again—though now in a different way—functions as the symbol of the *Pneuma*, the real life-force, which quenches man's deeper thirst and gives him plenitude of life, for which he is waiting without knowing it"[2] Thus it realizes what is said in the Prologue: "The Law was given through Moses; grace and truth came through Jesus Christ" (1:17).

The woman does not understand. Grasping only the superficial meaning of Jesus' words, she supposes the water to which the Master refers to be ordinary water and asks if he is greater than Jacob. In another of John's ironic touches, the Samaritan woman unwittingly implies that Jesus is truly greater than the patriarch who was responsible for the well. Desiring water for her own convenience, the woman is operating on a merely earthly level.

Jesus, consistent with his teaching regarding the purified temple (see 2:14–22), then alludes to the syncretic worship of the Samaritans, while condemning any adulteration of Judaism. The mention of the "fifth husband" could be a reference to the five pagan cities that in the eighth century BC brought their own gods to Samaria (see 2 Kings 17:24ff and Josephus, *Ant.* 9, 14, 8), thus leading the prophets and the Jews generally to consider the Samaritans idolaters, "adulterers." But both Jewish and Samaritan worship were to be superseded by the new worship "in Spirit and in truth" (4:23–24): Christ inaugurates a new relationship with God, a new worship symbolized by the wine of Cana, the living water, and the new temple he would raise up through birth in the Spirit.

As a consequence of Jesus' revelation, the woman confesses him as Messiah, the One who was to inaugurate a new order of

---

1. Benedict XVI, *Jesus of Nazareth*, vol. 1, p. 241.

salvation (see 4:25-26). From that moment to the end of the passage (see 4:27-39), John presents a double scene: Jesus speaks with his disciples, the woman with the people of her village. She becomes a witness of Christ, and her countrymen accept her testimony when they meet Jesus and have personal contact with him (see 4:40-42). The disciples, for their part, exhibit a lack of understanding concerning Jesus' food (see 4:31-33), like the woman concerning the water. Jesus, who gives life, needs no one to give him food. Besides, he lives to do the will of his Father, upon whom he as Son depends for everything. And it is God's will that Jesus should not only announce the work of mankind's salvation but carry it out through the transformation of all creation. What the Jews await at the end of time has become reality: "The fields are already white for harvest" (4:35).

2. In Jerusalem, a Discussion on the Authority of Jesus

In Jerusalem, Jesus cures the paralytic at the pool of Bethesda on the Sabbath. Called to account for that, he answers that, in curing, giving life, he does the same thing God is always doing. The authorities therefore decide to kill him, for he "called God his Father, making himself equal with God" (5:18). Now a long discourse of Jesus begins (see 5:17-47) in which he replies to this accusation.

Its first part (5:19-30) treats of the permanent action of God, who continues "working" even on the Sabbath because he is always governing the world. "Giving life" (healing) and "judging" (saving mankind) form part of that government and are manifestations of God's creative and royal power. The Son has authority to judge because he has authority to give life. "As the Father raises the dead and gives them life, so also the Son gives life to whom he will" (5:21). He can judge the world inasmuch as he is vested with power to give life: "He who hears my word . . . has eternal life; he does not come into judgment, but has passed from death to life" (5:24). Thus Jesus does what only God could do. Still, he cannot do anything by himself (see 5:19, 26–27), nor is he "making himself equal to God," in the sense that he is a second God in contrast to God. Jesus "is equal to God" insofar as he acts in absolute unity with the Father. The Son radically obeys the Father, and the Father loves the Son in a perfect way. Thus, all the Son does is done in union with the Father: There is an identity of will and action. And so he can give life and judge, which are actions of God. In conclusion, Jesus "is not equal to God" in the sense of being over against God but insofar as he has the same divine attributes.

The second part of the discourse (5:31–47) centers on the witness. From the Gospel's start, there have been references to the testimony of John the Baptist, Andrew, Philip, and Nathaniel (see 1:19–49). Later a new testimony by John the Baptist also appears (see 3:26). Following this is the testimony Jesus himself gave: He had come down from heaven, sent by God, and gives testimony to what he has seen and heard; anyone who accepts that testimony recognizes the truthfulness of God himself and has eternal life; to reject it is to deny the truth of God (see 3:31–34).

This theme persists in the present discourse, where Jesus affirms that the definitive testimony, above that of John (see 5:31–35), is that of the Father: It can be seen in the "works of God" (5:36). On the one hand is his power of giving life and judging; on the other hand is Scripture, which gives witness to Christ (see 5:39). To accept this witness, however, one must first have interiorly accepted the Word of God. The Scriptures in themselves are not sufficient. What is required is that one love God and seek his glory, not one's own. When all is said and done, the principal witness is the power of the "Word of God," which is shown in Jesus' words and actions and which one must accept interiorly. Those works of God are not just cures but the possibility of a new kind of life for those who accept Christ. This new life is found in the Church.

3. Jesus, the Bread of Life

The discourse in the synagogue of Capernaum (see 6:26–59) explains the sign of the multiplication of the loaves and the fishes at the beginning of chapter 6. Everything revolves around the Bread of life, symbolized in the bread with which Jesus satisfied the multitudes.

The discourse opens with an introduction in the form of a dialogue between Jesus and the Jews in which Jesus reveals the nature of the messianic goods he brings (see 6:25–34). The manna mentioned in Exodus 16, suggested by the multiplication of the loaves, is related to the promise of the Eucharist by a quote from Psalm 78:24: "He gave them bread from heaven to eat" (see 6:30). Hope that the Messiah would restore the gift of the manna was part of the Jewish tradition, and so those who were witnesses of the miracle ask Jesus to repeat the gift to confirm his messianic identity. But manna is a perishable food that "one consumes" (6:27). In contrast, Jesus says, one should work for a real and eternal food that he will give. He also tells the Jews that knowledge of the Torah (of which bread was a symbol) is not a real knowledge of the will of God. As the manna is not true bread, so neither is the Torah. God's bread, the true knowledge of God that gives life, is Christ. But like the Samaritan woman, his hearers remain at a merely superficial level and ask Jesus for that bread as food to satisfy their hunger: "They said to him, 'Lord, give us this bread always'" (6:34).

The discourse then continues with a revelation of Jesus as the Bread of Life insofar as God's word, revealed by the Father, nourishes man (see 6:35–47). Jesus says clearly that he is himself the Bread of God, the "Bread which comes down from heaven." It is therefore necessary that people come to him (see

6:35); that means believing in him as the One who is sent by the Father from heaven. His words in 6:36–40 recall the discourse of chapter 5. He is "the giver of life" (the vivifier), because the Father wants salvation to be accomplished through him, and he fulfills the Father's will by his perfect obedience. Whoever "sees" Christ with faith, whoever contemplates his glory, possesses eternal life now and is assured of the final resurrection (see 6:40). But those who listen to him now, as the Israelites listened during the Exodus, murmur against him (see 6:41–42). They take him for an ordinary man, Joseph's son, and declare that they know his father and mother (another example of John's "irony," by which the Evangelist is telling us precisely that Jesus did not have a carnal begetting). Jesus tells them he can be understood only by those who are "taught by God" (6:45), which is to say, those in whom the divine Word lives. The Father draws to him those who understand that he descended from heaven, for he is the only one who sees God, and it is this that gives eternal life. In short, whoever sees the Son has eternal life, while Jesus is the Bread of Life inasmuch as his revelation is a divine teaching that communicates the vision of God.

The verses that follow (6:48–59) contain the most specifically Eucharistic part of the discourse. Jesus shows that he now is food not only as the Word of the Father (the teaching of God) but insofar as his flesh and his blood are food for mankind. After recapitulating the previous ideas of the discourse (see 6:48–50), he affirms that he is the Bread and gives himself as Bread to be eaten. His hearers are surprised: "How can this man give us his flesh to eat?" But what he says can be understood in the light of his passion, death, and resurrection. Jesus gives his flesh and blood by dying for mankind, and this occurs sacramentally in the Eucharist. His words, "The bread which I shall give for the life of the world is my flesh" (6:51), are equivalent to those of the institution of the Eucharist: "This is my body which shall be given for you" (1 Cor 11:24). Drinking his blood is also an obvious reference to the sacrifice of Christ. Through his death, Jesus makes himself the Bread of Life for the world.

The incomprehension of Jesus' listeners in the wake of his words grew, since they thought the Eucharistic food to which he referred was his flesh in its actual, earthly state. But Jesus was speaking of how the flesh given as food would be after the Son of Man returned to heaven: that is, flesh animated by the Holy Spirit. This is what he meant in saying his words "are spirit and life" (6:63). They give the life generated by the Spirit to those who believe in him but produce no results for those who "do not believe" (6:64). Here is the judgment separating those with faith from those without it, as appears from Peter's confession and the reference to Judas the traitor (see 6:65–71).

4. Christ, the Light of the World

Chapters 7 and 8 essentially contain disputes between Jesus and the Jewish authorities arising from his appearance in Jerusalem as the Messiah. The material is organized in seven dialogues focusing on Jesus' messianic affirmations (see also chapter 5 of this book, § 3.4). At the heart of it is Jesus' revelation of himself as fountain of living water and light of the world, which underlines the rejection on the part of his hearers. The threat of death that now surrounds Jesus is present throughout (see 7:1, 13, 19, 25, 30, 32, 44; 8:37, 40, 59) and henceforth becomes more intense. The questioners are principally the Jewish authorities and the crowd present in Jerusalem for the Feast of Tabernacles. The seven dialogues can be organized as follows:

a) 7:14–24: The polemic with "the Jews" and "the crowd." Jesus says he has come from God, who sent him, and seeks only the glory of the one by whom he was sent.

b) 7:25–30: The polemic with "some of those from Jerusalem." Jesus speaks of his origin and destiny. His questioners think they know where he comes from, but they do not know his true origin as the One sent by the Father.

c) 7:31–36: The argument with "leaders of the priests," "Pharisees," and "Jews." Jesus speaks of his departure. Knowing neither where he came from nor where he is going, his listeners do not understand.

d) 7:37–52: On the last day of the feast, water was taken from the pool of Siloam and sprinkled on the altar of the temple, while rain was prayed for, and texts of Isaiah, Ezekiel, and Zechariah were read that fostered yearning for the coming of the Messiah. Jesus offers himself as the fount of living water, speaking of his glorification beside the Father and of the sending of the Spirit. His words give rise to diverse opinions, reflected in comments by the crowd, the temple officers, the chief priests, the Pharisees, and Nicodemus.

e) 8:12–20: Dispute with the Pharisees. From the first night of the feast, the temple court of the women is illuminated by four great lamps. It is perhaps in this context that Jesus reveals himself as the Light of the World. The theme of judgment in these chapters becomes more prominent. Light brings judgment, discriminating between those who prefer the darkness and those who choose light.

f) 8:21–30: Argument with the Jews. Jesus speaks of his death. Those who "are from below" die in their sins, while for him who "is from above," death is a return to the Father who sent him, an elevation (with a double allusion to the crucifixion and his exaltation). The cross will reveal the mystery of Jesus' identity.

g) 8:31–59: A polemic with the Jews who believed in Jesus but had insufficient faith. Jesus exhorts them to persevere in his Word. In this way they will come to knowledge of the truth and the freedom that results.

The subject of freedom gives rise to a discussion about Abraham and his descendants. Jesus is greater than Abraham and prior to him. To know the truth is to know him who has seen the Father. The true line of Abraham, the true children of God, are those who believe that Jesus is the One who has been sent. Those who accept him will not know death. As on other occasions, his questioners take this idea of not knowing death in a physical sense and therefore as something not attained even by Abraham and the prophets. Replying to this objection, Jesus reveals his divinity: "Before Abraham was, I AM" (8:58).

5. Jesus, the Good Shepherd, One with the Father

The discourse of chapter ten is divided into two parts. The first (10:1–21) deals with the shepherd and his flock; the second (10:22–39), during the Feast of the Dedication of the Temple, is a controversy, similar to that of chapters 7 and 8 about Jesus' messianic affirmations in Jerusalem.

The first part forms a unit with chapter 9, the healing of the man born blind and the controversy with the unbelieving Jews that followed, where the principal theme is light and the judgment it brings with it: "For judgment I came into this world, that those who do not see may see, and that those who see may become blind. . . . If you were blind, you would have no guilt; but now that you say, 'We see,' your guilt remains" (9:39, 41).

These words of Jesus lead to the discourse on the Good Shepherd. In its background are Old Testament passages presenting the chosen people as a flock, God as their shepherd (see Ps. 23), and the unworthy leaders of Israel as false shepherds (see Jer 23:1–6; Ez 34:1–31). Ezekiel pronounces a severe judgment upon the rulers of Israel who are not concerned about the people. Jesus similarly condemns the leaders of the Jews for expelling the man who was blind and dispersing the flock Jesus came to reunite. Ezekiel, on the basis of that judgment against the rulers, announces that God will raise up a single Shepherd, similar to David, who will pasture his sheep. Christ brings to fulfillment what the prophet announced. He is the Shepherd who not only knows and leads his sheep but "gives his life" for them (10:11), as is expressly seen in Christ's death as a vicarious sacrifice.

Earlier it was said that eternal life is a gift of Christ (chaper 3), which he gives by giving himself (chaper 6); now it is clear that eternal life is given by Jesus through his death, just as a shepherd saves his sheep by battling the wolf to the point of giving his life. The subject of the discourse, then, is judgment and a death that gives life. Those who reject life and the light condemn themselves. And although the rejection of Jesus leads to his death on the cross, through that death he will give life to the world even as his death judges it.

The second part of chapter 10 shows the consequences of this judgment. The discourse makes clear the attitude of those who willingly exclude themselves from the flock of Christ. The words "If you are the Christ, tell us plainly" (10:24) parallel those in the judgment of Jesus before the Sanhedrin, which the Synoptics give as "Are you the Christ, the Son of the Blessed?" (Mk 14:61). In both cases, Jesus' confession brings his condemnation to death (or an attempt to kill him, as we see in 10:31: "The Jews took up stones again to stone him"). The issue is whether Jesus is the Messiah. The answer is unfolded in three affirmations: "I and the Father are one" (10:30), "I am the Son of God" (10:36), and "the Father is in me and I in the Father" (10:38). Jesus is the Son who is one with the Father and who gives eternal life, as becomes clear with the resurrection of Lazarus in the next chapter.

6. The Glorification of Christ through His Death

After the anointing in Bethany (see 12:1–8) and the triumphal entry into Jerusalem (see 12:12–15), a brief discourse follows arising from the request to see Jesus made by some Greeks who had come to Jerusalem for the Passover (see 12:23–36). Jesus speaks of something seemingly imminent: "The hour has come" (12:23)—his death and resurrection, the passion and its meaning. The discourse begins with a reference to the grain of wheat that "if it dies, produces much fruit" (12:24) and culminates with Jesus saying he will draw all men to himself (see 12:32).

After speaking of the universal redemptive value of his death, Jesus teaches its meaning in the lives of his followers, using words very similar to those in the Synoptics: "He who loves his life will lose it" (12:25–26; see Mk 8:35 and parallel texts). He then refers to his glorification in a passage similar to the prayer in Gethsemane as given by the Synoptics and Hebrews 5:7–9, which speaks of how Jesus "offered up prayers and supplications, with loud cries and tears, to him who was able to save him from death, and he was heard for his godly fear."

John says, "Now is my soul troubled. And what shall I say? 'Father, save me from this hour?' No, for this purpose I have come to this hour" (12:27). Before the suffering that was drawing near, Jesus accepted the will of the Father: "Father, glorify thy name!" (12:28). God's glory would be shown in a definitive way in Jesus' death and resurrection. We have spoken of it earlier. Now it is clear that Jesus did not seek his glory; the glory was coming, united to a manifestation of the glory of God, and as a consequence of conquering of death (see 11:40). Now we are told that Christ's death is glorification, because it is a consequence of his act of voluntary self-giving. As a result of his death, the world is judged, and by this judgment the prince of this world will "be cast out" (12:31).

Not judgment, however, but the drawing of all to Christ is the ultimate end. "And I, when I am lifted up from the earth, will draw all men to myself" (12:32). The Son of Man's death on the cross produces this result. But his questioners do not understand what he says: The Messiah will be eternal, he cannot die (see 12:34), and so the Son of Man cannot be the Messiah. Yet Jesus affirmed that it is precisely the death of the Son of Man that is the means of exalting the Messiah: Death by crucifixion is a sign of the exaltation and glory of Christ.

The discourse concludes by returning to something said earlier. Christ is the Light, and one must believe in him: "While you have the light, believe in the light, that you may become sons of light" (12:36). Then, says John, Jesus "departed, and hid himself from them." The public ministry of Jesus has ended. The Light that came to the world has left to return to the Father, and those who did not believe in him remain in darkness.

In the following verses (12:37–50), an epilogue to the "book of signs," the Evangelist comments on what he has recounted (see 12:37–43), showing that he has explained and illustrated what the Prologue says: The Light came to its own, and its own did not receive it (see 1:10–11). The Evangelist closes this part of the Gospel with the principal element of Jesus' teaching (see 12:44–50), presented in a few verses introduced by "And Jesus cried out and said . . ." (see 12:44). We are not to suppose that Jesus left and then returned. This is just the Evangelist's way of recapitulating the teaching of Jesus' public ministry and so preparing for the second part of the Gospel, the "book of glory."

7. The Departure of Jesus

Several long discourses of Jesus to his followers precede the glorification of Christ (see 13:1—17:26). The "book of signs" has shown the rejection of the Light by his own; the "book of glory" shows how those who receive and believe in the Light are made sons and daughters of God (see 1:12). In the five chapters describing the Last Supper, only "his own" are present to hear Jesus' plans for them; and it is to them that he speaks in the discourses leading up to his departure. Afterward, in the three chapters describing his passion and death, Jesus is glorified and rises to the Father. By means of his death and resurrection, "his own" now have God as their Father. The Father is "their" Father, as Jesus says to Mary Magdalene when he appears to her after his resurrection: "Go to my brethren and say to them, 'I am ascending to my Father and your Father, to my God and your God'" (20:17).

Thus we can see that the "book of glory" illustrates the subject of the Prologue: "But to all who received him, who believed in his name, he gave power to become children of God; who were born, not of blood nor of the will of the flesh nor of the will of man, but of God" (1:12–13). Thanks to Christ's glorification "his own" are constituted anew—a new people, formed of those who believe in his name (the new Israel, the Church), whom Christ makes sharers in eternal life.

The content of the discourses is to a great extent John's version of Jesus' abundant private teaching to his disciples collected by the Synoptics. Many of the precepts, advice, and promises to the disciples (their mission to the world, the manner of life of the Christian community, the betrayal by Judas, the denial of Peter and the scattering of the disciples, future persecutions, the promise of divine protection, the assistance of the Holy Spirit), many predictions of Christ's death and resurrection, and predictions about the end and the Second Coming in the first three Gospels have parallels in these Last Supper discourses. Here, too, however, another theme is present in the first part of the fourth Gospel: the divine glory revealed in Christ, the knowledge of God, the divine Word that brings life, the relationship between the Father and the Son, etc. Everything centers on union with Christ and eternal life, to which the disciples are led by Jesus' death and resurrection. This life, a consequence of the mutual indwelling of Christ and his disciples that recalls the mutual indwelling of the Father and the Son, is a result of the love of God. If the key words in the first part are "life" and "light," in this part the key word is "love."

The structure is similar to that found elsewhere in the Gospel (chapters 5, 6, 9, 10). First, an action of Jesus is described (13:12–20), followed by dialogues (13:21—14:31). Then there is a long discourse (15:1—16:16), followed by a brief dialogue (16:17–33). The conclusion is a prayer of Jesus (17:1–26). His tone is that of someone between heaven and earth, already, as it were, ascending to glory. Jesus speaks as someone still on earth yet at the same time no longer of it, his words having timeless value as spoken to all who will believe in him now and in ages to come. The form and content are reminiscent of a testament or farewell address.

a) *The action of Jesus* (13:1–20). The washing of the feet is a sign explained and illuminated by the discourses. Among other things, it points to the consummation of the incarnation in the self-giving of his death and to the disciples' participation in this complex reality by means of baptism.

b) *The dialogues* (13:21—14:32). After the prediction of the disciples' betrayal and the departure of Judas (see 13:21–30), a dialogue commences between Jesus and his followers concerning the leave-taking and return of Christ—that is, his death and resurrection. It begins with a reference to the glorification of the Son of Man as something now occurring inasmuch as Jesus' passion has already begun (see 13:31–32). He says he will soon depart for a place (death) where they cannot accompany him. The disciples do not understand. Jesus tells them he is going to prepare a place for them and will return.

The departure Christ was to undertake, death, is his trip to the Father, with whom Jesus is one. Christ crucified is the way by which the disciples should travel to the same goal, the One who communicates knowledge and the vision of God. Yet he will still be with his own (see 13:33—14:14)—by listening to their prayers and sending the Spirit to be with them and in them (see 14:15–17). He will not leave them orphans, for after death he will return in a new way, while his disciples will have life through the knowledge of God that is a participation in the mutual indwelling of the Father and the Son (see 14:18–21). After Jesus' death, and thanks to it, his disciples will enter into union with their living Lord and, through him, also with the Father. Thus they will have eternal life. The whole of this process originates in God's love for the world. After the death of Christ, his disciples' mutual love should replicate the love the Father showed in sending his Son and the love the Son showed in surrendering his life. This is Christian love. And this love should be a revelation to the world, bringing it the faith and knowledge of God, of eternal life. The Spirit will guarantee this (see 14:22–26). Finally, as if in an appendix, these ideas are summarized (see 14:27–31).

c) *The discourse about Christ and his Church* (15:1—16:16). Subjects treated briefly in the previous dialogue—the mutual indwelling of Christ and his disciples, the work of the Paraclete—are developed more fully in this large monologue by Jesus about Christ and his Church that deals with the relationship of the members of the Church with the risen and exalted Lord (see 15:1–17), the disciples' situation in a hostile world (see 15:18—16:11), and the Spirit's action in the Church (see 16:12–16). The vine, a figure of the people of Israel in the Old Testament, with Eucharistic connotations, is used to represent the Church as the true people of God, now revealed by Jesus. But John specifies that Christ crucified and resurrected is the true vine including in itself all members of the true people of God like branches of a vine (see 15:1–8). This image points to the mutual indwelling of Christ and his followers, with love as its principle. Christ's love for his own mirrors the Father's love and has as fruit the loving obedience of his disciples. In this way, new light is again shed upon the commandment of love (see 15:9–17).

In contrast with that love, the Church is to endure the hatred of a hostile world. The disciples, by reason of their faith, are not of the "world of below," but belong to the "world of above" by their union with Christ. Therefore they suffer persecution, like Christ, whom the world also hated (see 15:18–21). This, however, is the judgment of the world (see 15:22–16:11): In rejecting Christ, the world condemns itself, since to reject Christ is to reject the Father.

In this context of judgment, Jesus introduces his teaching about the Paraclete. After the departure of Jesus, he is the "advocate" who defends Christians and the "consoler" who comforts them. In this judgment, he also assumes the role of public prosecutor and pronounces a final sentence upon the world (see 16:8–11). During his ministry, Jesus, the Light of the world, brought condemnation upon those who rejected the Light. After his death, his Spirit comes and affects a judgment of the world, by which the prince of this world is judged and expelled. The Spirit is, in addition, teacher of the Church and mediator of knowledge of Christ and the Father (see 16:12–16).

d) *From here until the end of the chapter* (16:17–33), the discourse is interrupted, as in chapters 13—14, by interventions by the disciples. This is like a résumé of the previous section, where the meaning of Christ's death and resurrection was explained as guaranteeing God's love, the indwelling of Christ, and the Church's power to judge the world. The discourse ends with the announcement of the victory (16:33) that will result from his death and resurrection.

e) *The prayer of Jesus* (17:1–26). This sublime conclusion to the farewell discourses is often called Jesus' "Priestly Prayer." In it Jesus consecrates himself for those whom he will send into the world (see 17:18–19). The prayer includes elements already discussed in the "book of signs" and in the previous farewell discourses.

Union with Christ, dead and resurrected, is now ratified by the prayer of intercession. By the obedient offering of his life, Jesus rises up to the Father, bringing with him all those for whom he intercedes—his disciples and those who will believe in him until the end of time.

In first place (see 17:1–8), Jesus asks for his glorification (that is to say, the glory he had before creation), inasmuch as he has fulfilled all that the Father gave him and has revealed the name of God. He therefore asks for acceptance of his sacrifice on the cross. This is not an egoistical prayer, since the aim of this glorification is that the Son properly glorifies the Father.

Next (see 17:9–19), Jesus contemplates his disciples in their situation in the world after his departure and prays for those whom the Father has given to him that they remain safe, while refusing to pray for the world (which, in rejecting Jesus, is a kingdom of evil). In contrast to a Gnostic Savior, Jesus does not ask that his disciples be taken out of the world, but only that they be protected from the evil one (who is the prince of this world). Asking that they be consecrated as he consecrated himself, Jesus sends them into the world to give testimony to the truth.

Finally (see 17:20–26), Jesus prays for those who in the future are to believe through the word of his disciples: that they be brought to the perfect unity of divine life, one with the Father and Jesus, who are one. This petition will be fulfilled in that the One making it will give his life for his friends.

Through these discourses, John prepares the way for an understanding in all its depth of the Passion narrative which follows.

Chapter 6

THE GLORIFICATION OF JESUS

AS IN THE SYNOPTICS AND THE LETTERS of St. Paul, in the fourth Gospel the cross is the culmination of Jesus' ministry. Distinctively, however, John teaches that the cross not only is the place of execution, as a necessary stage preceding the Resurrection, but is itself the throne of Christ's glory. For the fourth evangelist, Jesus' death is the commencement of his triumph, the first stage of his ascension to the Father, the moment of the glorification of the Son of God.

1. The Death of Jesus in the First Part of the Gospel

Although, as we have seen, it is the "book of glory" that deals with the death and glorification of Christ, one can say that no passage of the Gospel is untouched by the shadow of the passion, or, as the Evangelist might say, not illuminated by Jesus' death. In fact, many passages in the "book of signs" make direct reference to the glorious exaltation of Jesus on the cross. To better understand the account of the Passion, therefore, we need to look briefly at the passages in the first part of the Gospel alluding to the death of Jesus. Most have already been considered to some extent in discussing the discourses, but here we shall look at them together in order to provide a more unified vision of how John presents Christ's glorification.

The Hour of Jesus

A first group of texts is made up of those that speak of "Jesus' hour." As has already been suggested, the Evangelist uses this expression to refer to the time of Jesus' glorification on the Cross. This is the hour that reveals his majesty, as St. Augustine says: *Non qua cogeretur mori sed qua dignaretur occidi*, not forced to die but permitting himself to be killed.

In the fourth Gospel the word "hour" sometimes is used in a chronological sense to indicate a specific time of day: the tenth hour, the sixth hour, etc. But even then it suggests something more, as in 4:21, 23: "Jesus said to her, "Woman, believe me, the hour is coming when neither on this mountain nor in Jerusalem will you worship the Father. . . . But the hour is coming, and now is, when the true worshipers will worship the Father in spirit and truth, for such the Father seeks to worship him"; and 5:25: "Truly, truly, I say to you, the hour is coming, and now is, when the dead will hear the voice of the Son of God, and those who hear will live."

"Hour" here indicates the moment when something will occur, but it also has a transcendent dimension. The particular moment provides a glimpse of an "hour" with broader significance. In light of other references, it is clear that every "hour" is related to the "hour" par excellence, "the hour of Jesus," to which reference is made throughout the Gospel and which is consistently linked to the word "arrive." Moreover, everything in the fourth Gospel appears focused on that "mysterious hour" that is to come: "So they sought to arrest him; but no one laid hands on him, because his hour had not yet come" (7:30); "These words he spoke in the treasury, as he taught in the temple; but no one arrested him, because his hour had not yet come" (8:20).

As the narrative proceeds, it becomes increasingly clear that this hour is approaching and involves a crucial moment in Jesus' life. Thus, when some Hellenistic Jews wish to see him, he responds: "The hour has come for the Son of man to be glorified. . . . Now is my soul troubled. And what shall I say? 'Father, save me from this hour?' No, for this purpose I have come to this hour" (12:23, 27).

Evidently that "hour" will bring with it something repugnant to Jesus for which he nonetheless longs. This is why he is troubled. He knows he has come "for that hour" and accepting it will give glory to his Father; for the moment it is not said why that hour causes him to feel repulsion. Only a little later, at the beginning of the "book of glory," in the context of the Last Supper, does the Evangelist explain: "Now before the feast of the Passover, when Jesus knew that his hour had come to depart out of this world to the Father, having loved his own who were in the world, he loved them to the end" (13:1). Here is the first explicit statement of what the reader has already guessed: "Jesus' hour" arrives with his death.

But his death is not a failure. It is not the result of factors at once sad and unavoidable, but a moment voluntarily accepted, a manifestation of Jesus' love for his Father and for those for whom he dies. His death therefore will be a victory, the path that leads back to the Father. Thus the hour of Jesus is in itself an hour of glorification, as he makes clear at the start of his priestly prayer: "Jesus . . . lifted up his eyes to heaven and said, 'Father, the hour has come; glorify thy Son that the Son may glorify thee'" (17:1).

Jesus' death is his glorification and the glorification of the Father inasmuch as Christ, obeying the redemptive decree of God, brings to completion the work of salvation for the glory of God the Father. The cause of that glorification is love. The love with which Jesus gave his life manifests the value of the Father's love for his Son and for the world. The Father responds by glorifying him as the Son of Man—that is, in his humanity and through his resurrection and exaltation at the Father's right hand. In addition, with his death, Christ offers man the possibility of attaining eternal life in the knowledge of the Father and his only begotten Son, which redounds to the glorification of both.

This hour of Christ's glorification, the hour of the supreme manifestation of love, explains and is in turn illuminated by the other references to the "hour" in the Gospel. We cannot examine them all. But the first and last are closely related and can be understood in light of the significance of Jesus' hour as the occasion of his glorious return to the Father: "And Jesus said to her, 'O woman, what have you to do with me? My hour has not yet come'" (2:4); and "Then he said to the disciple, 'Behold, your mother!' And from that hour the disciple took her to his own home" (19:27).

In both cases, "hour" can be understood simply as a particular "moment." But viewed in relation to the Gospel as a whole, the "hour" of Jesus signifies a unitary process initiated in his manifestation to the world by signs that provoke acceptance and rejection and culminating in his death and resurrection. Jesus' hour is his entire ministry, all of which leads to his glorification. After his death, when he has been glorified, this hour is to become a reality among his disciples, and his mother will be the one who sees to it that the fruit of that hour reaches them. To her, as the New Eve, are entrusted his descendants, who must be protected against the enemy defeated by Christ in the hour of the cross.

"To Be Raised/Exalted"

Another group of three passages from the "book of signs" referring to Jesus' glorification speaks of Jesus who was soon to be "raised on high." The Greek verb *hypsoo*, "to raise," has a twofold significance in John. Literally, it means "to raise, to lift up." In its passive form, it can be translated as "to be crucified" (having been nailed to the cross, the crucified person is raised up). Its figurative sense is "to exalt, to honor." In the fourth Gospel the two meanings are joined. Thus the Evangelist indicates that the ignominious and cruel death of Jesus on the cross is at the same time Christ's exaltation/glorification. In the background is the figure of the Suffering Servant of the Lord in Isaiah: "Behold, my servant shall prosper, he shall be exalted and lifted up, and shall be very high" (Is 52:13). These words of the prophet, announcing that the Servant of God would be exalted by suffering, are seen by the Evangelist as fulfilled in Jesus' death on the cross.

The three passages have parallels in the three Synoptic announcements of the passion: "the Son of man must suffer many things . . . ," "will be delivered into the hands of men . . . ," "[they will] kill him . . ." (Mk 8:31; 9:31; 10:33–34). For John, those announcements are not only predictions of Jesus' death but declarations regarding his glorification. The three passages are as follows:

a) 3:13–15: "No one has ascended into heaven but he who descended from heaven, the Son of man. And as Moses lifted up the serpent in the wilderness, so must the Son of man be lifted up, that whoever believes in him may have eternal life."

This occurs in Jesus' dialogue with Nicodemus, the Pharisee who came to him at night. Jesus explains to him that one needs faith, and he compares his coming crucifixion to the bronze serpent that, at God's command, Moses raised on a pole as a remedy to cure Israelites bitten by the serpents in the desert (see Nm 21:8–9). To be saved, one must look at Jesus on the cross. He is salvation and life for those who look to him with faith, but a cause of judgment for those who do not believe in him. When Jesus dies, the Evangelist says, "They shall look on him whom they have pierced" (19:37). The words of the prophet Zechariah (see 12:10) are fulfilled and the words pronounced by Jesus about lack of faith or rejection of the crucified become a reality. The cross is the source of salvation.

b) 8:28: "So Jesus said, 'When you have lifted up the Son of man, then you will know that I am he, and that I do nothing on my own authority but speak thus as the Father taught me.'"

These words are spoken by Jesus in one of his disputes with "the Jews" (see 8:21–30). In the background is the theme of death. His hearers take his statement that he is leaving for a place where they cannot follow him as referring to his death and so suspect that he is referring to suicide. In response, Jesus says he does not belong to this world as they do but is from a world "above"; since his hearers were "from below," they could not follow him to his destination. And referring to the "raising of the Son of Man," he indicates that those he is speaking to will help him in his ascent to the world above by killing him. With his death, however, they will come to know his true condition—they will know "that it was he."

The expression "I am," which Jesus repeats in a number of places in the Gospel (see chapter 7 of this book) can mean simply, "It is I," or it can refer to the name of God as revealed to Moses: "I AM WHO AM" (Ex 3:14). This passage plays on the two meanings. Jesus appropriates the divine name, while at the same time designating himself. In this case, it is clear that his crucifixion will be his exaltation, since he will be truly known for what he is: the Son of God, one with the Father.

c) 12:31–34: "'Now is the judgment of this world, now shall the ruler of this world be cast out; and I, when I am lifted up from the earth, will draw all men to myself.' He said this to show by what death he was to die. The crowd answered him, 'We have heard from the law that the Christ remains forever. How can you say that the Son of man must be lifted up?'"

The context of this third passage is Jesus' announcement of the imminent arrival of his "hour" when the group of Hellenistic Jews asks to see him (see 12:20–37). He begins with the image of a seed that falls into the earth and, dying, produces much fruit, and ends with the declaration that he must draw all people to himself. Judgment and the condemnation of the evil one are emphasized. The final judgment of the world has already begun because the passion has already begun. With the death of Jesus—that is, with his exaltation—the definitive defeat of Satan will occur. But the judgment is not the last word. The final consequence of Jesus' glorification is that all humankind and the entire cosmos are drawn toward him, toward the "world above." This glorification is universal in its outreach: His death on the cross will be the means of attracting all people and all things. The cross is the foundation of the Church, which is universal.

"Giving His Life" / "Dying For"

Another set of passages referring to his passion and death affirms that Christ is giving his life (or his flesh) for others. One can distinguish four:

a) 6:51: "I am the living bread which came down from heaven; if any one eats of this bread, he will live forever; and the bread which I shall give for the life of the world is my flesh. . . ."

Jesus will give his flesh. To give is to surrender, and to surrender one's flesh or one's life is to die, just as "drink his blood" is an allusion to the shedding of blood and so to a violent death. Jesus' words are equivalent to his words instituting the Eucharist: "This is my body which is for you" (1 Cor 11:24). This shows the inseparable relation between his death on the cross and the Eucharist. Jesus, the Bread of Life, must be understood in the light of his crucifixion and death. He surrenders his life on the Cross, converts himself into the Bread of Life for the world by his death. His body crucified and his blood shed reach humankind through the Eucharist. That death, voluntary and vicarious, guarantees that eternal life, the true life, will remain in human beings.

b) 10:11: "I am the good shepherd. The good shepherd lays down his life for the sheep."

Christ gives life by giving himself. In the Good Shepherd discourse, he makes it clear that he is not only ready to die for his sheep, but will do so voluntarily and freely: "For this reason the Father loves me, because I lay down my life, that I may take it again. No one takes it from me, but I lay it down of my own accord. I have power to lay it down, and I have power to take it again" (10:17–18). Pope Benedict XVI writes:

> Just as the bread discourse does not merely allude to the word, but goes on to speak of the Word that became flesh and also gift "for the life of the world" (6:51), so too the shepherd discourse revolves completely around the idea of Jesus laying down his life for the "sheep." The Cross is at the center of the shepherd discourse. And it is portrayed not as an act of violence that takes Jesus unawares and attacks him from the outside, but as a free gift of his very self: "I lay down my life, that I may take it again. No one takes it from me, but I lay it down of my own accord" (10:17–18). Here Jesus interprets for us what happens at the institution of the Eucharist: He transforms the outward violence of the act of crucifixion into an act of freely giving his life for others. Jesus does not give *something* but rather he gives himself.[1]

c) 11:49–53: "One of them, Caiaphas, who was high priest that year, said to them, 'You know nothing at all; you do not understand that it is expedient for you that one man should die for the people, and that the whole nation should not perish.' He did not say this of his own accord, but being high priest that year he prophesied that Jesus should die for the nation, and not for the nation only, but to gather into one

---

1. Ratzinger/Benedict XVI, *Jesus of Nazareth*, vol. I, pp. 328–329.

the children of God who are scattered abroad. So from that day on they took counsel how to put him to death."

The text occurs in the account of the meeting of the Sanhedrin during which Jesus is formally condemned to death by the authorities (see 11:47–53). When the Evangelist quotes Caiaphas as saying that Jesus was to "die for the people," the deep meaning of this death is indicated. The Greek preposition *hyper* allows a double significance: "in the place of" and "for," or "in favor of." As Caiaphas uses it, the meaning is "die instead of the people." John points out that not only is he "dying instead of"—that is, so that the people of Israel do not die—but that he is Christ. With the death of Jesus, the nation will be saved.

Jesus was going to die not only in place of the true Israel, the universal Church, but for its salvation. In being exalted on the cross, Christ attracts and reunites the true people of God, formed by all believers, whether Israelites or not. This is the same idea expressed in the discourse on the Good Shepherd: "I have other sheep that are not of this fold; I must bring them also, and they will heed my voice. So there shall be one flock, one shepherd" (10:16). Here is a confirmation of the vicarious death of Christ that we also find in Mark 10:45: "For the Son of man also came not to be served but to serve, and to give his life as a ransom for many."

d) 12:23–24: "And Jesus answered them, 'The hour has come for the Son of Man to be glorified. Truly, truly, I say to you, unless a grain of wheat falls into the earth and dies, it remains alone; but if it dies, it bears much fruit.'"

The passage immediately precedes one we have already considered about the death and exaltation of the Son of Man, at the time the Hellenists sought to see Jesus. Humiliation is the path to exaltation. Death is the culmination of his self-surrender and the way by which Jesus' life acquires its full efficacy; it brings about the redemption of the human race. Jesus has made himself a grain of wheat that, in dying, produces much fruit. The cross is not failure: what is lost becomes gain (see 12:25), and without death there is no life.

"The Lamb of God"

A passage of special interest illustrates John's understanding of Jesus' death, which adds a sacrificial note. Presenting the testimony of John the Baptist, the Evangelist writes: "The next day he saw Jesus coming toward him, and said, 'Behold, the Lamb of God, who takes away the sin of the world'" (1:29). The following day, he again calls Jesus "the Lamb of God" (1:36). The Fathers of the Church saw in the reference to a lamb a symbol of innocence and integrity, expressing the pure innocence of Jesus.

The expression "Lamb of God" finds its later clarification and confirmation in the account of the passion, when John notes that Jesus was condemned on the eve of Passover, at the sixth hour (see 19:14), and that when he was dead, his executioners broke none of his bones (see 19:33, 36). The eve of the Passover was when everything necessary for the feast was prepared. At the sixth hour, midday, the lambs to be eaten at the paschal meal were ritually slaughtered. In conformity with the legislation set out in Exodus, none of the bones of the lamb to be eaten at the paschal meal was to be broken (see Ex 12:46). In light of these references, it seems clear that the expression "Lamb of God" refers to Jesus as the Paschal Lamb, sacrificed for the sins of humankind.

At the same time, however, the expression also suggests other realities. The most evocative of these is the figure of the suffering servant prophesied by Isaiah, especially in the fourth canticle, where the servant is presented as an innocent lamb that is sacrificed: "Like a lamb that is led to the slaughter, and like a sheep that before its shearers is dumb, so he opened not his mouth" (Is 53:7).

Considered in this light, the "Lamb of God" indicates the expiatory significance of Jesus' death—"He has borne our griefs and carried our sorrows" (Is 53:4)—and the character of the exaltation that accompanied it: "Behold, my servant shall prosper, he shall be exalted and lifted up, and shall be very high" (Is 52:13). The reference to the songs of the servant also is taken up by the German exegete Joachim Jeremiah, who thinks "lamb of God" may be a bad translation of the Aramaic, a language in which the words for "lamb" and "servant" sound almost alike. Thus John could have said, "This is the servant of God," in this way pointing out that the prophecy of Isaiah was fulfilled.

The expression could also allude to the *tamid*, the daily sacrifice in the temple of Jerusalem of a one-year-old lamb without defect. That would highlight the sacrificial character of Jesus' death while at the same time evoking the image of the Lamb of the Apocalypse, standing "as though it had been slain" (Rv 5:6, 12; 13:8), in whose blood the confessors of the faith wash themselves and make their garments white (see Rv 7:14). This would be an allusion to the free and triumphant manner in which Christ's sacrifice becomes manifest.

Nor can we exclude the possibility that the expression "Lamb of God" also refers to the sacrifice of Abraham (Gn 22:1–14). Isaac would then be a type of the beloved Son of God, with the difference that God did not spare Jesus the death that he freely accepted. Rabbinical thinking, reflecting a "theology of the bindings (*aqeda*)" of Isaac, emphasized the voluntariness with which Abraham's son prepared himself to be sacrificed. According to this rabbinical tradition, Isaac was a man of thirty-seven who tied himself up in order to be sacrificed. Since Abraham sacrificed a sheep—a ram—in place of his son (Gn 22:13), "Lamb of God" used in reference to Jesus was meant to teach that Jesus is the lamb sacrificed so that humankind would not die.

Evidently, then, the numerous allusions to the Old and New Testaments and to the Judaism of the day are not exclusive. Each sheds light on the meaning of the expression and in some way complements the others. The riches of the Gospel are inexhaustible.

Two Prophetic Signs

Finally, two scenes are directly related to the death of Jesus. Both occur close to a Passover. The cleansing of the temple (2:13–22) comes at the beginning of the Gospel, while the anointing of Jesus by Mary in Bethany (12:1–11) is just before the start of his passion.

In the Synoptic Gospels, the cleansing of the temple by Jesus at the beginning of his last week in Jerusalem is the immediate cause of his condemnation to death. In the fourth Gospel, by contrast, this incident is situated at the beginning of Jesus' ministry. As was said earlier, however, it not only explicitly announces the destruction of the temple—that is, the death of Jesus—but also marks for John the beginning of the process by which the Jewish authorities condemned Jesus to death. The Synoptics situate Jesus' condemnation on the night before his death; in John's version, it extends over the whole Gospel.

The anointing in Bethany in effect concludes the ministry of Jesus and comes immediately before his triumphal entry into Jerusalem. As noted above (chaper 4) in the analysis of the signs, the connection with his death is clear: Mary anoints the body of Jesus as one anoints a dead body, thus prefiguring his burial. The process of his condemnation to death that begins at the start of his ministry with the purification of the temple is verified by a sign at the end of the ministry, prefiguring what would occur through his exaltation on the cross.

2. The Supper with His Disciples

A more comprehensive study of the passion would require including Jesus' parting words to his disciples during the Last

Supper as part of the "book of glory." For brevity's sake, however, the content of those discourses was treated in the preceding chapter along with other discourses of Jesus (see chaper 5, § 8).

As we have seen, in this second part of the Gospel, the usual structure is reversed, so that the sign or action precedes the discourse: the discourses then explain the action—that is, the events of the passion. But these discourses also follow and explain a sign—namely, the washing of the feet, which has the peculiarity of anticipating the rest of the account. For Jesus' washing of the disciples' feet (see 13:1–20) is a prologue to the passion that embodies a summation of its significance.

The Word of God became incarnate, divesting himself of glory and taking on the human condition. After carrying out the purification (the work of redemption) by his death on the cross, Jesus resumes his previous condition and returns to the Father, bringing all mankind with him in his humanity. This reflects the movement of descent and ascent present in the entire Gospel. This action, itself charged with symbolism, is explained by the discourses following the washing in which Jesus speaks to the disciples of his departure and return, and makes it possible for them to grasp the meaning of the passion.

Completing the scene of the washing is the prediction of the disciples' betrayal (see 13:21–30). Once more the teaching of the Prologue appears: Jesus came "to his own" and they rejected him (see 1:11). Confronted with this treason, Jesus shudders, as he shuddered before the approach of his "hour" (12:27). Judas eats the morsel that Jesus offers him, accepting this proof of affection without changing his plans. He chooses Satan and loses himself in the night (see 13:30), for he loves darkness more than light (see 3:19). The hour of darkness has come. But the light will shine through the darkness on the morning after the Sabbath.

The Account of the Passion

A comparison of John's account of the passion with that of the Synoptics (leaving aside the Last Supper) shows common elements and a few differences. Certain episodes and details in the Synoptics are not present in John: for example, the prayer in the garden, the official session of the Sanhedrin, Simon of Cyrene's assistance, the brief appearance of Pilate's wife, the sympathy of the women of Jerusalem, the insults to the crucified, the darkness, the earthquake at the moment of his death, the tearing of the temple veil.

On the other hand, the fourth Gospel contains scenes or references not found in the Synoptics. Among these are the session before Annas, the long dialogues with Pilate, Jesus' words to his mother and the beloved disciple, the opening of his side by a lance, the seamless tunic, etc. Details, such as names of some persons and places and certain incidents and words, are in John but not the first three Gospels. Clearly, too, John adopts a perspective of his own in passages common to all four Gospels: that Jesus' arrest manifested his divinity; that Jesus voluntarily confronts his passion, drinking the chalice that the Father prepared for him until he knows that all has been accomplished and he gives up his Spirit; that Jesus' title of kingship was a political offense in the eyes of the Roman authorities; that the universal value of Jesus' death is suggested by the fact that the title which is the cause of his death was displayed upon the cross in three languages, etc.

John's account of the passion also is more emotional and more solemn than that of the Synoptics. In the fourth Gospel, as in the others, the passion is a fulfillment of Scripture, but John includes some citations not in the Synoptics: for example, "I am thirsty" (19:28; see Ps 69:21); "Not a bone of him shall be broken" (19:36; see Ps 34:20; Ex 12:46; Nm 9:12); "They shall look on him whom they have pierced" (19:37; Zec 12:10). Moreover, he also omits others, such as "My God, my God, why hast thou forsaken me?" (Ps 22:1).

In John, features proper to the suffering servant of Isaiah, emphasized in the first three Gospels by relating Jesus' terrible suffering and humiliations, received less emphasis. Instead of focusing on Jesus as victim, John stresses his majesty. When he is taken prisoner, accused before Annas, struck and crowned with thorns, interrogated by Pilate, and nailed to the cross, his royalty shines forth. Jesus is not carried along by circumstances that lead to his death. With calm dignity, he shows full understanding and control of what is happening: he knows all that is going to occur (see 18:4) and dies when all has been fulfilled (see 19:28). He acts freely and with authority, fulfilling his Father's will (see 18:11; 19:30). This is clear from the beginning of the Passion, when he is arrested in the garden. When he says "I am he," those who have come to arrest him, recognizing his divine majesty, step back and fall to the ground (see 18:6–8). Here is the majesty corresponding to his kingship and shown above all in the trial before Pilate and in the title placed on the cross proclaiming the cause of his condemnation. Jesus is a king reigning from the cross that is his throne. Consistent with what he has said throughout the Gospel, the cross will be the place of his enthronement and exaltation.

Five scenes can be distinguished in the account of the Passion: 1) the arrest (18:1–12); 2) the interrogation by Annas and Peter's denials (18:13–27); 3) the trial before Pilate (18:28–19:16); 4) the crucifixion and death of Jesus (19:17–37); and 5) his burial (19:38–42). There is a certain circularity to the narrative: when Jesus is seized in a garden, he is taken away bound; when he dies, he is bound by burial cloths and buried in a garden.

1. *The arrest* (18:1–12). This occurs in a garden on the other side of the Kidron valley (see 18:1). In the Synoptics, the place is called Gethsemane or Mount of Olives. The agitation described by the Synoptics at what is about to happen has already been described by John in 12:27–28, when some Hellenists wish to see him (see above § 1). Two figures stand out in relation to Jesus

at the time of his arrest: Judas and Peter. Both are linked to the theme of betrayal.

Jesus goes to meet Judas, who comes leading the group of captors. After he ate the morsel Jesus offered him, Satan entered him, and he disappeared into the night (see 13:27, 30). Now he comes by the light of lanterns and torches (see 18:3)—artificial light facing the light of the world whom he is betraying. In the face of the divine words "I am he" which Jesus pronounces, his adversaries fall to the ground. This is what happens in the Old Testament when God reveals himself: Those present fall to the ground on their faces. Here is the fulfillment of Isaiah's prophecy: "Whoever stirs up strife with you shall fall because of you" (Is 54:15). Thus John shows the divine character of Jesus, who has power to confront the darkness.

Jesus tells his captors not to harm his followers. He cares for his sheep and will let none perish (see 18:8–9; 10:27–28). He had declared as much in his prayer: "While I was with them I guarded them in your name. I have guarded those whom you gave me and none of them has been lost, except the son of perdition, so that the Scripture might be fulfilled" (17:12; see 6:39). Thus, to save his flock, he went to face his enemies as the shepherd faces the wolf.

Peter stands in contrast to Judas. Although he tries to defend Jesus, it is futile. The human means, the sword, can do nothing in the face of the divine will that the chalice be drunk. In the Synoptic account of Jesus' prayer in the garden, Jesus asks the Father that, if possible, he be spared this chalice (see Mk 14:36). Rather than being powerless against the treachery of Judas, he gave himself willingly to fulfill the will of his Father. He surrendered himself to God.

2. *Interrogation before Annas; Peter's denials* (18:13–27). Here, as in the previous scene, other figures—Peter and the Jewish authorities—are prominent along with Jesus. Jesus is arrested and bound, as Isaac was bound by his father Abraham

(see Gn 22:9), and is brought before Annas, who enjoyed great authority as former high priest. Peter is introduced by the "other disciple" (perhaps the beloved disciple) who is known to the high priest and is interrogated by the portress about whether he is a disciple of the one who has been brought there as a prisoner. In contrast with Jesus' "I am he" in the garden, we have Peter's "I am not" (i.e., a disciple of Jesus) said by Peter and the reference to the fire (see 18:17–18). This "no" beside the fire is repeated (see 18:25), and when Peter once more denies Jesus, the cock crows (see 18:27). Peter does not reappear until the morning of the Resurrection. Later, beside a fire on the shore of the lake, he expiates his denials with a triple declaration of his love for Jesus.

Jesus' interrogators ask him about his doctrine and his disciples, perhaps trying to learn if he is a false prophet. He denies nothing and points out that he has said nothing in secret (see 18:20). For saying this to Annas he is struck (see 18:22). Jesus asks the reason for this affront and gets no answer; though he is the one accused, he has the last word. Next he is sent bound to Caiaphas, the current high priest (see 18:24), but the Evangelist does not speak of another interrogation.

3. *Trial before Pilate* (18:28–19:16). John presents the judicial process before Pilate in a much more dramatic fashion than the other evangelists do. There are two settings: the exterior patio of the praetorium, the residence of the Roman prefect, where "the Jews" are present, and an interior room of that building. Many interpreters believe the trial took place in seven segments marked (explicitly or implicitly) by Pilate's exits and entrances in each of the two locations:

a) Outside: The Jewish authorities ask that Jesus be condemned as a criminal (18:39–32).
b) Inside: Dialogue between Pilate and Jesus about his kingship (18:33–38).

c) Outside: The Jewish authorities express their preference for Barabbas (18:38-40)
d) Inside: The crowning with thorns: Jesus, king (19:1-3).
e) Outside: The Jewish authorities insist that Jesus has claimed to be the son of God (19:4-8).
f) Inside: Dialogue of Pilate with Jesus about his origin and power (19:9-11).
g) Outside: The Jewish authorities succeed in having Pilate condemn Jesus (19:12-16).

The Evangelist situates the principal theme—Jesus is king (the Messiah)—in the center (d). The trial focuses on Jesus' kingship, as Pilate's interventions emphasize: "Are you the king of the Jews?" (18:33); "Do you want me to release to you the king of the Jews?" (18:39); "Shall I crucify your king?" (19:15). Jesus is enthroned in a mocking manner: "Hail, king of the Jews" (19:3). Pilate presents the disfigured "man" (19:5) to his "subjects," and questions his royal condition: "Where are you from?" (19:9).

At every moment, however, it is clear that Jesus' kingdom is not a political one. Thus the Jewish authorities recognize that they seek his death for having made himself out to be the Son of God. Pilate, on the other hand, refers to Jesus' kingship in the inscription he orders placed on the cross (see 19:19-22). In the trial, it is emphasized that Jesus is king and the true kingship is the reign of truth. Jesus is the truth (see 14:6), and he says the essence of his kingdom lies in "giving witness to the truth" (18:37). This means "giving priority to God and his will over against the interests of the world and its powers. God is the criterion of being. In this sense, the truth is the real 'King' that confers light and greatness upon all things"[2]

Human beings are judged by the truth, which is also light, and in the end it is the truth that those who judge Jesus, Pilate,

---

2. Ratzinger/Benedict XVI, *Jesus of Nazareth*, vol. 2, pp. 192-193.

and the Jewish authorities are themselves judged. This man who stands here in a state of humiliation, the *Ecce homo* (see 19:5), is in reality the Son of Man who comes to judge. Those like Pilate who fail to stand on the side of truth end as servants of the world (the Jewish authorities).

The solemnity of the moment is indicated by the place (see 19:13)—the Lithostrotos; the day—the Parasceve (eve of the Passover); and the hour (see 19:14)—about noon, the time of the sacrifice of the Passover lamb in the temple.

4. *Crucifixion and death* (19:17–37). John's account of the Passion does not mention Simon of Cyrene—Jesus carries the cross for himself (see 19:17), the point being that he carried out his mission voluntarily. In the prologue to his *Commentary on St. John*, St. Thomas comments that the Synoptics picture our Lord carrying the cross as a convict carries his instrument of torment, while in the fourth Gospel he carries it as a king carries his scepter. Pilate causes Jesus' royalty to be proclaimed in three languages (see 19:19–20), which indicates the universal scope of his kingship: Jesus is king of the universe.

The dividing up of his clothing among the soldiers fulfills Scripture (see 19:23–24). The seamless tunic (perhaps an allusion to that of the high priest) that they do not tear (see 19:24) symbolizes the unity of the Church, for which Jesus asked of his Father in his priestly prayer (see 17:20–26). The presence of his mother and the beloved disciple (see 19:25–27), together with the blood and water that flow from Christ's side (see 19:34), recalls the wedding feast at Cana (see 2:1–11). In designating his mother as mother of his disciples, represented by the one there present, Jesus inaugurates a new community of disciples who are mother and brother to him. His thirst (see 19:28) is a reminder of the chalice he must drink (see 18:11) to fulfill the Father's will to the end (see 13:1). It also recalls his meeting with the Samaritan woman (see 4:7) and his desire to save all souls.

With his death, "It is finished" (19:30)—that is, the work of salvation has been accomplished (see 4:34; 5:36; 17:4). The words "gave up his spirit" (19:30) indicate that Jesus really died and also suggests his sending of the Holy Spirit, so often promised during his public life (see 14:26; 15:26; 16:6–14). The water and blood that gush from his side evoke numerous signs and sayings in the Gospel and especially 7:38–39, where the water that flows from his body refers to the Spirit, not to be given until Christ is glorified, and the blood alludes to the "true drink" that Jesus promises (see 6:55). At the same time, his opened side symbolizes the Church and the believers incorporated into her by baptism and the Eucharist. Like the paschal lamb whose bones were not to be broken, he pours out all his blood in order to be eaten. Eternal life depends on Christ's death as a self-offering that fulfills the Father's will.

While the Cross is the culmination of Jesus' abasement, it is also there that the Son of Man is elevated above the earth to return to his Father. The crucifixion is his lifting up, his glorification. Jesus descends in order to rise.

5. *His burial* (19:38–42). Unlike the Synoptics, John makes no mention of the women who observed these events. Those who now step forward are two men: Nicodemus and Joseph of Arimathea. Christ's death already begins to draw everyone (see 12:32); Joseph, previously a hidden disciple, no longer hides, while he who came by night, Nicodemus, now comes in daylight. The service they perform for Jesus is extraordinary: The great quantity of aromatic spices used to prepare his body suggests a burial worthy of a king.

4. His Apparitions

In John, Christ's death cannot be separated from his resurrection. His exaltation begins with his death, inasmuch as it implies his resurrection. Thus a few brief references to the apparitions of the risen Christ are in order here.

Like the Synoptics, John does not describe the Resurrection. But he calls attention to the signs of its occurrence: the empty sepulcher and the peculiar disposition of the linens. Of course, these indications are not sufficient in themselves to cause belief in the Resurrection. Indeed, Mary Magdalene and Peter are witnesses of these signs yet do not say they believe. Rather, like Thomas, they believe after seeing him. On the other hand, the beloved disciple believes before seeing the risen Christ. Entering the sepulcher and coming upon the folded linens and the head covering by itself, "he saw and believed" (20:8). Therefore, they are blessed who, in imitation of the beloved disciple, believe because of the signs without seeing the risen Christ (see 20:29). But faith clearly is a consequence of love; loving more, he reached the tomb first.

Jesus appears to Mary Magdalene and, like the good shepherd, calls her by her name (see 10:3–4). The words of the Risen One, "Whom do you seek?" (20:15) and the title "*Rabbuni*" (Master) evoke the scene of calling the first disciples: "Jesus turned and, seeing that they were following him, asked them: 'What are you looking for?'" (1:38). This is a new beginning. And like Andrew and Philip, Mary, too, is sent to proclaim what she has seen. As a consequence of his resurrection and ascension to the Father, Jesus gives the power to become children of God to those who believe in him (1:12). No longer are they disciples, but brothers and sisters.

Christ's appearances in the cenacle show first of all that the Risen One is he who was crucified. This is apparent from the wounded hands and side he exhibits to the disciples (see 20:20). Now is the moment for gathering the fruit of his exaltation on the cross. The peace and joy for which the Jews looked in the last time, become real with his appearance (see 20:19–20), just as he had promised in his farewell discourse (see 14:27; 16:33; 16:20–22; 17:13). His sending forth of his Spirit (see 20:22) crowns the Johannine Pentecost and points to the link between the disciples' mission and the gift of the Spirit. This is the new creation: Just as God breathed the breath of life into Adam and man began to live, so Jesus now breathes his own Spirit upon the disciples, so that they have eternal life. His words to Nicodemus about the need to be born of water and the Spirit are fulfilled (3:5–8). A new humanity has been born. The Church has been born, in which Christ lives by his Spirit. The power he conferred to pardon and retain sins is a communication of his power. Jesus, judge of the world, communicates this power through the Spirit to his disciples, so that they exercise that judgment among men.

The appearance to Thomas makes it clear that, as was bound to happen, reports of appearances of the risen Jesus were met with unbelief. The evangelists all agree on this (see Mk 16:8, 14; Mt 28:17; Lk 24:11). Thomas wanted to see and touch (see 20:25): Not accepting the word of the others, he sought confirmation that something miraculous had happened. But Jesus reproached him for his lack of faith, as he did those who asked for a miracle in Cana: "Unless you see signs and wonders, you will not believe" (4:48). But then, face-to-face with Jesus, Thomas ceases to be an archetype of unbelief and utters the supreme confession of faith in Christ in all the Gospels: "My Lord and my God!" (20:28). This is an echo of the opening of the Prologue: "The Word was God" (1:1). In Thomas' recognition of the divinity of Jesus, the words of Jesus are realized: "When you have lifted up the Son of Man, then you will know that I am" (8:28).

Just before the first "conclusion" of the Gospel (see 20:30–31), already discussed (chap. 4 above), comes a final blessing. Future readers, believers of all times, shall be blessed for believing without having seen (see 20:29). No longer is theirs a faith based on miraculous signs, but a faith based on the word of others—in this case, on the word of the beloved disciple.

In the appendix (chapter 21), we find the appearance of the risen Jesus at the Lake of Galilee. Peter's role as head of the community of believers is underlined. The account is divided into two parts: the scene of the fishing (21:1–4) and the words of Jesus to Peter and the beloved disciple (21:15–23).

The miraculous catch of fish symbolizes the fruit of the apostolic mission—a mission without results in Jesus' absence, as night and the initial absence of the Lord both indicate (see 15:5). With Jesus present, however, the catch is abundant: When Peter removes the net from the water, it contains 153 large fish (see 21:11). The "taking" or "dragging" of the net once more recalls the glorification of Jesus: "And I, when I am lifted up from the earth, will draw all men to myself" (12:32)—a reference to the universality of his mission. The scene of the meal also has a Eucharistic symbolism: the lakeshore, the pan and the fish on the fire, the distribution of the bread and fish among the disciples all evoke the scene of the multiplication of loaves and fishes, which also took place close to the lake (see 6:1–13), and had Eucharistic connotations (the risen Christ is in the breaking of the bread).

The second scene (21:15–23) is likewise linked to the Passion. As Peter denied Jesus while close to a fire, so now, close to a fire, Peter is rehabilitated before the Risen One, who predicts his death and exhorts him to follow him to the end. Thus Jesus' words to him at the farewell are fulfilled: When Peter said he was ready to follow Jesus and to give his life for him, Jesus replied: "You shall follow afterward" (13:36). Like Jesus the shepherd (chapter 10), Peter will be shepherd of the community to the point of giving his life for the sheep. Death also will come to the beloved disciple, probably already dead when the Gospel was written (see 21:23). Clearly, no one should be followed, no matter how important, except Jesus.

The beginning of the Gospel presents the descent of the Eternal Word of the Father who became man. Jesus' whole ministry was to be an ascending, a return whence he had come, thus realizing the words of the prophet Isaiah: "For as the rain and the snow come down from heaven, and return not thither but water the earth, making it bring forth and sprout, giving seed to the sower and bread to the eater, so shall my word be that goes forth from my mouth; it shall not return to me empty, but it shall accomplish that which I purpose, and prosper in the thing for which I sent it (Is 55:10–11). Jesus accomplishes the mission given him by the Father. Here is the elevation of the Son of Man, who draws everyone to himself. This elevation culminates on the cross, his exaltation and glorification. Glorified, he returns to the Father and gives his disciples the Holy Spirit, who causes them be born from above (see 3:3, 5) and turns them into children of God and brothers of Jesus Christ (see 20:17).

Chapter 7

THEOLOGICAL QUESTIONS

AS WE HAVE SEEN, the fourth Gospel is sometimes called the "spiritual Gospel," while the Evangelist, given the way in which he soars up to the Word to contemplate the mystery of God, is spoken of as "the Theologian" for his soaring contemplation of the divine mystery. Thus, the theology of the fourth Gospel merits special attention. Clearly, however, its theology does not consist of formulations about God and the Christian life proposed by its author for belief. Rather, the fourth Gospel is more than anything a report, an account of faith generated by the Spirit.

Here, arising from apostolic testimony, the inspiration of the Paraclete, and the activity of the Evangelist, we encounter the figure and the mission of Jesus Christ, and the huge leap in our knowledge of the true God embodied in both. The Evangelist penetrates into the essential meaning of God's action in history and discovers the transcendent reality of his Person and its implications for the life of the Church and the individual Christian in his or her relationship with God. Drawing upon historical events and personal recollections, the theology of John carries the endorsement of the Church, which, with the assistance of the Spirit sent to it by Jesus, testifies to its truthfulness.

Along with the Evangelist's purpose, one must take into account the perspective from which he writes. The writer speaks from faith in light of the death and resurrection of Christ, and his accounts of Jesus' words and deeds therefore reflect two levels of understanding. One is the immediate level of those who saw him and heard him; the other corresponds to the understanding of the Evangelist and his readers after Jesus' death and resurrection. Those who heard and saw Jesus understood what he said and did according to the mentality of their time and place. But the Evangelist and those who read his Gospel in faith have a deep understanding of those same events. John does not transmit a bare account of Jesus' words and deeds but recounts them in depth after the death of Christ, according to his disciples' understanding of the deepest meaning of the Master's life as seen in the light of the Resurrection. He speaks of this in various places in the Gospel: "When therefore he was raised from the dead, his disciples remembered that he had said this; and they believed the scripture and the word which Jesus had spoken" (2:22; see also 12:16; 13:7; 16:13).

The reading of the Gospel also operates on two levels, one Christological and the other ecclesiological-sacramental. The Christological level of meaning derives from the level of historical fact and can be observed in passages in which Jesus' words or those of others have not only a meaning for the Jews of that time but also a properly Christian meaning based upon faith in Jesus after the resurrection. For example, John the Baptist's confession, "This is the Son of God" (1:34), is not an anachronism if read in the Old Testament sense, as Jews of that day would have understood it. But the expression has a much richer significance for readers of the Gospel than those original hearers could have imagined: at the Christological level, not only a messianic meaning but also the eternal Word of the Father become flesh, as in the Prologue, the meaning that emerged once Christ had risen.

The ecclesiastical-sacramental level of meaning also presupposes the level of historical fact. It appears especially in the events recounted against the background of faith in the risen Christ and also manifests circumstances of the life of the Church in which the Evangelist is writing, including its external relations. For example, the incident of the expulsion from the synagogue of the parents of the man born blind most likely mirrors the tensions with some Jews at the end of the first century. Other passages are related to the sacramental life of the Christians for whom John wrote: for example, the conversation with Nicodemus, in which the Church's teaching about baptism is implicit and the announcement of the "new commandment," insofar as it was the internal rule of life for the community.

On this basis, one can understand the Evangelist's relationship both with the Jesus of history and with the community he is addressing. The presentation of the history of Jesus aims to underline its significance for the life of the believer and of the Church. Also, insofar as the inspired apostolic witness constitutes a fundamental part of Christian revelation, it is a source from which to draw different theological aspects with special relevance for the faith.

1. Jesus Christ and the Father

The heart of John's theology is found in his Christology. Jesus is the eternal Son of the Father who became incarnate to give life to the world. This is a basic part of Christian faith unknowable by the human intellect apart from divine revelation. The Eternal Word of God has become flesh; Jesus of Nazareth, whose history we also know from the Synoptics, is God and man in a single unique Person. The extraordinary presentation of Jesus as a man who is at the same time equal to God is one of the fundamental features of the fourth Gospel.

Within the profound mystery of this relationship between the human and the divine in a single subject—in John's terms, between flesh and glory—Jesus' humanity and divinity are depicted in a splendid equilibrium. So delicate is this equilibrium that it is hardly surprising to find erroneous understandings whenever too much emphasis is placed either on Jesus' humanity or his divinity. The early heresies (docetist, ebionite, subordinationist, adoptionist, etc.) illustrate this. For Bultmann, the Jesus of John's Gospel is only a man whose humanity has nothing of the divine about it. For others, such as Käsemann, Jesus is a person of celestial faculties, whose humanity is merely a vehicle for exhibiting the glory of the only begotten Word of the Father, a kind of god passing through the world. But the picture arising from a calm reading in light of the tradition of the Church is very different: John presents Jesus as equal to God but also as a true man.

The divinity of Jesus is clear from the start of the Gospel. He existed before he was born: He is the Logos, the eternal Word of the Father, who is together with God (*pros ton Theon*). The rest of the Gospel only explains and confirms this truth. It can be observed in the fact that Jesus "knows" what is in men's hearts, in his performing of extraordinary deeds, his absolute dominion over events, his use of the prophetic words of the Old Testament to indicate that he comes from God, and, above all, his affirmations that he is the Son of God. The confession of Thomas confirms and ratifies what is declared in the Prologue: Jesus is "Lord and God" (*Kyrios* and *Theos*).

But even though these characteristics might seem to support the position of those who believe that the Evangelist considers Jesus to be solely a being of a heavenly kind, the fourth Gospel also makes it clear that Jesus' revelation is manifested through his flesh, through his condition of weakness as a human being. While the Gospel says from the beginning that the Word is eternal, from the beginning it also affirms that the Word became man (*sarx*). What follows simply confirms this reality. The Evangelist refers repeatedly to Jesus' human condition, showing him to be a true man who speaks, acts, and lives as such—one in whom the weakness of the flesh is radically demonstrated in his passion and death. For John, Jesus is not a god in human clothing but truly a man who was born, grew, and died like all the rest.

Certainly, though, that humanity cannot be understood or separated from his divine character. Any attempt to separate the flesh from the glory is bound to end in an incorrect understanding of John's Gospel. Jesus as he is depicted here is indivisible, at once human and divine. He is a man like other men and also fully divine. His "dependence" on God must be understood as the dependence within equality of a Son through his relationship with his Father. Only thus can we grasp the truth about Jesus and the message of salvation that he brought and the Gospel of John transmits.

The Revealer

The Gospel makes no bones about the fact that it intends for the readers to believe in Jesus as Christ the Son of God, and to have life in his name. Faith and life are united. Jesus has the power to give eternal life because he offers the world the knowledge of God. Even more, he shows not only how to come to know God, but that he himself is the channel of that knowledge inasmuch as he discloses to us the intimate mystery of God.

For John, Jesus is the revealer. His premise is clear: No one has ever seen God (see 1:18). Indeed, a human being cannot see God and continue living (see Ex 33:20). Yet there is an exception: there is One who has seen the Father, who proceeds from him (see 6:46) and introduces him to us. This is Jesus, who reveals himself as having come to lead humankind to life. Here is the heart of the remarkable news the Evangelist communicates. The whole Gospel of John revolves around this reality: Jesus is the revealer of the Father, God's final and decisive Word to humanity.

Jesus' revelatory function already begins in his manner of presenting himself to others as one who teaches. Those who first encounter him call him "rabbi," "teacher," and his whole life is devoted to teaching. He does this on the mountain (see 6:3), in the synagogue of Capernaum (see 6:69), in the temple (see 7:14, 28; 8:20), to the point that the Jews ask themselves whether he will go to the Diaspora to teach the Greeks (7:35). As teacher, he has disciples who listen to him and follow him. For his first hearers, we might say, Jesus is a master teacher of Israel.

Jesus not only teaches a set of truths in his own name, however, but also performs certain signs that prove he is a prophet, a new Moses, the prophet awaited by Israel (Dt 18:18). He is acknowledged as such by the Samaritan woman (see 4:19), by those who witness the multiplication of the loaves and fishes (see 6:14), by some in Jerusalem (see 7:40), and by the man born blind (see 9:17) among others.

But in a deeper sense, both when he gives instruction as a teacher and when he acts and is recognized as a prophet, he reveals—shows the face of God, makes his name known (see 17:25). In Jesus, all that he does—gestures, words, works—is revelation, the true revelation, since he himself is the truth. This is a very important concept in the fourth Gospel, closely related to Jesus' role as revealer.

In John, "truth" has the meaning it has in the Old Testament, where it is closely related to judicial testimony and to fidelity. But it also has elements in common with the concept of truth that developed in the Judeo-Hellenistic world, where above all it was understood to express something's correspondence with reality. In addition, it shares in the meaning "truth" has in the apocalyptic writings of the time, where it is often linked to the mystery of God. Borrowing from all these meanings, "truth" in the fourth Gospel uses them to refer to knowledge of God and of Christ.

Before Christ, knowledge of God was given by the Torah of Moses. After the Incarnation, "truth came through Jesus Christ" (see 1:17–18), which makes us truly know God. But truth cannot be reduced to intellectual knowledge. It is also the condition of the "life" that Jesus brought. Jesus is "the way, the truth, and the life" (14:6), that is to say, the path that leads to the Father inasmuch as he is truth and, in this way, communicates life. He who believes and accepts the word of Jesus is transformed by that truth and liberated from sin (see 8:32); whereas the devil "speaks deception," that is, denies divine reality, because "he is not in the truth."

In the end, along with having many shades of meaning, "truth" and "true" indicate the eternal reality revealed by Jesus Christ. The terms are linked to the revelation centered on the person of Christ and God's salvific plan. Christ himself is the truth. The truth "becomes recognizable when God becomes recognizable. He becomes recognizable in Jesus Christ. In Christ, God entered the world and set up the criterion of truth in the midst of history."[1]

He Who Was Sent

Jesus' position as a heavenly revealer is confirmed by the fact that he was sent by God. This is shown time and again in the Gospel, where verbs meaning "to send" (*apostellô* and *pempô*) are applied to Jesus more than forty times.[2]

As one sent by the Father, Jesus spoke the words of the Father (see 12:49; 8:26), did the works of his Father (see 10:25), fulfilled the will of his Father (see 4:34), to the point of likeness between the Father who sent and Jesus, the One sent: "He who has seen me has seen the Father" (14:9). What is more, that likeness is expressed in terms of presence: "It is not I alone . . . but I and he who sent me" (8:16; 16:32). That is, the likeness concerns an original, essential unity involving both Father and Son: "I and the Father are one" (10:30). This is what Jesus asks for his disciples: "That they may all be one; even as thou, Father, art in me, and I in thee" (17:21).

---

1. Ratzinger/Benedict XVI, *Jesus of Nazareth*, vol. 2, p. 194.

2. Other words signifying to "come from" are also used in relation to Jesus: "come from God," "come down from heaven," "come to," "return," "ascend to the Father," etc.

Although Jesus is at the center of the Gospel, it is clear at every moment that, because of his being sent by the Father, his mission is to reveal God who sent him and to whom he would return. Jesus' place is with him: "I came from the Father and have come into the world; again, I am leaving the world and going to the Father" (16:28) Jesus, as the One sent, is the presence and revelation of God who sent him. The content of Jesus' revelation is, then, God. But it is not a distant God. The God who reveals himself in Jesus is, in the first place, a Father; he is the Father of Jesus Christ. Jesus calls him this continually. John's Gospel is the only New Testament writing to use *páter* more frequently (one hundred twenty times) than *theós* (seventy-five times) to refer to God. And among the features that characterize the Father whom Jesus reveals, love is fundamental. The motive for sending Jesus is the Father's love toward mankind and his desire to save all: "For God so loved the world that he gave his only Son, that whoever believes in him should not perish but have eternal life" (3:16).

The Son

Throughout the Gospel, Jesus reveals himself as the Son of God, not simply "*a* son of God," as his contemporaries might have supposed, but "*the* Son"—the "Only Begotten" (see *monogenes*, 1:14, 18), the only One who is "truly the Son."

"The Son of God" is a messianic title rooted in the Scriptures of Israel and referring to a king chosen by God. Characters in the Gospel and sometimes its narrator refer to Jesus this way, speaking in light of the Scriptures of Israel. The title's use thus corresponds above all with the messianic status of Jesus, in whom God's promises to his people are fulfilled. Jesus is the Son of God, the hoped for Messiah.

However, the title "Son of God" is also intimately linked to another title to which Jesus alone refers and which better corresponds to the reality of his Person: "the Son." This is the most important title. John speaks of Jesus as "the Son" twenty times.

Jesus also refers more than 100 times to the Father and speaks more than twenty times of *his* Father. He uses the title "Son" to express his relationship to God. Jesus is not his own origin or end. He comes from the Father and returns to the Father, with whom he maintains a unity of being and will.

One cannot think of Jesus without the Father and the Father without Jesus. Their relationship is intimate and unique. God is Jesus' Father in a way different from his fatherhood of other men, as the risen Christ affirms: "I am ascending to my Father and your Father, to my God and your God" (20:17). What is more, there exists an identity between the Father and the Son: "I and the Father are one" (10:30; see 5:19, 21, 23, 26), so that the Son is in the Father and the Father in him (see 14:11). Still more, their identity includes and is defined by the love between them (see 5:20), a love in which the sending of the Son originates. The Father wills that salvation to come to humanity through the Son (see 3:36; 5:22; 6:40; 8:36). For that, the Father sent the Son (see 3:16–17), placing all power in his hands (see 3:35; 17:1–2).

The Pre-existent One

Jesus' identity with the Father and, therefore, his divine condition are confirmed by the Gospel's affirmation that he is pre-existent. John the Baptist expresses this when he says of Jesus: "After me comes a man who ranks before me." Here is confirmation of what is said in the Prologue: Jesus is the Word of God who existed from all eternity. He is the Logos, that is, the Word.

Logos is a term already used by Greek philosophers to indicate the ordering principle of the universe, but it was also attributed to divine Wisdom in the Wisdom books of the Old Testament (see Prv 8:22–31; Sir 24:1–22). Starting with this, Judaism in the time of Jesus had developed a theology of the Word (*memrá*), found, for example, in the translations of the Bible into Aramaic, where at times the properties of Divine Wisdom are applied to the Word of God. In addition, the

Judeo-Hellenistic philosophy of the day, including its greatest figure, the Jewish philosopher Philo of Alexandria, had elaborated a doctrine of the Logos as an intermediary between God and the world. For Philo, the Logos or Demiurge is the "eldest son" of God, the original idea and exemplar of the cosmos, while the cosmos is "the younger son" of God. (Plainly, Philo's concept of Logos is very different from John's, although they use the same terms.)

Logos in John has a meaning of its own. The fourth Gospel situates the Logos in a unified identity with the Father. Jesus is the eternal and creative Word of God who enjoys the plenitude of God in an equality of condition with him. As the Word, he is the source of everything created, now come to Israel in a new form, the Word that has become flesh in Jesus the Messiah. From this moment, Jesus' words are the words of God; his works are God's works; to see him is to see God. This is the mystery of which the Prologue and the whole of the Gospel speak. The yearning for the infinite can be satisfied only in the encounter with a person, Jesus of Nazareth, the Word of God made flesh.

"I AM"

The revelation of the divine filiation of Jesus therefore is shown as something absolutely new and radical: Jesus is equal to God. For Jesus himself to have declared this directly would have provoked scandal and rejection. Thus the Gospel shows him using indirect ways of affirming his intimate reality when revealing himself and God. This indirect mode can especially be seen when he uses the formulation "I am," which in the Gospel has a double significance: absolute, as an autonomous phrase with its own meaning; and predicative, in which "I am" is completed by affirming something of the subject.

The absolute use is found in cases such instances as, "I told you that you would die in your sins, for you will die in your sins unless you believe that I am he" (8:24); "Truly, truly, I say to you, before Abraham was, I am" (8:58); and others (see 8:28; 13:19). What at first might be taken for an incomplete phrase is seen to be a revelation of Jesus' divinity when one understands it as an allusion to the *ego eimi*, the name of God, found in the Jewish Scriptures and in the Judaism of that time. See, for example, Ex 3:14: "God said to Moses, 'I AM WHO AM.' And he said, 'Say this to the people of Israel, "I AM has sent me to you"'"; Is 43:10: "'You are my witnesses,' says the Lord, 'and my servant whom I have chosen, that you may know and believe me and understand that I am He.'" In using this formula, Jesus appears as the revealer of his divinity, manifesting it as God did in the Old Testament.

Something similar occurs in the two uses of "I am" where it appears that a predicate should be understood. In the account of the storm on the lake, Jesus says to his disciples, "*I am*, do not fear" (6:20); while at his arrest in the garden, when he says to those who are about to seize him, "*I am* he" (18:5), they fall to the ground. Both incidents recall the solemn and extraordinary manifestations of God in the midst of his people found in the Old Testament theophanies.

We see the predicative use of "I am" when Jesus says of himself that he is the bread of life (see 6:35, 51), the light of the world (see 8:12), the door (of the sheepfold) (see 10:7, 9), the good shepherd (see 10:11, 14), the resurrection and the life (see 11:25), the way, the truth, and the life (see 14:6), and the (true) vine (see 15:1, 5). The basis for these affirmations is found in the absolute use of "I am" and also has parallels in the Old Testament, where "I am" is used in describing God's action on behalf of man: "Say to my soul 'I am your salvation'" (Ps 35:3; see Ex 15:26). In short, by using images drawn from the Old Testament and the traditions of Israel, applies to himself certain features that reveal his identity. "When Jesus says 'I am he,' he is taking up this story [the manifestation of God to his people] and referring it to himself. He is indicating his oneness. In him the mystery of the one God is personally present: 'I and the Father are one.'"³

The Son of Man

So far it might seem that, for the Evangelist, Jesus was solely a divine being. Yet John clearly is testifying to a reality that he and others have seen (see 19:35; 21:24). To the eyes of his contemporaries, Jesus was a teacher, even a prophet, and, even more, simply the "son of Joseph" (1:45), a man like any other: "Is not this Jesus, the son of Joseph, whose father and mother we know?" (6:42). True, consistent with John's irony, those who say this do not know Jesus' true origin (his virginal birth, according to the testimony of the Synoptics). But Jesus does not contradict them either, since he also had a human origin and indeed refers to himself as "Son of Man."

This title can be understood as meaning simply "man," since that is what the Aramaic *bar enash*, "son of man," means. Yet, by this self-description, Jesus was saying more about himself, simultaneously affirming his human condition while also indicating that he was a revealer from heaven, like the figure of the Son of Man in Daniel (see 7:13), and in Jewish apocalyptic writing (mainly, the Book of the Parables of Enoch and 4 Esdras), where the expression refers to a figure with a human appearance who comes from heaven full of majesty. Thus, by employing the image of the Son of Man, Jesus says of himself that he is a celestial figure who descends from and ascends to heaven: "No one has ascended into heaven but he who descended from heaven, the Son of Man" (3:13; see 1:51; 6:62).

Jesus also uses "Son of Man" in the Synoptics above all to refer to his role as judge at the end of time and to predict his sufferings. In the fourth Gospel however, the expression has some special nuances.

---

3. Ratzinger/Benedict XVI, *Jesus of Nazareth*, vol. 1, p. 348.

Certainly the eschatological judge is present in John: "Truly, truly, I say to you, the hour is coming, and now is, when the dead will hear the voice of the Son of God, and those who hear will live. For as the Father has life in himself, so he has granted the Son also to have life in himself, and has given him authority to execute judgment, because he is the Son of man" (5:25–27). But there is less emphasis in John on eschatological judgment, since for the Evangelist judging has already begun with the Incarnation. Jesus is the judge whose acceptance or rejection lead to condemnation or salvation.

In the fourth Gospel, then, the title "Son of Man" above all emphasizes Jesus' human condition. Rather than present a "Son of Man" who is a purely celestial being or adopt mistaken or inadequate ideas of Christ, John uses this title to make the point that the revelation from on high took place in the flesh of the Son of Man, that is to say, in his weakness. In fact, John brings together principally the sayings of the Son of Man that refer to Jesus' death (see 3:14; 6:27, 53; 8:28; 12:23, 34; 13:31), thus emphasizing his human character. Lest some suppose "Son of Man" refers only to a divine being, the Evangelist emphasizes that the title is a direct result of the Incarnation and is related to his death. For this reason, John uses it almost exclusively to designate Jesus' earthly ministry (Francis Moloney).

At the same time, nevertheless, the title cannot be separated from his condition as a celestial revealer. This is clear in his talks about the Eucharist, where his celestial condition as Son of Man, "the bread which has come down from heaven" (see 6:33) is linked to the offering of his life (his flesh and his blood given as food (see 6:51–58). In short, the Johannine Christology can be understood in the light of the character of Jesus as revealer. The revelation is no less than the manifestation of Christ and his relation with the Father. It reaches its climax in the cross and is understood as revelation for the salvation of humankind. It communicates not knowledge but life.

2. The Holy Spirit

The Spirit is progressively revealed in the fourth Gospel, beginning with the baptism of John the Baptist and culminating after the Resurrection with the breathing out of the Spirit upon the disciples. Earlier, at the Last Supper, Jesus promises the Spirit and explains its action.

In the first sections of the Gospel, John the Baptist testifies to having seen the Spirit descend and "remain" upon Jesus (1:32–33). Unlike his own baptism with water, Jesus "baptizes with the Holy Spirit" (1:33). Later, Jesus says the Spirit will be poured out upon those who receive baptism: "Unless one is born of water and the Spirit, he cannot enter the kingdom of God" (3:5). The relationship between water and the Spirit reappears in 7:37–39, during the Feast of Tabernacles, when Jesus affirms that rivers of living water will well up in those who believe in him (or, according to another reading, that rivers of living water will well up from within him, that is, from Christ). The Evangelist adds: "Now this he said about the Spirit, which those who believed in him were to receive; for as yet the Spirit had not been given, because Jesus was not yet glorified" (7:39). Finally, at the moment of his glorification, when all has been fulfilled on the Cross, Jesus gives up his spirit (see 19:30). This is a way of indicating his glorious death, since, once risen, he will infuse the Spirit into his disciples: "Receive the Holy Spirit" (20:22).

Before his glorification, Jesus speaks at length about the Holy Spirit at the Last Supper, especially in reference to his function in the Church. In his farewell discourse, Jesus says that, like himself, the Spirit also will be sent by the Father, from whom he proceeds. The Father will do this in response to Jesus' prayer. In addition, both the Spirit and Jesus are the "truth," and both come to teach (reveal), although the Spirit receives from the Son what he has to declare: "When the Spirit of truth comes, he will guide you into all the truth; for he will not speak on his own authority, but whatever he hears he will speak, and he will declare to you the things that are to come. He will glorify me, for he will take what is mine and declare it to you. All that the Father has is mine" (16:13–15).

Jesus calls the Holy Spirit "the Spirit of truth" (14:17; 15:26; 16:13) and "Paraclete" (consoler, witness, advocate, spokesman— see 14:16, 26; 15:26; 16:7). As "the Spirit of truth," one with God and with Jesus, who is the truth, the Spirit performs the function of delivering the truth (the revelation of God in Christ) to people. By what he does, people are led from ignorance to truth. As "Paraclete," a word that etymologically means "called next to one" (in order to accompany, console, protect, defend), the Spirit acts among the disciples. He will always be with those who believe in Christ, dwelling in them (see 14:17). Thus, as the Spirit manifested himself above Jesus at his baptism, indicating that he was with Jesus, so his coming will make it possible for Christians to be personally in Christ.

The Spirit comes to the disciples and remains with them, guiding them to the full truth and teaching them what pertains to the mystery of salvation. He reminds them of what Jesus taught them and gives them light to understand the true meaning of those words (see 14:26). That is, the Spirit continues the mission of Jesus when he returns to the Father, thus making possible the continuation of Jesus' mission in the Church. The Spirit is Christ's witness to the disciples, who in turn witness to Jesus before the rest of men (see 15:26–27). On the other hand, by continuing the presence of Christ in the world, the Spirit acts as judge of a world dominated by evil and hostile to God. How he judges depends on whether the world accepts or rejects Christ and his revelation, and his judgment will shed light on the world's true situation.

In brief, everything said of the Holy Spirit in the fourth Gospel is said first of Jesus. Thus John indicates the role of the Spirit in the work of salvation after Christ's death and resurrection.

Sent by Jesus, the Holy Spirit is like the Son's personal presence among believers after his glorification, guaranteeing the effects of the work of salvation. For John, one might say, God's revelation in Christ is carried out in two stages: 1) God becomes incarnate in a real human form to draw all to him (he is visible and limited in time and space) and 2) free of limitations and invisible, he completes the work of the visible stage, extending his presence to all humanity by means of the Holy Spirit. This is to say that the Spirit continues the revelatory work begun in Christ and makes it possible for people to take advantage of that revelation.

The pouring out of the Spirit guarantees the link between Jesus and the life of the Church. The Spirit is needed to interpret revelation and make it possible for the truth of revelation, transmitted by the preaching of the apostles, to be received and spread by others. Revelation otherwise would be obscure and mysterious.

3. Eschatology

The arrival of the "day of the Lord" will not, as many thought, mark God's definitive intervention in history, bringing with it the last judgment and definitive reward and punishment. The resurrection of the body and the establishment of God's imperishable reign (the Kingdom of God inaugurated by the Messiah) constitute the essential elements of the eschatological doctrine of the Old Testament. The last times are to come with the dramatic arrival of a Savior from above. Then history will end and a new, definitive era will begin.

This vision changed with the coming of Christ. The Christian conception assumes the eschatological understanding of the Old Testament but modifies it by affirming that salvation and the last times are already realized with the death and resurrection of Jesus, while history will continue until Christ's second and final coming, bringing with it God's definitive judgment and the resurrection of bodies.

The fourth Gospel shares this perspective about the final things and, like other New Testament writings, affirms that all the hopes of salvation rest upon Christ. Nevertheless, a careless reading could give the impression that, according to John, the last times are already present with Jesus, leaving nothing more for which to hope. The emphasis on the idea that the goods of salvation are realized—something that Jews of that day looked to happen in the end times—seems to render superfluous a Second Coming, and with it the final judgment and the resurrection of the body. Thus the fourth Gospel might be taken as the expression of an eschatology made present or realized: the end times have arrived, and one need no longer look for another coming of Christ. Moreover, this understanding would seem to be confirmed not only by the identity between Jesus and the glory of God (see 1:14), but above all by the emphasis on the judgment pronounced by Jesus by his presence and by the reward attached to this judgment, eternal life, which is obtained through faith in him.

But any such interpretation is partial. True, the fourth Gospel attaches less importance to the Second Coming of Chris than the other Gospels do: John concentrates more on Christ's coming in the flesh than on his future coming. But the goods he brings are not exclusively for this life. Not only does Jesus not deny the reality of death, but he takes it for granted as a condition for attaining fullness of life: "He who believes in me, although he has died, shall live" (11:25). In fact, Jesus affirms that his death and resurrection are the path he must travel to prepare the final dwelling place for those who believe in him: "When I go and prepare a place for you, I will come again and will take you to myself, that where I am you may be also" (14:3). There they will see his definitive glory: "Father, I desire that they also, whom thou hast given me, may be with me where I am, to behold my glory which thou hast given me in thy love for me before the foundation of the world" (17:24). In addition, passages in the Gospel speak expressly of the Second Coming and of a judgment: "The hour is coming when all who are in the tombs will hear his voice and come forth, those who have done good, to the resurrection of life, and those who have done evil, to the resurrection of judgment" (5:28–29; see also 6:39–40, 44, 54; 12:48). According to the fourth Gospel, then, there is also a final judgment.

Certainly the Gospel insists on the judgment Jesus brings to the world. Even more, it affirms that Jesus himself is the judgment evoked by his coming: "This is the judgment, that the light has come into the world" (3:19). But that judgment is not the definitive one. Faith in Jesus separates the children of the light, those who believe, from the children of darkness, those who do not believe. Those who believe already participate in divine life: "He who believes in the Son has eternal life" (3:36; see 3:18, 5:24; etc.); those who do not believe already receive God's condemnation: "He who does not believe is condemned already, because he has not believed in the name of the only Son of God" (3:18; see 3:36). Judgment is a consequence of one's response to the revelation of Christ. But although Jesus affirms: "For judgment I came into this world, that those who do not see may see, and that those who see may become blind" (9:39), this judgment is not the same as final condemnation. Jesus is the occasion of a judgment, but men and women must decide in regard to him— they must choose between accepting or rejecting his revelation. Judgment and the consequent "division" caused by the preaching of Jesus (see 10:19–21) continue in the subsequent times of the Church. He who believes already has eternal life, life with God, which anticipates the resurrection on the last day when the final judgment will take place.

4. Faith as a Response to the Signs

The fourth Gospel presents an array of signs that Jesus performed. The Evangelist recorded them with the aim of maintaining and increasing his readers' faith. In his conversation with Nicodemus, Jesus declares that faith, as a response to the love of God manifested in Christ, is the condition for eternal life: "For God so loved the world that he gave his only Son, that whoever believes in him should not perish but have eternal life" (3:16). The idea of faith is thus fundamental in John and runs throughout the Gospel. Unlike the Synoptics, where faith above all means trust in Jesus' ability to perform a particular miracle or cure, in John faith has more to do with adhering to his person, to the mystery of his divinity, and so, to his revelation.

The process of having faith in Jesus begins with his signs (see 2:12) but is not limited to them. In fact, Jesus also complains of a lack of faith that consists in concentrating on the sign's miraculous aspect without understanding its real significance (see 2:23–25; 6:26). As we saw in chapter 3 above, although the signs make visible the complete salvation present in Christ and confirm the message of Jesus, they create a situation that requires taking a stand. They are not of themselves sufficient for belief. Confronted with the signs, one can react by remaining at the level of wonderment in the face of something marvelous, or one can move to the point of believing and, beyond that, to a personal encounter with Christ. The signs illuminate the minds of those who witness them, but by themselves they do not persuade or convince. They are an interior invitation to believe. But definitive adherence requires divine assistance, since faith is a free gift of God (see 6:37) and people cannot believe unless the Father moves them (see 6:65). At the same time, faith is a free action of man. For that reason, Jesus frequently exhorts people to believe in him, for as free beings, people can reject that gift (see 3:36; 8:24; 15:22).

Testimony is fundamental to the process of believing. The testimony that Jesus gives concerning himself is a way of expressing the revelation he brings, for it manifests his consciousness of his relationship with his Father. And it is a true testimony because it is born of that relationship. The contents of that revelation-testimony are the words of Jesus and the teaching drawn from those words.

But other testimonies (of John the Baptist, of the signs, of Scripture) are also divine revelation in Jesus and about him. This revelation is transmitted by the testimonies of the disciples who saw and heard Jesus (see 21:24). Thus, to believe means to accept the revelation transmitted by testimony. In fact, in the fourth Gospel the words "to believe" and "to know" seem to be related or interchangeable (6:69; 17:8). Revelation brings one to deeper knowledge, but only after one has accepted it through a personal and total act of submission.

In summary, faith is a result of God's action causing testimony about Christ to reach one through apostolic preaching and supplying the interior grace required for its acceptance, and it also is a result of the free act of a human being who recognizes the truth of God's testimony and voluntarily and joyfully gives himself to Christ. With personal adherence to Jesus Christ, one obtains eternal life—that is, salvation—which embraces an array of goods: divine filiation, eternal life that frees one from death, truth and the freedom that comes with being liberated from the slavery of falsehood, joy, and so on.

5. The World

"Johannine dualism" is a typical feature of the fourth Gospel. This expression refers to the antithetical elements that frequently appear in the Gospel: God (Jesus)–the world; light–darkness; truth–falsehood; flesh–spirit; death–life; belief–nonbelief, and so on. Some interpreters think the Evangelist adopted this device under the influence of the Qumran writings, where one often finds opposed terms. But such dualism is not peculiar to Qumran. It is found also in Jewish apocalyptic literature of the period, suggesting that it is not a property of only one Jewish group. Nor is there any reason to attribute it to some supposed Gnostic sources, as Bultmann suggests. Rather, John speaks in a manner common to the

Judeo-Hellenistic milieu of his time, where this antithetic terminology was often employed.

Nevertheless, for John, dualism does suit his central conviction: salvation is found only in Jesus. Unless one accepts the Savior, there is no salvation. Here is the context for the antithetical terms found in the Gospel.

Space is lacking to deal with all of them here. But one occupies a special place: the "world," in opposition to God. "World (*kosmos*) in John is very rich in meanings and nuances. It is used at times in a neutral or positive sense to refer to creation and within it in particular to humanity, which is the object of God's love (see 1:10; 3:16; 13:1); but "world" also often has a negative sense, insofar as it refers to those who reject Christ and whose prince is the devil (see 1:10; 7:7; 15:18–19; 16:8–11; 17:16). Understood in this second way, "world" suggests the rebellion of human beings who wish to live independently of their Creator, thus blighting their own existence. Yet even so, God does not seek the annihilation of the world but its salvation. Here, then, is the reason for the Incarnation, as explained by a text with the double meaning—positive and negative—of the word "world": "For God so loved the world that he gave his only Son, that whoever believes in him should not perish but have eternal life. For God sent the Son into the world, not to condemn the world, but that the world might be saved through him" (3:16–17; see 12:46).

Where the definitive work of salvation has not yet become operative, Christians live in a world that is opposed to God and in slavery to sin: "If the world hates you, know that it has hated me before it hated you. If you were of the world, the world would love its own; but because you are not of the world, but I chose you out of the world, therefore the world hates you" (15:18–19). But one who accepts Jesus can overcome the seductions that come from the world prior to Christ's glorious return, since believers are already in the "world of God" by virtue of their union with Christ, as the branch is in the true vine. In addition, Christians can be confident that they can live in this world of seductions until the coming of Christ because Christ has prayed for them: "I am praying for them; I am not praying for the world but for those whom thou hast given me. . . . I have given them thy word; and the world has hated them because they are not of the world, even as I am not of the world. I do not pray that thou shouldst take them out of the world, but that thou shouldst keep them from the evil one" (17:9, 14–15).

6. The Church and the Sacraments

What the Gospel of John says about the Church and the sacraments does not involve a special vocabulary with a greater or lesser resemblance to that employed in the other New Testament books. To grasp the rich ecclesiological teaching of John, one needs to take into account his intention in writing and the perspective he adopts when presenting the teaching.

The Church

John's selectivity leads him to include some things and omit others, but it does not follow that he is unaware of what he does not mention. For example, he does not explicitly tell of the choice of the Twelve and the mission of preaching and curing recounted in the Synoptics, nor does he speak expressly of the New Covenant constituting the new people; but that does not mean he is ignorant of them.

John presupposes the choice of the Twelve. ("Did I not choose you, the twelve?" (6:71; see 13:18; 15:16) and speaks of the following of Christ as "coming" with him, which implies staying with him, as he indicates to the two disciples who sought him: "Come and see" (1:39). He also speaks of the *mission* of the disciples, stating explicitly that just as the Father sent the Son and the Holy Spirit, so Jesus was sending his disciples to the world (see 17:18; 20:21). He also refers to the *alliance* that was the basis of the new people, though using terminology different from that of the first three Gospels. When the risen Jesus says: "I am ascending to my Father and your Father, to my God and your God" (20:17), he alludes to the formula of the covenant found in Leviticus: "I will be your God, and you shall be my people" (26:12; see Ex 6:7). The mediator of the New Covenant is Jesus, as the Prologue affirms: "The law was given through Moses; grace and truth came through Jesus Christ" (1:17).

While the Gospel gives great emphasis to the believer's personal relationship with Jesus, that bond does not exclude the Church. The relationship is not individualistic but exists within the sheepfold, the flock (see 10:1–16), and as a participation in the life of the vine and its branches (see 15:1–7). Thus it implies the existence of a community, the Church, within which one is permanently united to Jesus. Chapter 17 of the Gospel presents a stirring vision of the communion of faith and life with the three divine Persons enjoyed by the members of the community. John stresses here that the unity of believers in the Church arises from the unity of the Father and the Son (and of the Holy Spirit, if, the word "glory" in 17:22 is taken, as several Fathers of the Church take it, as referring to him: "The glory which thou hast given me I have given to them"). This prototype of the relationship of unity that should exist among believers is a unity in love. Love characterizes the community (the Church) and expresses the unity of those who believe in Jesus. Love is a heavenly reality made present among humans. Unity in love actualizes divine life. Love is the commandment of the new community.

In addition, the use of "we" and "us" in the Gospel's Prologue and epilogue (1:14, 16 and 21:24) underlines the disciple's union with Christ within the community of the Church as the ecclesial context of the entire narrative.

In this community there are ministers with specific functions. Although the Evangelist does not mention specific offices, this does not mean they do not exist. Jesus' closest disciples took on the role of church leadership, as can be seen by the tasks carried out by the Twelve, who are sent as apostles to gather the harvest (see 4:35-38; "apostle" in Greek means "one who is sent"). In addition, Jesus entrusts the flock to Peter (see 21:15-17)—a fact of great significance in view of the prominence of the beloved disciple in the fourth Gospel.

Yet Peter also plays a prototypical role in this Gospel. On the one hand, his depiction here shares certain elements with the Synoptics: the name of Cephas, or Peter, his membership in the Twelve, his presence in certain episodes of the Passion and Resurrection; he also is spokesman for the Twelve at the discourse on the Bread of Life (6:67-69), which is an echo of the messianic confession of Peter in the three first Gospels (see Mk 8:27-30; Mt 16:13-20; Lk 9:18-21). On the other hand, Peter's relationship with the beloved disciple shows his position as leader. The deference of the other in letting Peter enter the sepulcher first is directly relationed to the function of shepherding the lambs and sheep of Christ conferred on him by the risen Jesus (see 21:15-17; 10:1-18). Peter is called to follow Jesus as the only authentic "shepherd" in order to continue his pastoral mission. There is neither a true mission nor a true community of faith without Peter.

The Sacraments

While John does not mention the institution of sacraments to which the Synoptic Gospels refer (though without always agreeing in their accounts), or does not speak of them in the form they have in today's Church, this does not mean he was unaware of them and their institution by Christ. Here, too, we must allow for the Evangelist's perspective and purpose. Authors such as Oscar Cullmann see in the fourth Gospel numerous allusions to the sacraments, while others like Rudolf Bultmann deny practically all of them (or else take them to have appeared at a later date), but most writers find clear indications to support the view that John knew and alluded to some of the sacraments, and especially to baptism and the Eucharist.

The practice of baptism is taken for granted in John. Although he does not speak directly of Jesus' baptism, he does repeat John the Baptist's testimony to the overshadowing of Jesus by the Spirit at the Jordan (see 1:32). This is a reference to the baptism of Jesus, present in the background of the institution of sacramental baptism. Moreover, the statement that John baptized "with water" (1:26, 31, 33), as opposed to Jesus' new baptism with the Spirit, would not be easy to explain apart from the practice of Christian baptism—the birth of the children of God of which Jesus speaks: "Truly, truly, I say to you, unless one is born of water and the Spirit, he cannot enter the kingdom of God" (3:5). Similarly, Jesus' insistence on the need to drink the water of eternal life—a reference to the Spirit that will be poured on those who believe in him—should be understood in relation to baptism (see 4:13–14; 7:37–39). The cure of the man born blind, who washed in the pool of Siloam (see 9:7–11), and the washing of the feet of the disciples (see 13:1–11) undoubtedly contain allusions to sacramental baptism.

John's perspective in speaking of the Eucharist also differs from that of the Synoptics. While he does not describe its institution at the Last Supper, he undoubtedly knew of it, since the doctrine of the Eucharist in the discourse at Capernaum (see 6:26–59) can be understood only in light of the sacrament's institution by Jesus. His words in the synagogue there refer to the words of institution: The Eucharistic bread is the true bread of heaven that replaces the manna (see 6:32), while the Eucharistic wine expresses the New Covenant in his blood established by Jesus (confirmed in the episode of the marriage feast of Cana and the description of the vine in chapter 15). Furthermore, where the Synoptics narrate the institution, John recounts the washing of the disciples' feet by which Jesus expresses his total self-giving for love and sheds profound light upon his words in the institution of the sacrament: "Do this in my memory" (Lk 22:19). The Eucharist is not just the repetition of a ritual action but the renewal of Jesus' death on the Cross for humankind, itself the basis of Christians' self-giving for others: "I have given you an example, that you also should do as I have done to you" (13:15).

7. Mary, the Mother of Jesus

The role of Jesus' mother stands out above those of the other women who appear in the Gospel. We find her at the beginning and the end of his ministry: the wedding feast of Cana (see 2:1–11), when Jesus performs his first sign, and the crucifixion (see 19:25), when his death is the last and definitive sign of faith. In both places, Jesus addresses his mother as "woman" (2:4; 19:26) and in both there is a reference to the "hour" of Jesus. The hour that had not yet arrived (see 2:4), when the water had yet to become wine, is fulfilled at the hour of his death ("it is consummated"), when the wine of messianic times is realized in the blood flowing from the side of Christ (see 19:34).

Mary is a figure of the people of Israel who gave birth to the Messiah. She is the perfect disciple who believes from the beginning and shows his disciples the path of faith ("Do whatever he tells you"). She is the woman, the new Eve, the mother of the new humanity born from the side of Jesus, which is the Church, represented in the beloved disciple. Origen wrote in his commentary on the fourth Gospel:

> We make bold to say that the Gospels are the first fruits of all of Scripture and that among the Gospels, the first fruits correspond to the Gospel of John, whose meaning no one can understand if he has not rested on the breast of Jesus and has not received Mary from Jesus as his mother. And to be another John, it is necessary that, like John, Jesus refers to us

as though we ourselves were Jesus himself. Because, according to those who have a sound opinion of her, Mary has no other children than Jesus; therefore, when Jesus says to his mother "Behold your son," and not "Here is this man, who is also your son," it is as if he were saying: "Here is Jesus, to whom you have given birth." In effect, anyone who has attained perfection, "I no longer live, it is Christ who lives in me" and, since it is Christ who lives in him, of him he says to Mary: "'Behold your son,' Christ."[4]

---

4. Origen, *In Ioannem*, 1, 23.

Part II
THE LETTERS

Chapter 8

THE LETTERS OF JOHN

THE TRADITION OF THE CHURCH attributes three letters to the author of the fourth Gospel. Two of these letters of John, the second and third, are the work of a writer who refers to himself as "the Priest." In addition to the initial greeting and farewell, they contain nearly identical formulations and expressions. But these two documents—and especially the second—also contain ideas and ways of speaking that appear in the first letter, so that one can say there is not a verse in the second letter of John is not found also in the first letter. As for the latter, it shares some content and expressions with the fourth Gospel. Thus it is hardly surprising that they should be regarded as coming from the same tradition and should be attributed to the same author.

Their place in the canon, following the letter of James and the two letters of Peter, perhaps reflects the order in which the "pillars" of the Church (James, Cephas, and John) are named by Paul in Galatians 2:9 ("When they perceived the grace that was given to me, James and Cephas and John, who were reputed to be pillars, gave to me and Barnabas the right hand of fellowship"). That, aside, there is a parallel with the conclusion of the fourth Gospel, where we find Peter and the beloved disciple together, as if to emphasize that those two are inseparable.

I. The First Letter of John

1. Witnesses of Tradition

That the first letter of John was rapidly disseminated and came rapidly to be regarded as authoritative is shown by the fact that St. Polycarp and St. Justin (*Contra Tryphon* 123) knew it as early as the second century, although they do not indicate its authorship. Not much later, however, witnesses appear who affirm that John the son of Zebedee wrote the Gospel and the first letter that bears his name. Around the year 180 St. Irenaeus of Lyon assumes in his *Adversus Haereses* that the letter was written by the apostle John, for he cites passages attributing them to "John, the disciple of the Lord" (3, 16, 5.8). Clement of Alexandria, around the year 200, also cites it frequently in his writings, assigning it explicitly to the apostle St. John (see *Stromata* 2, 15, 66; 3, 4, 32; 3, 5, 44; 3, 6, 45). So do Origen (184–253), according to the testimony of Eusebius in *Historia Ecclesiastica* (6, 25, 8), and Tertullian (c. 160–c. 222) (see *Adversus Praxeam* 15, *Scorpiace* 12; *Adversus Marcionem* 5, 16). From the fourth century on, it was habitually cited as the work of the evangelist John. Eusebius of Caesarea, in his *Historia Ecclesiastica* (see 3, 24, 17), echoes this tradition in classifying 1 John among the "recognized" or canonical (*homologoumena*), works usually appearing in the lists of canonical books since the third century. The Canon of Muratori, possibly from the second century, testifies that the author of the letter is John, the author of the fourth Gospel.

2. Transmission

These references show the authority enjoyed by this document as an apostolic testimony. Ancient manuscripts such as P^9 in the third century and the great codices of the fourth century show that the text we have has been faithfully transmitted. Only in the past was there concern about the authenticity of a passage in the Clementine edition of the Vulgate (1592). The debate about the so-called Johannine comma (*"inciso joanico"*) is hardly more than a footnote now, but in past times it was a burning issue.

The Clementine edition of the Vulgate introduced into the text of 5:7–8 an addition saying: "There are three witnesses *in heaven: the Father, the Word and the Holy Spirit and these three are one: and there are three who give testimony on earth:* the Spirit, the water, and the blood; and these three agree."

The addition in italics is a dogmatic Trinitarian reflection on the briefer original text. Its first appearance incorporated into the text was in a Latin treatise of the fourth century. From the fifth and sixth centuries on, it appeared with greater frequency in Old Latin (*Vetus Latina*) manuscripts and, from the ninth century on, in the Vulgate. But in fact it is lacking in the Greek manuscripts and in those of the oriental tradition. It is present in only two Greek manuscripts, the oldest of the fourteenth or fifteenth century, and as a later edition in the margins of two others, the oldest from the eleventh century. No Greek Fathers cited it in the Trinitarian controversies of the fourth century (Sabellianism and Arianism), an inexplicable omission had they known of it. We can therefore conclude that it does not belong in the original text. Yet the heated polemics over its authenticity persisted until the Congregation of the Holy Office issued a Declaration on June 2, 1927. The official Latin edition, the Neo-Vulgate, does not include it.

3. Content and Structure

The letter begins with a prologue indicating the author's intention: to give witness concerning the Word of life so that the letter's readers will be in communion with God, with Christ, and with their brethren (see 1:1–4). After announcing that "God is light," it develops the demands of Christian life, presented as a path in the light, which guarantees communion with God and with Jesus Christ, whose blood cleanses from sin (see 1:7-7). To maintain this union with God, it is necessary to recognize oneself as a sinner and to fight against sin, for not to recognize sin is to make God a liar (see 1:8-2:2). In addition one has to keep the commandments—especially that of fraternal love—and thus perfect one's love of God.

This commandment of love is a new commandment because it has still not been completely put into practice in a world freed by Jesus from the power of darkness (see 2:3-11). The Christian cannot love the world and should struggle against it and its attractions—luxury, the temptation of the eyes, and a pretentious style of life—staying on guard against the Evil One (see 2:12-17).

The presence of the Antichrist, which has been realized in the false teachers, shows that the final times have come. Those false teachers are liars and have left the community. They are recognizable by their denial that Jesus is the Christ who has come in the flesh (see 2:18-23). The recipients of the letter, on the other hand, have been anointed by the Holy One; therefore they have no need that the false teachers teach them, if they remain in the truth that leads to eternal life (see 2:24-27). Those who do the works of justice enjoy union with Christ, the just One, but full union will arrive with the Second Coming. What matters is that the Christian is a child of God (see 2:28-3:3). Moreover, he has been born of the seed of God and therefore is struggling against sin (see 3:4-10).

Then, returning to the opening theme, the author exhorts his readers to practice fraternal charity, since one who does not love his brother is a murderer like Cain, and it is necessary to put the commandments into practice (see 3:11-24). He indicates the criteria for discerning true from false spirits. One who confesses that Jesus in the flesh is of God and produces good fruit (see 4:1-6). Immediately, he turns to fraternal charity, basing his exhortation on the fact that God is love, as is shown by his sending his Son to the world to save us. Christians can love because God has loved them first. They should demonstrate that love by loving their brothers. If they do not do this, they are lying (see 4:7–21).

Those born of God have faith in the fact that Jesus is the Christ and follow his commandments. With that faith in Jesus, they conquer the world (see 5:1–5). And the Spirit, the water, and the blood give testimony of this faith (see 5:6–8). The testimony of God leads to belief in his Son and to attaining eternal life in him (see 5:9–12). This is why this letter has been written: so that its hearers will believe in the Son of God and thus have eternal life. This faith sustains confidence that God hears prayer for sinners (see 5:13–17). To know God and the truth is the guarantee that the Son of God has come and has brought us eternal life (see 5:18–20). The document ends with a warning against idols (see 5:21).

As can be seen from this summary, although the thematic content of the letter allows for a certain schematization, the document's structure is enormously complex. Although transmitted as a "letter of John," it does not have the format of a letter of that time—greetings, a body, a farewell. No sender is indicated nor is it said to whom it is directed; the customary greetings are lacking. The recipients are generic, and it is basically a polemic. Some interpreters hold that it was a homily or a religious treatise (Raymond Brown, Hans-Josef Klauck, Josep-Oriol Tuñí). This suggests that it was a kind of circular sent to the Christian communities of a region. While this explanation may reflect the original intention, however, it would also be difficult to prove.

The language is direct and simple, with a limited vocabulary and rather elementary syntax (with a predominance of phrases connected by the conjunction "and"). Nevertheless, due principally to brusque changes of style and content, the letter's logic is not always easy to understand. It is not surprising, then, that there have been many attempts to describe the text's structure, but none of them has been really satisfactory. Most recognize a prologue in 1:1–4, and many find an epilogue or conclusion in 5:13–21. But opinions regarding the body of the letter vary a great deal according to the approach. Some authors suggest dividing it into two parts (for example, 1:5–3:10 and 3:11–5:12), others in three (for example, 1:5–2:17; 2:18–4:6; 4:7–5:12), and others into four or more.

Lack of a clear structure and genre has led some exegetes to interpret this document as an elaboration of various sources. In consequence, they have proposed as a basic source some phrases (in some cases just a few, a larger number in others, depending on the author) or some prior writings (Ernst von Dobschütz). The original basic text has then been extended and corrected by other texts in light of various considerations. For example, in line with his theory regarding the composition of the fourth Gospel, Bultmann, in various studies of the letters, expressed the view that 1 John was developed from a basic text of twenty-six double verses with a Gnostic source. There are several variations on this proposal (François-Marie Braun and John C. O' Neill). Another view suggests a progressive process of composition, but with a single author involved (Wolfgang Nauck).

But despite all these hypotheses about the intervention of various hands, the text's homogeneity of style and vocabulary is undeniable. In any case, none of the hypotheses about the origin of the letter has prevailed. In the face of this tangle of proposals, we must ask ourselves whether it is not perhaps easier to understand this document as a set of "thoughts" of someone in authority (that is, the beloved disciple), set down without a precisely logical order and gathered together at a moment when the situation called for a correct understanding of doctrine, or simply as a testimony and record of what was written by someone who enjoyed authority at one time or another. The letter would thus be a way of expressing the mind of someone who was at the head of the community and from whom these thoughts were received—a collection of texts of the beloved disciple, gathered together as a precious testimony.

4. Relation to the Fourth Gospel

The relationship of 1 John with the fourth Gospel is undeniable. A detailed analysis of the letter's style, sentence structure, vocabulary, and ideas shows notable resemblances and a few differences.

Similarities

Both documents use certain characteristic terms: *ginoskein* ("to know"), *martyria*, *martyrein* ("witness," "to bear witness"), *pater* ("Father," referring to God), *kosmos* ("the world"), *terein* ("to guard"), *menein* ("to remain"), *phanerothenai* ("to manifest"), *aletheia* ("truth"), *sarx* ("flesh"). There are also typical turns of phrase: "be born of God," "be of God," "remain in God," "abide in the truth," "walk in the light," "to do truth," "guard the commandments," "keep one's word," "to have sin," "to free from sin," "to be of the world," "to do good," etc. So, too, there is in both a frequent use of antitheses, characteristic of John's thinking and also found in Qumran: "light–darkness," "truth–falsehood," "love–hate," "life–death," "God–the Devil," "justice–sin."

Furthermore, both texts manifest an interest in particular doctrinal subjects, as they are reflected in certain expressions. Some significant examples are:

a) *Ways of referring to Christ*
- *the Logos*

    1 Jn 1:1: "That which was from the beginning, which we have heard, which we have seen with our eyes, which we have looked upon and touched with our hands, concerning the word of life."

    Jn 1:1: "In the beginning was the Word, and the Word was with God, and the Word was God."

- *the Only Son*

    1 Jn 4:9: "In this the love of God was made manifest among us, that God sent his only Son into the world, so that we might live through him."

    Jn 1:18: "No one has ever seen God; the only Son, who is in the bosom of the Father, he has made him known."

- *the Savior of the World*

    1 Jn 4:14: "And we have seen and testify that the Father has sent his Son as the Savior of the world."

    Jn 4:42: "They said to the woman, "It is no longer because of your words that we believe, for we have heard for ourselves, and we know that this is indeed the Savior of the world."

b) *On the reality of the Incarnation (see the Prologues of the letter and the Gospel) and its redemptive value for the forgiveness of sins:*

1 Jn 3:5: "You know that he appeared to take away sins, and in him there is no sin."

Jn 1:29: "Behold, the Lamb of God, who takes away the sin of the world!"

c) *On the Christian life*

- *"passage from death to life"*

    1 Jn 3:14: "We know that we have passed out of death into life, because we love the brethren. He who does not love abides in death."

    Jn 5:24: "Truly, truly, I say to you, he who hears my word and believes him who sent me, has eternal life; he does not come into judgment, but has passed from death to life."

- *"being born of God"*

  1 Jn 3:9: "No one born of God commits sin; for God's nature abides in him, and he cannot sin because he is born of God." see also 4:7; 5:1; 5:4.

  Jn 1:13: "who were born, not of blood nor of the will of the flesh nor of the will of man, but of God;" see also 3:3.

- *becoming "a child of God"*

  1 Jn 3:1: "See what love the Father has given us, that we should be called children of God; and so we are. The reason why the world does not know us is that it did not know him."

  Jn 1:12: "But to all who received him, who believed in his name, he gave power to become children of God."

- *"to have life"*

  1 Jn 5:12: "He who has the Son has life; he who has not the Son of God has not life."

  Jn 3:36: "He who believes in the Son has eternal life; he who does not obey the Son shall not see life, but the wrath of God rests upon him."

- *keeping the commandments, which are "his word"*

  1 Jn 2:5: "but whoever keeps his word, in him truly love for God is perfected. By this we may be sure that we are in him."

  Jn 14:21, 23: "He who has my commandments and keeps them, he it is who loves me; and he who loves me will be loved by my Father, and I will love him and manifest myself to him. . . . If a man loves me, he will keep my word, and my Father will love him, and we will come to him and make our home with him."

- *exercising fraternal love in fulfillment of the new commandment*

  1 Jn 3:11: "For this is the message which you have heard from the beginning, that we should love one another."

  Jn 13:34: "A new commandment I give to you, that you love one another; even as I have loved you, that you also love one another."

Differences

Along with these similarities and other more fundamental ones, the letter also is different from the Gospel in some ways.

a) About ten percent of the letter's vocabulary does not appear in the Gospel. That includes some significant terms. For example: "communion," "antichrist," "false prophet," "*Parousia*," etc. There are also significant words in the Gospel that do not appear in the letter: *anabainein* ("to rise"), *katabainein* ("descend"), *doxa, doxadsein* ("glory," "glorify"), *krinein* (to judge"), etc.

b) The letter has only one explicit reference to the Old Testament (Cain), while the Gospel has abundant citations.

c) Some expressions in the letter that have a meaning different from their meaning in the Gospel. "The beginning" in 1 John 1:1 and 2:14 (the beginning of revelation in the human life of Jesus) is not equivalent to "the beginning" of the Gospel's Prologue in 1:1 where it signifies the pre-existence of the Word.

d) Eschatology is more emphasized in the letter than in the Gospel. The letter speaks of the "*Parousia*" and the "day of judgment" (2:28; 3:2; 4:17), stressing the Parousia as the moment when an account of one's Christian life must be given (and also as the moment when one becomes fully united with Jesus). The Gospel places greater emphasis on the judgment and retribution as already accomplished in Christ.

e) The presence of the Spirit as a person receives less emphasis in the letter than in the Gospel. The letter does not use the term "Paraclete" in reference to the Spirit, but in 2:1 it refers to Christ as the "Paraclete" or advocate.

f) The letter attributes to God features that the Gospel attributes to Jesus. For example, 1 John 1:5 says that God is light, while in the Gospel Jesus is the Light. In 1 John 4:21 it is God who proclaims the commandment that we love one another, while in the Gospel Jesus does this (13:34).

5. The Author

These differences have led some to conclude that we are dealing here with two different authors, and the author of the letter was a disciple of the Evangelist (Windisch, Dood, Schnackenburg, Barrett, Zumstein, Brown, Smith, Klauck). There is no consensus, and the question remains open. What is certain is that both letter and Gospel reflect a Johannic community with a common tradition. Behind that tradition is an apostolic personage vested with authority, the beloved disciple (one of the "we" of those who have heard and seen Jesus, who knows the meaning of his life and death). As in the case of the Gospels, the tradition is antecedent to the writings we possess and gave rise to them. The works linked to John appear to be a theological response to the specific circumstances of their intended audience. In this way it is possible to explain the differences between the letter and the Gospel, without positing an unknown period of time between the composition of one and the other. In any case, it seems more likely that the letter was written after the Gospel (although the question also is discussed whether the letter might have been written when the Gospel had not reached the final form in which it has come to us). If true, this would help explain some differences between the two texts.

An explanation of the authorship of the letter according to the "Johannine school" (mentioned in the introduction to this book) might resemble that proposal regarding the composition of the Gospel. That is to say: As the Gospel originates in the testimony of the beloved disciple, put into writing by perhaps one or several of his disciples, so in the face of circumstances perhaps endangering the unity of the community, a document was produced containing the beloved disciple's testimony on this matter. (The explanation does not rule out the possibility of the document's being a compilation of various written testimonies by the disciple.) This would explain why the document was traditionally presented as a letter of John.

6. The Occasion for the Letter

Considering the similarities between the Gospel and the letter and so proceeding on the assumption that they are products of the same milieu, it is clear that the letter does not reflect the same tensions between Christians and the synagogue found in the Gospel. The letter does not refer to "the Jews" or the temple, with its feasts, customs, and traditions. Instead the criticisms directed by Jesus in the Gospel against some Jews are now applied to people who are putting the faith of the community in danger (they are called "liars," "sons of the devil," and "murderers").[1] It is they, and the need to unmask their errors, that are the motivation for writing.

It is also said of them that they are "false prophets" (4:1), who "came out from among us" (2:19) but are no longer in full communion with the writer. In other words, this is a schismatic

---

1. Compare 1 John 2:4; 3:8, 10; 3:15 with John 8:44: "You are of your father the devil, and your will is to do your father's desires. He was a murderer from the beginning, and has nothing to do with the truth, because there is no truth in him. When he lies, he speaks according to his own nature, for he is a liar and the father of lies."

group. Their expulsion seems to have been recent, since their situation is not said to be of the past and none of them "is of our own" (2:19). It would seem that they were numerous, since "the world listens to them" (4:5) and, being seducers (see 2:26; 3:7) who attract with their doctrines and trickery, they are causing disorder in the community. They are dangerous, moreover, inasmuch as they claim not to have a different faith and say they know God and are in him (see 2:4, 6), live in communion with him and love him (see 1:6; 4:20), are in the light and do not have or commit sin (see 2:9; 1:8, 10). But as the letter shows, the reality is much different. This therefore is a critical juncture for the community, so grave in fact, that in the writer's judgment it is a sign that "the last hour" has come (2:18)—that is, the last times announced by Christ (see Mt 24:15–28), when the conflict between good and evil, the children of light and the children of darkness, is to become evident and "antichrists" will arise (2:18; see 2 Jn 7) who will oppose the Son of God.

The indications contained in the letter suggest that the errors being proposed by this dissident group were of a moral kind, though probably grounded in a Christological view of a Docetist nature.

a) They denied that Jesus is the Son of God (see 2:22–23), that he is the Christ (see 2:22), and above all did not accept that he had come in the flesh and lived a true earthly life (see 4:2–3). In consequence, they also denied that his Passion and death were expiatory (see 1:7; 2:2; 4:10), contenting themselves with saying Jesus had come "in water"—apparently a reference to baptism—as if the only thing important for salvation was to believe that Christ had come to the world as one sent and a Savior, and all that was necessary was to believe in his word. At the same time, they ignored the earthly life of Jesus and especially his death on the Cross as an act of love and expiation through which sins are forgiven (see 2:12).

The author of the letter insists, however, that Jesus has come not only with water, "but with water and with blood" (5:6). This seems to be an allusion to the blood and water that flowed from Christ's side (see Jn 19:34). Therefore, while those who alter the doctrine say they are led by the Spirit, the author indicates that the true Spirit is the Spirit of truth that proceeds from God. This is the Spirit that he, the author of the letter, has and those who follow him (see 4:5–6), who have received the anointing of the Father and of the Son (see 2:27). To confess that the Son of God has come in the flesh is the guarantee of knowing God and knowing the truth (see 5:20).

b) The letter declares that, as a practical matter, the proponents of those ideas engaged in conduct incompatible with faith. They were walking in darkness, since no matter how much they boasted of being in communion with God and not committing sin, in fact they were not keeping the commandments (see 2:3–5) and committed sin even though they did not recognize it (see 1:8, 10). Not confessing Jesus in the flesh and what he did on earth, but instead teaching and believing in a kind of salvation by knowledge (see 4:8), they were not leading a moral life in conformity with the true faith. That was shown by their failure to practice love for neighbor. And without love for one's brethren, there is no true faith, nor are there true children of God.

Many efforts have been made to identify those who held these doctrines with a heresy known from other sources, but this has produced no satisfactory result. Some interpreters believe the error might have arisen under the influence of a kind of incipient gnosis, born perhaps in a Jewish or Judeo-Christian setting. Still, we know little of this heresy as it was then, since our sources are later ones. Moreover, it is not clear when Gnosticism began, considering that there was a great variety of Gnostic currents and it is better to speak of "Gnosticisms." Nor is it known whether they were of Jewish, Christian, or oriental origin, though probably they combined elements taken from various religions. In any case, their common denominator was the affirmation that salvation comes from a person's own knowledge (*gnosis*), not through the redemptive sacrifice of Christ. That aside, what the letter has in view is a kind of Docetism, upon which most of the Gnostic movements drew from the second century on. This doctrine denied that Christ is truly man. Ignatius of Antioch (ca. 110) battled it.

The possibility cannot be excluded that the errors of those unmasked by the letter reflect the teaching of Cerinthus (against whom, says St. Polycarp, John wrote his Gospel). But little is known about him, and various ancient Christian writers attributed different errors to him. In his account of the Gnostics, St. Irenaeus says that, besides holding erroneous views of creation, Cerinthus also took Docetist positions in saying Christ was a spiritual being who descended upon Jesus, an ordinary man, after his baptism and left him before the crucifixion.

One cannot dismiss the possibility that the errors mentioned in the letter might have arisen from exaggerating certain aspects of the fourth Gospel: for instance, its insistence on Jesus as the Light that saves (perhaps somewhat obscuring the salvific significance of the Cross), or its reduced emphasis on moral themes in comparison with the Synoptics. In any event, the error might originate in a mixture of erroneous Christological theories of a Docetist sort, perhaps arising from faulty interpretation of the Gospel.

7. Date

Since Polycarp and Justin knew 1 John, it must have existed before 150 AD. The most likely date of composition is after the fourth Gospel, around the year 100. Some authors locate 1 and 2 John in the decade following the composition of the body of the Gospel but before its final redaction after 100 AD.

8. Teaching

The teaching is uniform and is repeated in similar or even identical words. It is grounded in a basic and specific doctrine that might be synthesized as follows.

Before addressing the problems raised by the schismatics, the author declares it necessary to be in communion with God, that is, in communion with the Father and the Son. This communion is based on confessing the true faith, which centers on belief in Jesus as the Son of God, the Messiah, who came in the flesh and died for our sins. That faith demands living charity, loving as God loves, as a child of God.

Developing the message further, the writer says the basis for being with the Father and the Son lies in remaining in communion with the transmitters of the faith and accepting their teaching. To be in union with God is "to know God;" "to be in God" or "to be in the light"; "to have the Father" or "to have the Son," and so "to have eternal life," and, above all, "to remain" in God.

God the Father gave testimony about his Son and commands us to believe in the name of his Son Jesus Christ. This is the only possible way of being in union with the Father and possessing eternal life. The condition for being united to God is therefore to confess Jesus as the "Son of God" (2:23; 4:15; 5:5; etc.), the "Word" (1:1), the "only Son" (4:9), "the Christ" (5:1). That faith implies confessing Jesus as Savior of the world, the one who truly came in the flesh, in order to take away the sins of humankind. By this faith, the Christian is united to Christ and through him to the Father. But for that he should live as Christ lived, "take the way of the Way" (2:6). And the very heart of Christ's Way on earth is love. "God is love" (4:8, 16) and revealed that love by sending his only begotten Son to the world (see 4:9). The communication of divine love is realized by means of supernatural rebirth in baptism, by which the Christian "is born of God" (3:9).

Love of God is shown in keeping the commandments, not loving the world insofar as it is an enemy of God, living justice, and struggling to purify oneself of all sin. But above all, it is shown by living the new commandment: to love one another, giving one's life for others as Christ "laid down his life for us" (3:16). Thus we must love with deeds and in truth. God's children are recognized as such from the fact that their charity is intimately related to divine filiation. "Everyone who believes that Jesus is the Christ is a child of God, and everyone who loves the parent loves the child" (5:1). Divine filiation is the consequence of God's great love for humanity (see 3:1).

II. THE SECOND AND THIRD LETTERS OF JOHN

As has been said, the so-called second and third letters of John have many points in common with the first, but, due to their brevity, are less mentioned by the Fathers and ancient Christian authors.

St. Polycarp may have known 2 John, for in his *Letter to the Philippians* 7:1 he seems to allude to 2 John 7: "For many deceivers have gone out into the world, men who will not acknowledge the coming of Jesus Christ in the flesh; such a one is the deceiver and the antichrist." Tertullian also alludes to this passage in *De Carne Christi* 24. The first explicit reference to the Evangelist as author of the letter comes from St. Irenaeus, who expressly attributes 2 John 7:11 to "John, the disciple of the lord" (*Adversus Haereses* 1, 16, 3; 3, 16, 8).

On the other hand, we have no references to 3 John until the third century. Eusebius of Caesarea, in line with Origen's (third century) statement that not everyone considered these two letters canonical, places them among the questioned writings of the New Testament, and St. Jerome makes the same point. From the fourth century on, however, 3 John appears in the lists of canonical books until its definitive confirmation by the Council of Trent.

1. The Author

The writer of the two letters does not give his name but identifies himself simply as "the Presbyter" (or "the Elder"). The title indicates someone with dignity or a person who enjoyed authority among those to whom the letters were addressed. There are various possibilities as to who this was. The title could refer to the fact that the beloved disciple was one of the apostles, since "presbyter" sometimes was used as a synonym for "apostle" (for example, in 1 Pet 5:1, Peter calls himself *sympresbyteros* or "presbyter like them"; and Papias in Eusebius, *Historia Ecclesiastica* 3.39.4 calls Philip, Thomas, James, John, and Matthew "presbyters"). It could also be understood as the title of an official of the Church (in the same way as "bishop"). Several authors have identified the "Presbyter" who wrote the letter with "John the Presbyter," the disciple of the Lord cited by Papias of Hierapolis (second century), according to the testimony of Eusebius of Caesarea; he had authority and did not belong to the group of the Twelve. Others confine themselves to the general statement that he was a disciple of the disciples of Jesus.[2]

The two letters are the work of the same writer, as can be seen by comparing their salutations and farewells, which use nearly identical formulas. As has been said, both—especially the second—are very close to 1 John. For example, in 2 John the author uses expressions or formulations identical with or very similar to 1 John: "loving the truth;" "knowing the truth;"

---

2. In the sense of a disciple of Jesus who was not part of the group of the Twelve, Papias uses the term in relation to Aristion and "the *presbyteros* John." "Presbyter" as a disciple of the disciples of Jesus is found in Irenaeus, *Adversus Haereses* 4.27: "I heard of a certain presbyter who had listened to those who had seen the apostles and those whom they had taught."

"remaining in Christ" or "in the teaching of Christ;" "possessing the Father and the Son." He also refers to the first Christian teaching as that which "you have heard from the beginning." He insists on the keeping of the commandments and in a special way on fraternal love. Whoever does not confess that Jesus Christ has come in the flesh is said to be a "seducer" or "antichrist." These and other features strongly suggest that the letters, if not from the same hand, are at least products of the same milieu.

In any case, whether or not the three are by the same author, 2 John's close resemblance to 1 John and 1 John's to the Gospel indicate that within the communities linked to the beloved disciple, the Presbyter was the guardian of the disciple's legacy, administrator, so to speak, of the tradition received from John, the son of Zebedee (see Ratzinger/Benedict XVI, *Jesus of Nazareth*, vol. 1, p. 226). In this sense, it might also have been he who collected the material of the beloved disciple that we find in 1 John and who may have taken part in the final writing of the Gospel.

2. Content and Circumstances

The two letters follow the format of letters of that day: a greeting, identifying the sender and intended recipients, body, containing the reason and principal content of the letter, and final farewell with various greetings.

a) The second letter of John, addressed to "the elect lady and her children" (2 Jn 1), is very likely a way of designating a local church, certainly in Asia Minor, as is also suggested by the fact that the author refers at the end of the greetings to "the children of your chosen sister" (2 Jn 13). This symbolic designation "chosen lady" referring to a local church is more probable than the identification of the chosen lady as a specific woman in Greek called Chosen (*Elekte*) or Lady (*Kyria* was also a proper name), or as a woman whose name is omitted and who is designated by honorary titles.

After indicating the sender and addressees and giving the opening greetings, the letter recalls an essential element of the doctrine included in 1 John—namely, the practice of charity and communion with the Father and the Son—and speaks of the existence of schismatics with whom the letter's recipients should not have contacts. The farewell expresses the desire to visit those to whom the letter is addressed.

From its content, one concludes that the Church to which the Presbyter is writing is in a delicate situation due to the appearance of people who seek to indoctrinate its members with teachings that differ from those they have received. The designation of those people as "seducers," who do not confess Jesus Christ "as having come in the flesh" and therefore are "antichrists" (2 Jn 7), implies that they are the ones against whom 1 John was written (see 1 Jn 2:22; 4:3). It is said of them that "they are leaving" or "going beyond" the doctrine of Christ and not remaining in it. They oppose the teaching of 1 John, which has been transmitted "from the beginning" (11:1–4). It is this doctrine of which the Presbyter reminds them, synthesizing it as faith in Christ's incarnation and in the need to walk in the commandment of love so as to guarantee communion with the Father and the Son.

b) The third letter of John is directed to a specific person, Gaius, of whom we know nothing. A document of the fourth century, the *Apostolic Constitutions*, has a list of bishops in which Gaius and Demetrius (who also appears in the letter) are referred to as bishops of Pergamum and Philadelphia respectively (VII, 46), but the historical value of this information is doubtful.

Following the greeting, the Presbyter praises Gaius for being a true Christian, as he demonstrated in showing hospitality to the envoys of the Presbyter. In contrast with this is the attitude of Diotrephes, who did not respect the authority of the Presbyter, in that he did not accept what was indicated in writing, or receive his envoys; he even expelled them from that community. The Presbyter also mentions a certain Demetrius as a person of trust. The final greetings, very similar to those of 2 John, express the Presbyter's desire to visit Gaius and speak with him.

The letter's occasion seems to be a crisis of obedience more than a doctrinal question, although obviously the two things are related. Diotrephes does not acknowledge the Presbyter's position of authority or accept other Christians who probably were sent by him. Both may have been heads of house churches, but Gaius is unlike Diotrephes in receiving the Presbyter's envoys. Demetrius, who is in communion with the Presbyter, may possibly have been a recognized missionary who carried the letter or who was thinking of visiting Gaius a little later. Not much more can be said about any of them. Attempts to identify Diotrephes with a Monarchist bishop whom the Presbyter opposed because his elevation implied the institutionalization of the Church as opposed to a charismatic Church defended by the Presbyter (Adolf Harnack), or with a Docetist bishop who had excommunicated Christians without the permission of the Presbyter (Walter Bauer), or with an orthodox bishop representing the official Church, who had acted against the Presbyter, excommunicating him for his Gnostic tendencies (Ernst Käsemann), or in someone with authority who was combating the schismatics in a way the Presbyter did not agree with (Raymond Brown), are too hypothetical.

In any case, what is clear from this letter are the authority and dignity (apostolic or derived from the apostles) of the Presbyter. It is a testimony to their veneration for him that, in circumstances in which the development, growth, and institutionalization of the Church were difficult, the recipients of his correspondence collected and preserved it.

3. Date of Composition

Given the lack of other data from tradition, one can suppose that 2 John was written at about the same time as 1 John, in a moment when the heresies did not appear as dangerous as the first letter indicates. But it might also have been written as an introduction to the first letter, summarizing its principal points; or else after it, recapitulating its essentials. In any case, it is believed to have been written some years after the Gospel, although perhaps before its final redaction.

The third letter of John reflects a situation later than to the other two. Some interpreters consider it more or less contemporaneous with the final redaction of the Gospel, at the time of the pastoral development reflected in chapter 21, around the year 100 AD.

Part III

REVELATION

Chapter 9

THE REVELATION OF JOHN

1. The Last Book of the Bible

REVELATION (OR THE APOCALYPSE) is the final book of the New Testament and the Bible. As the last book of the New Testament, it presents the culmination of the saving work of Christ. The Gospels recount the central moment in the working out of salvation by Jesus, the Word incarnate, who gathers his disciples and conquers death by his passion and resurrection. The Acts of the Apostles and the apostolic letters describe the action of the risen Christ guiding the Church in history through the Holy Spirit. Revelation concentrates on the definitive victory of Christ and his followers over the powers of evil, which culminates in the end of time when he will return again.

As the final book of the whole Bible, Revelation presents itself as a kind of closing word on human history. The beginning of that history is described in the accounts of Creation found in the Book of Genesis, while its development is traced through the Old Testament in the history of God's chosen people of Israel and in the New Testament, which testifies to the coming of the Messiah and the inauguration of the new people of God, the Church.

The Book of Revelation narrates the end of that history and the coming of a new world—new heavens and a new earth: The beginning of the scriptural narration finds its fulfillment here.

Revelation's images of an earthly paradise (see 21:1–5; 22:1, 14) recall those of Genesis, and, in the context of both, suggest to the reader a panorama of history from its beginning to its end.

Despite popular perceptions, the book does not announce the coming of enormous catastrophes and misfortunes. Read attentively and interpreted as its author intended, it is a book communicating joy, encouragement, and hope. "Blessed are they who read it and practice what it contains," it says (1:3; 16:15; 22:7). True, it tells the reader that the end of this world will be marked by evil and rebellion against God, described with an impressive realism; at the same time, however, it announces a happy end for the just, with a happiness surpassing what man could imagine based only on what has happened so often in history—the seeming triumph of evil. The enormously realistic author of Revelation is well aware of this; but above all he believes that God's goodness and mercy, shown in the death and resurrection of Christ, are stronger than evil and death, and that good is winning out in history and will be totally victorious at the end.

2. Its Canonicity

The Christians who received and preserved Revelation saw in it a teaching about Jesus risen and glorious, in harmony with the Gospels and the letters of the apostles, and a stimulus to live the Christian life with fidelity and authenticity, as the apostles had urged from the beginning. Read in the early Church, it was eventually taken to be part of the authentic apostolic tradition, and so to be integrated into the New Testament.

Nevertheless, this process was not without difficulties. Revelation is one of a group of books called deuterocanonical, that is, writings that for some time were not received as sacred by all the Christian communities. Its use by some ancient heretical sects to support their teachings may have caused its authenticity to be doubted in some sectors of the Church, especially in the East. But the ambivalence of some writers of the Eastern Church was mitigated by the witness of the Latin Church, which soon accepted it as canonical, as we see from the second century Muratorian Canon, which included Revelation in its list of the sacred books.

Arguing in favor of its canonicity was the widespread, though not universal, belief in the early centuries that its author was the apostle St. John. The first explicit testimony to this effect is found in St. Irenaeus around the year 185. Today there are diverse views on this subject. While the author of Revelation does introduce himself with the name John, he does not speak as an apostle in the manner the Twelve did but as a prophet speaking in the name of the glorified Jesus. Revelation speaks with the voice of one who writes what he has received from our Lord in heaven in a mystical, supernatural, and personal experience meant to fortify the faith and hope of the entire Church represented by seven specific churches.

The Old Testament contains a book with the same literary features and a similar content as Revelation. This is the second part of the Book of Daniel (chapters 7 to 12), which tells of visions the prophet had concerning how and when the times in which the writer lived would end. In the Gospels, too, we find some discourses of Jesus dealing with the end of the world and his Second Coming (see Mk 13:1ff and the parallels Mt 24:1ff; Lk 21:5ff), and the letters of St. Paul and St. Peter speak frequently of the Second Coming of Christ, universal judgment, and the renewal of this present world, though without describing these things as richly as the Apocalypse does.

3. Apocalyptic Literature

To understand the language and cosmic vision in which the Christian message of Revelation is expressed, we need to consider a series of Jewish works produced before and at the time of this book's writing. Since the middle of the nineteenth century their similarity to the "apocalypse" of John has caused them to be referred to as apocalyptic literature, and many have been called "apocalypses."

The meaning of "apocalyptic" is not well defined, from either a literary or sociological-religious point of view. Some writers, considering as a literary genre, take it to refer to a revelation of celestial mysteries. Others focus more on content, especially eschatological teaching. Following John J. Collins, *apocalyptica* is here used to signify a literary genre containing revelation, presented in the framework of a narrative, in which the revelation normally is mediated by a being from another world and directed to a human addressee to whom it discloses a transcendent reality while at the same time pointing to an eschatological salvation linked to a world that transcends the present one (see *The Apocalyptic Imagination*, p. 4).

The extent of the body of literature corresponding to this description is by no means clear, since these works were not originally designated by the term "apocalypse." Nor, except for some books attributed to Enoch, were they transmitted together. Rather each circulated independently, and each had its own particular way of expressing its message in line with the religious spirit of one or another Jewish group. Still, they do have some common features that they share to a great extent with the Apocalypse or Revelation of John.

The writing of apocalyptic literature extends over a long period of time, from the third or fourth century before Christ until after the second Jewish war in 130 AD. These books were written in difficult circumstances, when the identity of the people was seriously threatened, as during the persecution by Antiochus Epiphanes around the year 175 BC. Numerous works presented as being direct revelations of the hidden mysteries of God, made first to their ancestors and now put into writing, appeared in this context of persecution. All corresponded to particular historical, social, and religious circumstances moving the authors, speaking on God's behalf, to show their readers the meaning of their situation and the attitude they should maintain in the face of what was thought to be an imminent end. Apparently these things were not so easily determined, since these works often gave more emphasis to what was transpiring in heaven and would happen at the end of the world than the events at the time they were written. All the same, the situation of the author and his readers is clear enough, as in the case of the Apocalypse or Book of Revelation.

To a great extent, this kind of literature had its roots in prophetic literature. The prophets had already announced the definitive intervention of God, the "day of the Lord" (see Am 5:18–20; Is 2:12–21; 13:6–9; Jer 30:5–7; Jl 1:15; 2:1–17), when the world will be judged, the impious condemned, and the just exalted in intimacy with God. Moreover, to communicate their message the prophets made use of visions and symbolic images (see Am 7:1–8, 3; Hos 13:7–8; Jl 2:10–11; Ez 1–2).

But prophetic literature was not the only inspiration for apocalyptic literature. The wisdom books also were influences, their visions mingling with moral exhortations, calls to reflection, and promises of future blessedness or punishment.

Particularly noteworthy among Old Testament apocalyptic precedents are some passages in the Book of Isaiah (chapters 24–27), a large part of the Book of Zechariah (especially chapters 9–14) and, above all, the Book of Daniel (especially chapers 7–12).

In Daniel, God's intentions are disclosed to the prophet by means of heavenly visions, interpreted by an angel. Images are employed that had great impact on later literature and to some extent were taken up in the apocalypse of John. Especially notable is the contemplation of universal history as a whole, divided into successive periods, and the announcement of its approaching end, marked by the inauguration of a new world in which even those who have already died will participate in virtue of their resurrection. Common to all the visions is the author's conviction, based on what has been revealed to him, that he lives in the time just before the end. That ending is prefigured in previous history, narrated in the form of prophecy to make it clear that what was being said would surely come since it is predestined by God. This eschatological conclusion will come about through God's immediate and brilliant victory over the powers of evil incarnated in the persecutors of his people as well as and through the resurrection of the just and their ascension to heaven, where they will shine like the stars.

The largest body of apocalyptic literature is found, however, in a group of books that are not part of the biblical canon. Among these the most ancient, the so-called 1 Enoch, is also the first work we have in the form of an "apocalypse." Written in the fourth or third century BC, it provides the basis for this type of religious and literary expression in the future, though with new elements added and different purposes in view at different times.

I Enoch itself is a collection of five books coming from different eras, with the oldest being the Book of the Watchers. Here, in the face of evil more powerful than humankind, there is an appeal to a new revelation of Enoch, who saw and wrote what would happen in the heavens. The other books of I Enoch are the Book of Astronomy, the Apocalypse of the Animals, the Epistle of Enoch, and the Apocalypse of the Weeks. In them Enoch is carried to heaven and there contemplates God in his true temple. In Enoch as in Daniel, it is assumed that the final outcome predestined by God is imminent.

Another influential book is the so-called Book of the Jubilees, at the beginning of the second century BC. Here the revelation is given in the name of Moses, with the intention that readers will begin to fulfill the Law with full fidelity and more rigorously than the Pentatuch's treatment of the Law of Moses indicates.

In the Qumran literature (second century BC to first century AD) one finds compositions of an apocalyptic type that are strongly echoed in the Apocalypse of John: for example, in speaking of final battles, of the heavenly liturgy, and of the New Jerusalem, with its temple and serenity.

After the destruction of Jerusalem in the year 70, this type of literature continued to appear in the Jewish world in numerous works. These include the Apocalypse of 4 Esdras (2 Esdras), containing a series of visions in which the human person, unable to overcome the evil in his heart, awaits a mighty intervention from above; 2 Baruch, which sees the destruction of the temple as the final act before the day of judgment; the Apocalypse of Abraham, dealing with the problem of the reign of evil in the world, especially in the form of idolatry; the Apocalypse of Moses, telling of God's revelations to Adam and Eve concerning their descendants and the resurrection awaiting Adam after his sin; and books III and IV of the Sibylline Oracles, which, although not strictly apocalyptic, have elements in common with the Apocalypse of John in regard to Rome's condemnation for immorality and arrogance and also in the use of the legend of the return of Nero.

All these apocalyptic books show a profound religious attitude and an unbreakable faith in the God of Israel. They seek to console those suffering persecution and encourage them, as the case may be, to passive resistance or armed struggle, in the hope that God will give them victory. Perseverance in faith in the midst of persecutions and a renewal of hope that God will not leave things that way but will make his terrible punishments fall upon the enemies of Israel or sinners are among the principal outcomes this body of writings has in view.

4. The Formal and Doctrinal Features of Apocalyptic Literature

Apocalyptic literature is a new way of perceiving and transmitting divine revelation in the face of the Jewish belief that prophetic activity ended with Malachi at the return from exile.

Persecution was the usual context in which these works were written. Later, too, we find the schematic presentation of history as a whole together with the expectation that the final end is close at hand. This message is presented as a revelation of the secrets guarded in heaven, which now, with the arrival of the end times, are revealed in these apocalyptic books.

These works typically take the form of the "pseudo-epigraph," a writing attributed to a notable person of the past (Noah, Lamech, Enoch, etc.) or at least of the exile as represented in Scripture (Baruch, Daniel, Esdras), with whom the writers wish their message to be associated. This person is usually transported to heaven and there shown mysteries that must later be explained. In the face of these revelations, the seers often are troubled, fade away, or fall to the ground on their faces. Frequently, the one who interprets the message is an angel (angels are basic features in many of the apocalyptic works).

The language of these books is marked by a repetitive character and the inclusion of long discourses. The use of numbers and lists predominates, and number symbolism recurs frequently (seven, twelve, 1260, "a time plus two times plus half a time," half of seven) as do animals, beasts, symbolic dragons, heavens, winds, strange mountains, trees of life, and so on.

Teaching is often transmitted through images, in the manner of the prophets (the throne of God in Isaiah; the heavenly chariot, the sword or the cutting of a cedar in Ezekiel; horses, the measuring of the city, or the candelabra and the two olive trees in Zechariah, etc.). The images are used in speaking of God and his power at the end times, his transcendence, and his triumph over his enemies. In the absence of actual experience of that final moment in history, the symbols give an account of it drawing upon the great actions of God described in Scripture: creation in its positive aspect (new creation) or negative (the original disorder), the flood that comes unexpectedly, the punishment by fire that wiped out Sodom and Gomorrah, the

Exodus, accompanied by the great punishment visited upon the Egyptians and the Jews' path to safety through the sea, etc. This kind of language is naturally congenial to apocalyptic literature, whose transcendent and supernatural message requires the use of analogy and simile to prompt and stimulate a profound intuitive grasp, rather than exact knowledge, of what is being said.

The content of these books is highly varied, but very briefly one might say the revelations they transmit deal principally with resurrection, the imminence of the new era, and the great crisis looming in world history. Where the ancient prophets, inspired by God, revealed the profound and radical change in history that would occur with the coming of the Messiah, that change is now linked to the end of the world as it presently exists. This world and history are seen as giving notice of a destiny already determined by God, whose imminent accomplishment will happen through terrible cosmic battles. In general, these books consider this world to be under Satan's power and without possibility of regeneration; thus they place their hope in a new world that God will create, with humankind contributing little more than prayer. In this sense, they reflect strong deterministic tendencies: for all this is already written, leaving very little room for freedom and conversion.

All the same, this eschatology of restoration starts with the idea God is good, that he controls history, and that he will not tolerate evil indefinitely. In the end, he will destroy evil. Someone who knows how to read the signs of the times—cosmic battles between good and evil, the resurrection of the dead or of the just, the role of the Messiah, the renewal of the temple, the reunion of the twelve tribes, the domination of the Gentiles by Israel, etc.—will also come to know what will follow these events.

5. The Uniqueness of John's Apocalypse

Scholars seeking to establish the literary genre of St. John's Apocalypse have found it to be something more than the works we call "apocalyptic." It is a complex book using and referring to various sources, so that readers can place the emphasis on one or the other. Speaking in the apocalyptic context, one can say it combines the prophetic (1:3; 22:6–20), the epistolary (2:1–3:22), and the liturgical (4:8, 11; 5:9–14; 11:17–18;) genres.

An important feature distinguishing it from the apocalypses of that time is that these latter are characterized by containing divine revelations disclosed to famous persons of the past, while the Book of Revelation does not include this feature, and its author presents himself as John. This and other facts that we shall address below suggest that the best way of describing this book's genre may be to call it a prophetic apocalypse or an apocalyptical prophecy.

Certainly the characteristic aim of the apocalyptical writing of the time was to sustain faith at difficult moments and foster hope in the coming of the Day of the Lord and the kingdom of God by a set of revelations. And even though the Book of Revelation opens by indicating that it is a "revelation" of Jesus Christ given by God to John (see 1:1), this does not necessarily mean the book must be understood as an apocalypse. Undoubtedly, many of the images used to refer to the past, present, and future are typical of apocalyptic literature beginning with the Old Testament. But the book's second sentence indicates that we have here a prophecy as well: "Blessed is he who reads aloud the words of the prophecy, and blessed are those who hear, and keep what is written therein" (1:3). John plainly is conscious that God has delegated that the writing of that prophecy to him (see 22:7, 10), so that he considers himself a prophet in the line of the prophets of the New Covenant. This is suggested by the circumstance that the angel who shows him the visions calls John "a fellow servant" and tells him that "the testimony of Jesus is the spirit of prophecy" (19:10; see 22:9). In other words, the Holy Spirit, who inspires the prophecy, enables the prophets to testify to the revelation that Jesus brought and is bringing, according to what is said at the beginning of the book: John is the one "who bore witness to the word of God and to the testimony of Jesus Christ, even to all that he saw" (1:2). This testimony includes God's word about the history of humanity in the present and future.

True, the Revelation of John, like other apocalypses, speaks of "what must soon take place" (1:1). But what is going to take place is a consequence and culmination of what has already happened (the victory of Christ risen under the image of the slain lamb) and is now happening (the reign of Christ in heaven and the adoration being given to him, as well as the patience and prayer of the saints). And where other apocalypses, after organizing previous history according to periods (Jubilees) or engaging in numerological calculations regarding just when the end will come (Daniel), present that coming as imminent, the "soon" of Revelation is not so immediate or so specific. John refers by symbols to the end; and since he does not know when the end of time will come, the Book of Revelation, like Jesus in his eschatological discourse, invites readers to a hopeful vigilance, without trying to establish either the when or the how. In fact, while other apocalyptic writings do not allow for a lengthy period between the moment in which the oracle is pronounced and the end, John offers the symbolism of "a time, two times, and a half a time." This signifies the process of history: it is half of seven which signifies fulfillment. Like other apocalyptic works, Revelation is concerned with the end, but it presents it according to a new schema.

Those to whom John was writing considered this book different from other apocalypses. The Jewish apocalypses were directed to Israel as the chosen people or to the descendants of the patriarchs (for example, the Testament of the Twelve Patriarchs), but John's was directed to the Church as a whole, represented by the seven churches to which his letters are addressed. It is Christ, living and glorious, who speaks in the liturgy of his

Church, which is suffering persecution (see 1:4–10) and experiencing temptation (external hostility and the risk of perverting the gospel). Christ and his promises are the response to the yearnings and problems of each church. The seven letters end with Christ's promise "to the victor": salvation that is eschatological and transcendent, not worldly: entrance into paradise (see 2:7); escaping the "second death" (2:11); admittance to the banquet (a pebble with a new name, 2:12); participation in the reign of Christ, as described in Psalm 2, "He shall rule them with a rod of iron" (2:26–28); communion with God and the saints (see 2:12); sharing in the kingship of Christ (see 3:21).

The Book of Revelation also has a different way of presenting the enemies of God. In other Jewish works, they are given very concrete features (Antiochus Epiphanes or the antichrist described physically in the Apocalypse of Elias), but the Revelation of John uses symbols like the Beast, the false prophet, or the prostitute city, which can be interpreted as referring to different enemies of God and humankind at different moments in the Church's history. And while in other apocalypses the motive for God's definitive intervention is that the Jews are not fulfilling the Law or the persecutors have outdone themselves in oppressing the people, in the Revelation of John it is above all the prayers of the saints rising to the throne of God that summon divine intervention.

Thus, despite having features in common with the Jewish apocalyptic literature of the time, Revelation differs profoundly. It is similar to the Jewish apocalypses in being presented as a revelation, granted by God through visions and journeys to heaven. But this is the revelation-testimony of Jesus Christ transmitted through one of his witnesses, John, interpreting history in the name of God. Similar Christian books somewhat later than Revelation, such as the Shepherd of Hermas and the Ascension of Isaiah, also belong to Christian prophecy.

6. The Language and Style of Revelation

Stylistically, Revelation differs notably from ordinary Greek and contains many errors of vocabulary and grammar. The vocabulary is meager, although its semantic density is rich. In this sense, it has the same limitations of vocabulary as the other Johannine works. Some believe they see in its use of Greek the hand of someone who does not know the language well. Others attribute its errors to the author's semantic situation: while writing in Greek, he either thought in Hebrew or was strongly influenced by the Hebrew Scriptures. Almost all scholars agree that the author of Revelation has a Semitic mentality.

The book's symbolic images are taken mostly from the prophetic books of the Old Testament. Some are objects: the golden candelabra with seven arms (see 1:12; Zec 4:2), the book with the seven seals (see 5:1; Ez 2:9), the two olive trees (see 11:4; Zec 4:3-14), etc. Others are gestures: marking the foreheads of the elect (see 7:3; Ez 9:4), eating the book of the prophecy (see 10:8-10; Ez 2:8), measuring the temple (11:1; see Ez 40-41), etc. Some cities have symbolic meaning: Zion or Jerusalem, Babylon, Armageddon (see 14:1; 21:2; 14:8; 18:2; 16:16, etc.). Numbers also are given a symbolic value: three refers to the supernatural and divine; four to what has been created; seven and twelve to plenitude. Something similar occurs in the case of colors: white symbolizes victory and purity; red, violence; black, death. Images of fantastic animals and beasts are plentiful.

The narrative often is not straightforward, with new themes appearing within a principal theme. Historical sequences, generally of a symbolic character, are interwoven with heavenly visions. Not uncommonly, an event is anticipated briefly and later developed at length. At times, an account is interrupted by a passage meant to console the just.

7. Date and Place of Composition

There are two principal theories regarding the date of composition: immediately after the persecution of Nero (68–69) and at the end of the reign of Domitian, about the year 95.

Advocates of the first theory hold that Revelation shows knowledge of the persecution suffered by Christians under Nero but not of the destruction of the temple of Jerusalem. The use of the name "Babylon" for Rome points to a date after the year 70 AD when Jewish sources did the same. It appears, too, that Christians began calling the first day of the week *Dies Domini,* the Lord's Day, after that date. Some authors also hold that the communities of Asia Minor as described in Revelation are more developed than are the churches described by other writings at an earlier date.

Those who hold the second view rely on the testimony of St. Irenaeus, considered credible by specialists. The Bishop of Lyons put the writing of the Book of Revelation at the end of the era of Domitian, about the year 95 (*Adversus Haereses* 5:30). So do Victorinus (*In Apoc.* 1:11 and 17:10) in the third century or at the end of the second, St. Jerome (*De vir. Illust.* 9), and Eusebius (*Hist. Eccl.* 3, 18, 4). This date is consistent with the character and content of the book, especially the description of the antichrist as another Nero.

The place of composition is Patmos (see 1:9), a small island in the Aegean Sea, not far off the coast of Ephesus. The revelation it contains took place on a Sunday, "the Lord's day" (1:10). An ancient tradition, to which Tertullian attests, states that the beloved disciple was exiled to that island because of his preaching and apostolic ministry.

8. Audience and Purpose

The book is directed to the "seven churches that are in Asia" (1:4): Ephesus, Smyrna, Pergamum, Thyatira, Sardis, Philadelphia, and Laodicea. As the Muratorian Canon indicates, the number seven is symbolic; the book is meant for the universal Church. This can also be inferred from some general expressions: "Blessed is he who reads aloud the words of the prophecy, and blessed are those who hear, and who keep what is written therein" (1:3); or from the repeatedly sounded cautionary note: "He who has an ear, let him hear what the Spirit says to the churches" (2:7, 11, 17, 29; 3:6, 14, 22).

The book seeks to alert Christians to serious dangers for the faith while at the same time consoling and encouraging those suffering from the hostility of both the authorities and their fellow citizens (see the Introduction to this book, § 2). In the face of injustices and outrages, John tries to comfort the Christians, so that they will retain a lively hope in Christ's final triumph and remain faithful to him—to death if necessary (see 2:10).

Starting from this historical situation, the seer presents the situation of the Church at that moment along with a broad panorama of the end times. Yet, he understands that those final times have already begun with the coming of Jesus Christ. Thus the book provides a certain perspective for current events and the hope of final triumph, depicting a cosmic struggle between good and evil while also taking for granted Christ's definitive triumph.

Referring to the vision of the Woman in chapter 12, Benedict XVI writes:

> This Woman represents Mary, the Mother of the Redeemer, but at the same time she also represents the whole Church, the People of God of all times, the Church which in all ages, with great suffering, brings forth Christ ever anew. And she is always threatened by the dragon's power. She appears defenseless and weak. But while she is threatened, persecuted by the dragon, she is also protected by God's comfort. And in the end this Woman wins. The dragon does not win. This is the great prophecy of this Book that inspires confidence in us! The Woman who suffers in history, the Church

which is persecuted, appears in the end as the radiant Bride, the figure of the new Jerusalem where there will be no more mourning or weeping, an image of the world transformed, of the new world whose light is God himself, whose lamp is the Lamb" (General Audience, August 23, 2006).

9. The Author

In four places (1:1, 4, 9; 22:8), the author of the book calls himself John. He does not present himself as "apostle," as, for example, Paul sometimes does, but as "servant" of Jesus (1:1), "brother" and "participant" in the sufferings of those to whom he is writing (1:9), and "prophet" (see 10:11). Tradition since the second century identifies this John with the apostle, the son of Zebedee. The first to do so was St. Justin, who converted to Christianity in Ephesus in the year 135 and relates that "a man called John, one of the apostles of Christ," received the revelations contained in the Book of Revelation (*Dialogue with Trypho*, 81). Other witnesses to the same effect include Papias, St. Irenaeus, Origen, Tertullian, and Melito of Sardis.

Nevertheless, Eusebius reports disagreements on the part of others, for example, a Roman priest named Gaius, who thought Revelation had been written by Cerinthus, a Gnostic of that era (*Hist. Eccl.* 3, 28, 3). St. Epiphanius says some writers of that time, called *álogoi* for denying that Christ was the Logos, also denied that John had written the book (*Panarion* 51, 1–35). But the most important testimony against Johannine authorship is that of Dionysius of Alexandria, in the middle of the third century. This bishop, opposing Millenarianism, which found support in the Apocalypse (Revelation), sought to show that the book should not be interpreted literally and could not have been written by John the apostle. According to him, its poverty of language and its differences from the letters and the Gospel of John point to different authors (*Hist. Eccl.* 7, 25, 2). From the fourth century, some Fathers (St. Athanasius, St. Basil, and St. Gregory of Nyssa) accepted the Johannine authenticity of the book, while others, above all the representatives of the Antiochian school (such as St. Cyril of Jerusalem, St. John Chrysostom, and Theodoret) resisted doing that.

Most authors now believe Revelation could not be by the author of the fourth Gospel in light of the notable differences of style, vocabulary, and thought between Revelation and the Gospel and letters. Besides the numerous solecisms and barbarisms, the number of common words is very limited, and some key words in the Gospel are either virtually absent from Revelation (and vice versa) or, if they appear, are not the same (for example, "lamb"—in the Gospel, the Greek word *amnos* is used, in Revelation, *arnion*).

These differences between Revelation and the fourth Gospel in vocabulary and style suggest that they are from different hands. But taking into account the similarities between the two, the very ancient tradition of Johannine authorship, and the fact that the differences can be explained by differences of subject matter and purpose, one cannot rule out the possibility that the Gospel and Revelation share the apostolic authority of John the apostle, the beloved disciple, and come from the same community. In any case, specific similarities permit us to trace them to a single community.

Some similarities of vocabulary are significant. After the designation of Jesus as "Logos," "Word of God" (Jn 1:1–14 and Rv 19:13), the most notable maybe that both texts use certain specific terms: for example, "traversed," inspired by Zechariah 12:10 (Jn 19:37 and Rv 1:7), which does not appear elsewhere in the New Testament, in the Septuagint, or in the tradition of Theodosius; and the verb *skênôô* (Rv 7:15; 21:3, and Jn 1:14) in reference to God's dwelling among his people, which also appears nowhere else in the New Testament. And despite the difference in terminology mentioned above, both attach great importance to the paschal lamb (Rv 5:6–13; 6:1, 16; 7:9–17; Jn 1:29, 36).

But it is their basic message more than particular features like these that especially link Revelation and the fourth Gospel. To appreciate that, it is best first to consider Revelation, then indicate the theological similarities between the two texts (see chaper 10, section 5). This will serve to show the Johannine character of the book as it has come to us in the tradition of the Church.

Chapter 10

THE MESSAGE OF REVELATION

AS WAS SAID ABOVE, popular perceptions notwithstanding, Revelation's purpose is not to announce catastrophes or foretell great calamities in the end times. The book has the form typical of a literary genre of its era, the apocalyptic, but contains true Christian prophecy concerning the meaning of history.

A modern reader unfamiliar with the times in which it was written and with little biblical training undoubtedly finds it difficult to understand. Considerable knowledge of the Old Testament, especially prophets and Jewish literature from the third century BC to the first century AD, is required to appreciate many of its affirmations and their nuances. But even so, admitting that reading Revelation is a challenge, the book's message can be grasped clearly enough by any reader once its images and symbols are understood and the development of its theme has been made clear. Its message of consolation is ever timely, especially at critical moments in the history of the Church and humanity.

1. Content

Revelation begins with a Prologue (1:1–3) presenting the book—a revelation of Jesus Christ of a prophetic character—and its author. By way of introduction, John greets the seven churches of Asia Minor (Ephesus, Smyrna, Pergamum, Thyatira, Sardis,

Philadelphia, and Laodicea), which represent the Church as a whole (see 1:4–8). He then declares that in Patmos on the Lord's Day, he had a vision of Jesus Christ: appearing to him in a glorious form in the midst of seven golden candelabra (the churches) Jesus directed him to write in a book what he saw and send it to the churches (see 1:9–20). Next come messages to these communities (see 2:1–3:22), referring to their specific situations, noting their qualities and in some cases their deficiencies, and promising a future reward for those who overcome evil. Adhering to a pattern, these messages begin with instructions to the angels of the churches to write and ends with a warning to attend to what the Spirit is telling them. The past is mentioned and contrasted with the present, and threats and promises are given, ending with an exhortation to penance and conversion.

Next comes the recounting—in a very different tone—of a vision in heaven that serves as an introduction to those that come after. Using images and symbols drawn from the Old Testament, John describes God's majesty and the praise God receives in heaven. God is seated on a throne; around him are twenty-four ancients on their thrones (the heavenly Church, which includes the old and new Israel—the twelve tribes and the twelve apostles), seven flaming lamp stands (which symbolize the seven spirits of God), and four living beings (seraphim who praise God) (see 4:1–11). God holds a sealed book (symbol of mysterious salvific plans) that can only be opened (revealed) by the Lamb, standing and sacrificed (Christ dead and resurrected), who is at the throne of God. The Lamb's power is represented by his seven horns, his knowledge by his seven eyes, identified with the seven spirits that he sent to the Church. The Lamb also receives the praise of the ancients, the four living beings, the angels, and all creation (see 5:1–14).

Now the Lamb begins to open the seven seals of the book—the disclosure of history's meaning in the light of Christ. With the opening of the first four, there appear four horses with their riders. The first horse is white; its rider is perhaps the victorious Christ who controls what follows. The second is red; its rider is war. The third is black; its rider is famine. The fourth is a pale color (the plague); its rider is death. The divine punishments announced in the Old Testament are personified by means of these images (see 6:1–8). With the opening of the fifth seal, the glory of those who suffer persecution is revealed (see 6:9–11). An earthquake and great natural catastrophes accompany the sixth. These events precede the "day of the wrath" of the Lamb, the great judgment of God from which absolutely no one can escape (see 6:12–17).

As a way of creating suspense before opening the seventh seal, John describes a calm created when angels prevent harmful winds from blowing (see 7:1). Two visions are part of it. The first shows the divine protection of those sealed by God and who belong to him. They make up the great multitude of the saved: 144,000 (twelve times 12,000), a number indicating fullness that can represent Christians drawn from Judaism or the new Israel (see 7:2–8). The second vision is of an innumerable multitude of people dressed in white robes. Representing the glorious situation of those redeemed by Christ through his death, they recall a baptismal procession (see 7:9–17).

After this, the seventh seal is opened. Silence falls, evoking perhaps a liturgical silence in preparation for what follows. The seven angels are given seven trumpets (representing the execution of God's judgment on the world), and the prayer of the saints rises (see 8:1–6). The sounding of the trumpets is the voice of God announcing and meting out punishment for the sins of humankind.

The first four punishments recall the plagues of Egypt. They fall upon "a third part" of the earth, the seas, the sweet waters, and the stars (see 8:7–12). After an intermediate vision, in which an eagle pronounces three woes of horror and compassion regarding what is to come (see 8:13), the fifth trumpet sounds, announcing a punishment affecting not nature but man. The vision includes the fall of a star, the "angel of the abyss" (in Hebrew *Abaddon* and in Greek *Apolion*), which frees the forces of evil, symbolized in a terrible plague of scorpions that torments mankind for five months (a limited time). Thus the first "woe" ends (see 9:1–12). With the sounding of the sixth trumpet, the angels of death who are near the Euphrates (the place from which invasions that devastated Israel usually came) form an enormous army on horseback that causes the death of a third of humanity (see 9:13–19). In spite of the medicinal character of the punishments, which are a call to conversion, those who survive do not repent of their sins (see 9:20–21).

Before the seventh trumpet sounds, there is another interval in which expectation grows. John finds himself once more on earth. An angel offers him a small open scroll to eat. The vision, similar to a description by Ezekiel (see Ez 2:9–3:2), shows the prophetic character of John, whose prophecies affect all creation. If John would seal—maintain in silence—the divine plans announced in "seven peals of thunder" (10:4) that he hears, he must prophetically proclaim the contents of the small scroll given him to eat (see 10:1–11). After this, he is given a rod to measure the temple and the altar, thus indicating divine protection of the Church. Its persecution will not be definitive, but will be for a limited time (1,260 days—three-and-a-half years, that is, half seven). Even so, the two witnesses (the Christians), shown with the features of Moses and Elias, are not spared suffering and death. In the end, however, they will participate in the resurrection of Christ and their enemies will perish. Thus ends the second "woe" (see 11:1–14).

The final confrontation pitting Satan and the powers of evil against Christ and his Church begins with the sound of the seventh trumpet. Before the combats are described, there is an anticipation of the end in which the definitive triumph of Christ's kingdom is proclaimed in another consoling parenthesis. God's plan for the world has been accomplished, and so the triumph is already a present reality. The appearance of the Ark, in the manner of the theophany of Sinai, heralds the fulfillment of messianic times (see 11:15–19).

After this, two signs appear representing those who will take part in the final combat: the woman and her descendants (Israel, the Church, the Virgin Mary), and the red dragon (the devil) with seven heads and seven crowns (the power to make war) and ten horns (represent the kings who are enemies of the people of God). The dragon stalks the woman, who gives birth to a son with messianic features. The Son is snatched up to heaven and the woman flees to the desert. There then takes place a great combat in the heavens: Satan against the Messiah who was born of the woman, and against Michael and his angels. Satan is conquered and thrown to earth, where, although deprived of his power, he continues to fight against the woman and the rest of her children (the devil is still struggling against the projects of God and his people). But God will always protect the woman.

The attacks of the devil become more and more terrible (see 12:1–18). He carries them out by means of two beasts to whom he communicates his power. The first, which comes out of the sea, is described as having the features that the prophet Daniel attributed to the empires that would invade Israel (see 13:10); in Revelation, the beast symbolizes the Roman Empire and all political power that wants to supplant God. The weaponry of the second beast, which arises from the earth and is at the service of the first, is seduction by means of deceptive prodigies in the manner of the prophets (see 13:11-18), probably symbolizing the divinized Roman emperor and all who try to take the place of God. As a counterpoint, the Lamb appears, and preparations are made for judgment in anticipation of his victory. The Lamb comes with his followers—those who share in his salvation and sing a new song (see 14:1–5). Following this, three solemn interventions of angels announce the arrival of the hour of the final judgment (see 14:6–13). The judgment that the Son of Man will accomplish draws nearer with two new visions: a grain harvest and a grape harvest (see 14:14–20).

Now a new sign appears, that of the seven angels who spread seven plagues. First, those who are saved sing a song of victory (see 15:1–4). Then the angels come out of the tent (the presence of God) and receive seven golden cups filled with God's wrath (see 15:5–8). As they pour out the cups, they inflict the punishments, interrupted by a brief exhortation to vigilance and faithfulness.

The four first cups, related to elements of nature, are a version of the plagues of Egypt: ulcers on the earth, the sea and the rivers turned into blood, a blistering sun. The fifth (darkness on the throne of the beast) and the sixth (drying up of the Euphrates to allow the passage of the terrifying peoples of the East) are related to the forces or powers acting in history (see 16:1–12). The kings of the earth directed by the dragon, the beast of the sea, and the beast of the earth (the false prophet), gather in Armageddon for the final battle against God (see 16:13–16). When the seventh cup is poured, however, all are defeated. The theophany and earthquake that accompany the punishment indicate the severity of what will happen to them, for the sentence against the great Babylon (Rome) has been decreed (see 16:17–21). In a new vision, an angel tells of the fall of the city. Rome is presented as the great harlot riding on a beast of seven heads and seven horns. The angel explains that the harlot (Rome) sits upon seven hills, which at the same time are seven kings (the emperors), together with the kings allied to Rome, represented by the ten horns of the beast. These give their power to a Roman king, now identified with the beast: they all are to turn against Rome (the harlot) and will persecute the Church without success because Christ will conquer. The harlot will be devoured by those same kings (see 17:1–18).

Following this, a new vision shows the fall and ruin of Babylon (Rome, personifying the enemies of God) as if it had already occurred. God's people are called to separate themselves from her and from the evil she does, while, to the joy of the just who suffered there, the laments of those who became rich from the city and its evil actions are heard (see 18:124). Justice has at last been done. The just sing a song of praise because the harlot has been defeated and the definitive establishment of the kingdom of God is at hand, manifested in the wedding feast of the Lamb and now witnessed prophetically by John (see 19:1–10).

This song is followed by a vision of Christ glorious and triumphant, mounted on a white horse, the color of victory, at the head of an army of riders in white on white horses (see 19:11–16). After this we see an angel who calls the birds of the sky to prepare to fall upon the spoils of Christ's enemies—those who followed the beast and the false prophet—when they are defeated. The army of Christ captures the beast and the false prophet and throws them into hell, while the kings are killed by the sword (see 19:17–21). The dragon is captured by an angel and chained in the abyss for a thousand years (deprived of power for a time), which coincides with the reign of the saints with Christ. Later they will have power before their definitive end to attack the saints and the beloved city (the Church) in an especially intense way, but only for a short time. We see how God defeats them and throws them for all eternity into a pool of fire and sulfur (see 20:1–10). Then follows the universal judgment (with an image of the white throne and the books that are opened: some for judgment, another for life) and the condemnation of the impious (see 20:11–15).

With God's enemies, including death, destroyed, John has a vision of new heavens and a new earth. Here is the new creation, foretold by the prophets at the coming of the Messiah, where renewed humanity, the New Jerusalem, will be forever in communion with God, as guaranteed by the eternal and all powerful Word of God. In the vision, the New Jerusalem, descending from heaven, is shown as the Spouse of the Lamb and described as a splendid and perfect city (indicated by using the number twelve in reference to the elements of which it is built and its dimensions), based upon the twelve apostles. The presence of God and the Lamb dwell permanently in it so that it does not need a temple. The river of life (the Holy Spirit) vivifies it, and the blessed who live in it will see God because they belong to the Lord (see 21:1—22:5).

The visions conclude with John's testimony to the truthfulness of his prophecy. He has written it in the name of God, and it should be made known to all men. The certainty of its fulfillment is sealed with a solemn warning and a blessing (see 22:6–15).

Similar solemnity attends a concluding affirmation of the book's authenticity in words attributed to Jesus. Following these, the Church joins in prayer that the Lord come (see 22:16–17). Before the farewell, the author refers to the immutability of what has been written. It is a revelation of God, to or from which no one may add or subtract anything (see 22:18–19). The book ends with a hopeful prayer: "Come, Lord Jesus!" and the final farewell (see 22:20–21).

2. Structure

This summary may suggest that the Book of Revelation is a more or less structured work, with a prologue, an introduction, a worked-out development, and a conclusion. While these elements are certainly present, there is no self-evident logic to the structure, and the reader is likely to have difficulty keeping track of events. To cite obvious examples: the visions that follow the letters have no clear fixed plan, and while certain subjects are repeated (the punishments preceding the end, the triumph of the elect, the fall of Babylon, etc.), others appear to break the narrative thread or seem better suited to the book's ending or some other point.

Various hypotheses have been proposed to account for this lack of continuity. Some interpreters think Revelation was assembled from various sources, others that it was written by a number of authors, or was revised from two apocalyptical writings composed at different times, or was the product of several rewritings, etc. But although there may be some truth to such speculations, it is undeniable that the book's vocabulary and style are clearly unified, and the work as a whole can be understood as a well-defined unit. In any case, to understand it better, it will help to try to establish a structure for the text as it stands, no matter how it was composed.

The possibilities are numerous, and none is totally convincing. Some interpreters seek to structure the work by using the number seven as a key (Raymond Loenertz, Ernst Lohmeyer, Giancarlo Biguzzi). This number frequently appears in relation to actions repeated seven times—the so-called septenaries (the seven letters, the seven seals, the seven trumpets, the seven cups)—or in naming realities or objects linked to the actions or elements of the septenaries (seven churches, seven spirits, seven stars, seven lamp stands, seven horns, seven eyes, seven angels, seven thunders, seven heads, seven crowns, seven plagues, seven hills, seven kings). A number of proposals along these lines then divide the work into seven parts.

Certainly seven is very important, and each of the septenaries forms a unit, but, as is usually the case with reductionism, proposals according to which the key to the structure is the number seven seem to force things a bit. For example, it is not easy to find a clear principle of unity after the seventh trumpet (see 11:15). From this point on, symbolism predominates. Nor is it clear that, apart from the four explicit septenaries, one can speak of a septenary of visions or voices from heaven or anything else, as has sometimes been done.

Many agree in dividing the work into two large sections: the letters (1:9–3:22) and the rest (4:1–22:5), but there is no agreement about how this second part is organized. One rather widespread proposal (Ugo Vanni) divides it into five parts: an introductory part containing the vision of the throne of God and of the Lamb (4:1—5:14), followed by a part on the seals (6:1—7:17), another on the trumpets (8:1–11:14), another on the signs (11:15—16:17), and a concluding part (16:17—22:5). Other authors believe they recognize an interweaving or concentric structure (Elisabeth Schüssler Fiorenza) in which the entire work revolves around the center of this second section (10:1–15:4), where the book's climax is located. What follows this symmetrically reflects what precedes it (A B C D C' B' A'). Still others, such as André Feuillet, see a progressive development, with everything tending toward the final consummation of the Church.

All these proposals are valuable in understanding what the author is saying. As has been said, many agree that the book has two large sections of unequal length, the first (chapters 1–3) located on earth, the second (chapters 4–22) in heaven. But although they deal with two different subject matters, the two sections do not stand in isolation from each other. What happens on earth and affects Christians living in the time when John writes has meaning in light of what "happens" in heaven. The book presents a dramatic conflict between Christ and the powers of evil that grows until its final outcome in the victory of Christ. But the process does not move in a straight line. Each vision contains a synthesis of the conflict, with its development and its outcome, that is assumed in some way in the next vision. The tension thus increases, and for that the author also employs literary devices that maintain suspense by prolonging or delaying what he has announced will happen.

In view of this, as well as the content described above, the book could be structured as follows.

Prologue (1:1–3). The book is presented as a revelation to the author of what is going to happen in the future; this is known to God the Father, and also to Jesus, who, as Son, shares in that knowledge.

Introduction (1:4–20). John describes how he received the revelation and the command to communicate it.

First part: Letters to the Churches (2:1–3, 22). Exhortation to remain firm in the faith and not to identify with the pagan world in the historical circumstances in which those whom the book addresses found themselves.

Second Part: Eschatological visions (4:11—22:15). Prophetic manifestation of God's plan for humanity and the Church, as shown to the author in visions.

Introductory vision (4:1–5, 14). The author is brought to heaven and contemplates God in his glory, who from there directs the destinies of the world and the Church. These constitute a mystery that only the Lamb, the risen Christ, can reveal, since he alone can open the seven seals—that is, he is the only one who can give meaning to history.

First section (6:1–11, 14). This includes the visions up until the sounding of the seventh trumpet. As the seals are opened, they reveal the events preceding the final culmination. The opening of the first six seals concerns the arrival of the day of God's definitive coming, which will be preceded by divine punishments (see 6:1–17). When the seventh is opened, trumpets sound, again announcing that coming and the carrying out of God's judgments on the world (see 8:1–9, 21). The misfortunes that will befall humanity are a call to conversion before the Second Coming of Christ.

The exposition is like an upward spiral. Ideas and sayings recur to emphasize movement toward the end. Interruptions function as pauses (the vision of the saved and of the two witnesses), showing divine protection of Christians, consoling those who remain faithful to God (see 7:1–17, 10:1–11, and 11:1–14) and ensuring their victory.

Second section (11:15—22:15). The victory of Christ and the glorification of the Church. The final trumpet announces the arrival of the kingdom of Christ, the culmination of human history. As it approaches, it will be preceded by more intense clashes between the devil and the doers of evil on the one hand and the Church and Christians on the other. This is a contest between Satan and Christ.

As those to whom the book is addressed find themselves persecuted by the Roman Empire, which divinizes the emperor, so, throughout history up to the Second Coming of Christ, the Church will be stalked and persecuted by states and individuals who wish to take the place of God and arrogate his power; this is symbolized by the beasts (11:15—13:18). But the Christians can be sure of victory. As in the previous section, the author intersperses visions anticipating the end with passages offering consolation and reaffirming that the triumph belongs to Christ who will judge all humankind (14:1—15:4).

With the pouring out of the seven bowls with the seven plagues, the last chance for conversion is proclaimed. The final victory over the enemies of the Church, symbolized by the harlot and the beasts, belongs to Christ. He is superior to their power, and his triumph—already begun with his death and resurrection—will culminate at the end of time. Those faithful to God will participate in his victory (15:5—19:21).

The end, in which everything said up to now is embraced, brings the climax of the book and transmits its definitive message. Although after the death and resurrection of Jesus, the snares of the enemy become very intense, and with Christ's second coming at the end of time, the devil will disappear definitively, the final judgment will take place, and then will come the final establishment of the kingdom of God. There will be a new creation, in which renewed humanity will form part of the heavenly Church living with God for all eternity (see 20:1–22, 15).

Conclusion (22:16–21). Paralleling the introduction, the book's prophetic character is confirmed and ratified by the prayer of the Church, by John, and by Christ.

3. God the Father, Jesus Christ and the Church

As we have seen, the fundamental objective of the Book of Revelation is to reveal the meaning of history in the light of the death and resurrection of Christ. The key to that interpretation is the vision of the throne of God in his glory and of the Lamb who stands before the throne on which God sits.

God the Father

As also in the apocalyptic works of that day, the point of departure for understanding what is happening in history is God's goodness and omnipotence. He, the Lord of history, will not permit evil to rule over his elect. God is "the Alpha and the Omega, the beginning and the end," from whom all proceed and toward whom all creation is directed, "that which is, that which was, and that which is to come," the God of the present, the past, and the future, the *Pantocrator*, "the All-Powerful," who is acting at all times to effect salvation (1:8). God is also the Father of Jesus Christ (see 1:6), and will be Father of those faithful to him: "I shall be his God, and he shall be my son" (21:7), for he is a merciful God who listens to the cry of the martyrs (6:8–11). God is also "he who is seated on the throne" (4:2), the Lord of history. Nothing escapes his providence. He is the universal judge, to whose judgment everything is subject (see 20:11–15). In the end his creative power and his infinite love will lead God to restore everything and create a new world, where there will no longer be sorrow or tears, because all of the old has passed away (see 21:1–5).

God himself guarantees these things in his first intervention in the Book of Revelation: "'Behold, I make all things new.' Also, he said, 'Write this, for these words are trustworthy and true.' And he said to me, 'It is done! I am the Alpha and the Omega, the beginning and the end. To the thirsty I will give from the fountain of the water of life without payment. He who conquers shall have this heritage, and I will be his God and he shall be my son. But as for the cowardly, the faithless, the polluted, as for murderers, fornicators, sorcerers, idolaters, and all liars, their lot shall be in the lake that burns with fire and sulfur, which is the second death'" (21:5, 8). With these words God confirms his absolute lordship over creation and over the history of which the book speaks. Though the book's author and readers find themselves still in a world of sorrow and suffering, God meanwhile is here and now making a new world. Present human suffering and the future world emerging through God's mercy are mysteriously linked.

The Lamb

Jesus is the Lamb sacrificed but standing (see 5:6) that is, Christ dead and risen. There has been much discussion about the Greek word *arnion,* which the Book of Revelation uses for the Lamb, together with *amnos,* which appears in the fourth Gospel. Setting aside the problem this raises for the common origin of both, *arnion* suggests not only the sacrificial character of the immolated lamb but also his power; since *arnion* also means ram, it more readily allow for the expression of the Lamb's power symbolized in his horns. That he is standing (has risen) indicates his exaltation. In the Apocalypse, as in the Gospel of John, Christ, in whom are fulfilled Isaiah's prophecies concerning the Servant of the Lord, is the paschal lamb that sheds his blood for humanity and by so doing is raised up to the right hand of God. Christ, he "who was pierced" (1:7) and by his victory on the Cross and Resurrection is "the first-born of the dead" (1:5), participates in God's saving power. He is the Lamb, dead, defenseless, yet nevertheless erect, who holds in his hands the history of the world. The hope of those who suffer is based upon him. Although appearing to be a weak Lamb, he is the victor.

To Jesus, "the Christ" (1:1), belongs the glory of God through his death and resurrection. There at the throne together with God, he receives the same worship offered by all creation: "To him who sits upon the throne and to the Lamb be blessing and honor and glory and might for ever and ever!" (5:13). For this reason, he is shown with attributes expressing this unique relationship with God. He is "Son of God" (2:18), the "Amen" (3:14), vested with divine prerogatives: His seven horns and seven eyes signify the omnipotence and omniscience of God (see 5:6). The Lamb already reigns in this world for he is lord of history, the one who can open the seals and execute the plans of God. Though not directly identified as "the Son of Man," he appears in the initial vision with the features that the prophet Daniel used to describe this heavenly figure (see 1:12–20) who possesses the power of judging all of humankind (see 14:14).

In addition, he is "the Word of God," the "Faithful and True," the horseman with a coat dyed with blood, who rides on a white horse, a sign of his victory, and as "King of kings and Lord of lords" triumphs over all his enemies with his Word (19:11–16). And he is "the Shepherd" (7:17), whose mission is to lead the Church to its final union with God. For this reason he also bears the title "Spouse" (21:2).

Christ dead and exalted speaks to the Church by means of his Spirit. From the beginning it is said that Jesus has "seven spirits" (3:1), the same seven spirits as before the throne of God (see 1:4), and it is the Spirit who speaks to each of the seven churches (see 2:7, 12, 17, etc.). This expresses the power of God, his omniscience and his intervention in the events of history. God acts through his Spirit, who has been communicated to Christ, and who Christ communicates to men. The Spirit is "the font of living water" (21:6; see 22:17) who has been given to the Church. Through him, the Church has divine life. John, in his task of communicating the revelation of Jesus Christ, shares in that Spirit, for "the testimony of Jesus is the spirit of prophecy" (19:10).

The Church

The message of hope of the Book of Revelation responds to a historical situation in which the Church on earth is suffering at the hands of the world and the enemies of God. The seven churches of Asia Minor, to which John wrote on God's behalf at the end of the first century AD, were experiencing a crisis. The Christians were faced with the choice of adoring the political power of the state, to which divinity was attributed, or God. Marginalization and even martyrdom threatened. It is reasonable to suppose that, in these deeply troubling circumstances, Christians would wonder about the meaning of their suffering. In this grave situation, John, speaking for God, exhorts his readers to remain firm in the faith and not give in to the strong pressure being brought to bear upon them by the pagan world.

Among other reasons, the motive for fidelity is that those to whom John wrote were the people of God, the Church, bought with the blood of the Lamb. Thus the saints sing: "Worthy art thou to take the scroll and to open its seals, for thou wast slain and by thy blood didst ransom men for God from every tribe and tongue and people and nation" (5:9; 7:9). Thanks to Christ's sacrifice, Christians have become members of a priestly people (see 1:6; 5:10), a people chosen by God, on pilgrimage on earth without being accomplices of the sins of the pagan world (see 18:4) and striving to be faithful to the Lamb in the midst of persecution (see 2:2, 19; 3:4).

But this people are not alone nor present only on earth. The people of God also exists triumphantly in heaven, where a multitude of those who "have washed their robes and made them white in the blood of the Lamb" (7:14) praise God before his throne, singing a new song (see 14:1-5). The Church is therefore the community of the elect, considered in their full and indissoluble union with Christ on earth and in heaven. The source and explanation of that union is the beloved Spouse of God, bedecked like a bride for the wedding of the Lamb. It is also the Holy City, the new Jerusalem, the "beloved City" (20:9), which is next to God and characterized by its perfection, as can be seen from its dimensions and the splendid materials of which it is built. And it is the temple of God, built upon the victors (3:12), where God is worshipped by the countless multitude of the elect (7:1-17).

The Church is also the "woman" of chapter 12. At the point of giving birth, she faces the serpent, Satan, who wishes to eliminate her descendants. This woman first of all represents the people of Israel from whom the Messiah comes. But the snatching up of her Son and his elevation to the throne of God, while the Woman is persecuted by the dragon, indicates that this Son is Jesus Christ and this Mother is the new people of God, the Church. She is described with the features of her final glorification: "clothed by the sun," because she participates in the divine light and is filled with God; "the moon at her feet," because she is queen of history and all that takes place (the calendar of the Jews was lunar); "on her head a crown of twelve stars," the twelve tribes of Israel, because with the coming Messiah this people has been reconstituted in the twelve apostles. In addition, recognizing that the struggle between the Woman and the serpent is an allusion to the promise of salvation after the fall of our first parents (see Gn 3:14-15), it is logical that the Woman should also represent the Mother of the Messiah, Mary, who like a New Eve inaugurated the line of those who were to crush the head of the infernal serpent. That is how the passage has been understood in the tradition of the Church.

4. The Last Times and the Struggle against Evil

The end times have begun with the death and resurrection of Christ. He has conquered death and already gained the victory. The churches to which John writes are awaiting his definitive manifestation, when he will come as judge and establish his lasting kingdom.

Christians who find themselves in a critical situation are anxious that the work of salvation be accomplished soon. Thus the revelation that John writes on behalf of Christ turns on "what is going to happen soon" (1:1), namely, Jesus' glorious return. John does not say that what he is announcing will happen immediately—he does not specify a date. He simply affirms that it will occur; indeed, in a certain sense is already happening. In the face of this yearning of the Church, Christ himself says, "Yes, I am coming promptly." The idea is repeated seven times in the book (see 2:16; 3:11; 16:15; 22:7, 12, and 20), indicating the firmness and sureness of the promise. Meanwhile, Christians are to remain faithful in anticipation of that coming, not becoming careless, but displaying vigilance by means of penance and conversion (2:1—3:22).

Still, the author reminds those to whom he writes that the enemies of the Church will remain active until the Second Coming of Christ. The infernal serpent and his instruments for harming the followers of the Lamb do not tire. Two beasts stand out among those instruments opposed to God and the Church. They are symbolic beings, which "that ancient serpent, who is called the Devil and Satan" (12:9) launches against Christians. The first has seven heads and two horns, the second two horns similar to those of a ram (*arnion,* the same term as Lamb). But it speaks like a dragon and seeks to cause the inhabitants of the earth to adore the first beast.

The description of these beasts has its source in Daniel, where the beasts signify the persecutions of the Jews in the times of Antiochus IV (second century BC). In the Book of Revelation, it refers to the persecutions the Christians are suffering at the hands of the authorities of the Roman Empire and those non-Christians hostile toward them. The beasts do not signify one emperor in particular; rather, they represent powers that historically embody the forces of evil in one way or another. The first symbolizes political power aggrandized to the point of supplanting God. The second represents the forces of evil that defend, justify, and propagate this deification of power, representing it as something good. It is the false prophet, symbolic of the propagandistic pressure of governments that reject God and falsely exalt man—a prophet of falsehood, as it were.

This second beast is said to be recognizable by a number: "Let him who has understanding reckon the number of the beast, for it is a human number, its number is six hundred and sixty-six" (13:18). That is, 666 determines its identity. The author seems to be using a procedure of Hebrew numerology called *gematria* that consists in substituting the numerical value of a name's letters for the name itself. In Hebrew as in Greek, the letters of the alphabet were given a numerical value: A = 1, B = 2, C = 3, etc.). Both in antiquity and in more recent times, therefore, names have been proposed (from "Euanthas" or "Teitan," according to St. Irenaeus, to others without foundation, such as the Pope, Luther, and Napoleon in more recent times). Up to now, none of these identifications has been convincing. Supposing 666 to be the encrypted name of a person known to the readers of the letter, most authors are inclined to identify him as an emperor. "Nero Caesar" (written in Hebrew characters), is possible as a prototype of the persecutors of Christians, although it presents difficulties. The reading "616" in some ancient manuscripts could point to "Caesar god" or to "Gaius Caesar" (Caligula), an emperor who persecuted the Jews and could stand as representative of the enemies of God's people. Some interpreters think the author of Revelation meant this number but "rounded off" as 666.[1] In any case, none of the suggestions is certain.

What is certain is that Satan will be definitively defeated. But before then, according to the visions of the final combats, he will be imprisoned for a thousand years. Then he will be very active for "a short time" (20:3), as opposed to the "thousand years" of the reign of the saints with Christ (20:4–7). The text is as follows:

> Then I saw an angel coming down from heaven, holding in his hand the key of the bottomless pit and a great chain. And he seized the dragon, that ancient serpent, who is the Devil and Satan, and bound him for a thousand years, and threw him into the pit, and shut it and sealed it over him, that he should deceive the nations no more, till the thousand years were ended. After that he must be loosed for a little while.
>
> Then I saw thrones, and seated on them were those to whom judgment was committed. Also I saw the souls of those who had been beheaded for their testimony to Jesus and for the word of God, and who had not worshipped the beast or its image and had not received its mark on their foreheads or their hands. They came to life, and reigned with Christ a thousand years. The rest of the dead did not come to life until the thousand years were ended.

---

1. This "rounding off" might reflect a desire to mark its opposition to the name of Jesus, whose letters add up to 888. According to this, both 666 and 888 can be seen in relation to 777, which means fullness par excellence. Thus, 666 is the imperfect number (7-1 three times), and 888 the number that transcends fullness (7+1 three times). Strangely, the triangular number of 8 (that is to say the sum of 1+2+3 . . . up to 8) is 36, and the triangular number of 36 is 666. As can be seen, this is all very speculative.

This is the first resurrection. Blessed and holy is he who shares in the first resurrection! Over such the second death has no power, but they shall be priests of God and of Christ, and they shall reign with him a thousand years. And when the thousand years are ended, Satan will be loosed from his prison (20:1-7).

The meaning of the passage is obscure and need not be understood as describing a series of events. The combination of numbers may be no more than a way of symbolically expressing the superiority of Christ to Satan—it is as "a thousand years" are to a "short period of time"—and the idea that the devil's power will end for good, though at times his presence may be strongly felt.

In any case, the reference to the millennium has always been a problem for interpreters. Some, such as the ancient "millenarists" or "chiliasts" (from *khilioi,* "a thousand" in Greek), have taken it literally and believed that after the resurrection of the dead, Christ will reign on earth for a thousand years. More recent groups (some Protestants, Jehovah's Witnesses, Mormons, etc.) share this view with variations.

But like most of the numbers in the book, "a thousand" should be interpreted in a symbolic way. John could be referring to the time of the Church, not a future time but the time in which the Church now lives until the Second Coming of Christ. In this time, the faithful can already enjoy the life of God in Christ (in the sense of the fourth Gospel) while awaiting the Parousia. John thus combines two Jewish concepts of the period: that which took the end times as a messianic reign here on earth, and that which considered it to be something occurring in the future, with the appearance of new heavens and a new earth. For John, with the incarnation, Christ inaugurated the kingdom of God and showed his power against the demon; his kingdom will be fully established and the devil definitively defeated with his second coming.

St. Augustine interpreted this passage along these lines. For him, the "thousand years" extend from the Resurrection to the Parousia. During this time, the demon's activity is limited (he is "chained"), for Christ has already begun to reign. As a consequence, the "first resurrection" (20:5) is understood as the resurrection of the dead worked by baptism: the Christian has passed from death to life in Christ (see Jn 11:25–26). The "second death"—eternal condemnation, that is—does not have power over the baptized (20:6). The second resurrection, not mentioned as such in the Book of Revelation, is that which will occur at the end of time.

In any case, Christians who experience the presence of evil in their lives can be sure that, with Christ, there is nothing to fear. The powers of evil are not stronger than he is. The Book of Revelation is thus a great book of consolation and a song of hope. It therefore ends on a note of hope with a prayer invoking our Lord's definitive, victorious coming: "Come, Lord Jesus!" (22:20). The reader can say with the seer of Patmos, "Come, Lord Jesus!" and can exclaim in the words of Benedict XVI, "You have already come, Lord! We are sure of your presence among us. It is our joyous experience. But come definitively. . . . Come, Jesus! Come and transform the world! Come today already and may peace triumph! Amen!" (General Audience, August 23, 2006).

5. The Johannine Character of the Book

As we saw in chapter 9 of this book the formal differences between the fourth Gospel and the Apocalypse are notably substantial, so that they seem not to have been written by the same hand. But their basic similarities make it likely that Revelation originated in the same community in which the Gospel of John was written and so has the apostolic authority of the beloved disciple. This is how it has been understood in the tradition of the Church.

The fourth Gospel has sometimes been likened to a symphony that opens with a prelude (the Prologue) and continues, harmoniously connecting its different movements. Something similar can be said about Revelation. As Louis Bouyer remarks in his book *The Bible and the Gospel* which I basically follow in the paragraphs below, the last book of the Bible is a symphonic poem, with various repeated and interweaving themes that alternate with choral and orchestral pieces. Both begin in a similar way: chapter 1 of the fourth Gospel shows Christ as he appears in the world, the living Word directed to Israel, the Shekinah, the luminous and vivifying presence of God; chapter 1 of Revelation shows Christ as the Son of Man revealed to the seer-prophet in his resurrection. Following this, the two books develop a common theme: the war of the children of darkness against the children of light, who by accepting Christ have received divine filiation and already in this world enjoy eternal life. The Book of Revelation shows the opposition between the world of darkness, that of the beast (the actual world, the Roman Empire), and the world of the light, the future world (heaven, where God is glorified ceaselessly by the angels). The basic theme is the same, while the differences reflect the different circumstances in which the readers find themselves. The Gospel is a mystagogical catechesis directed to Christians who have already received new life in Christ; Revelation is a consoling message to Christians suffering tribulation by persecution.

Both books show the consequences of the incarnation, death, resurrection, and glorification of Christ. As in the fourth Gospel where the Word, sent by the Father, gives life to the world and returns to the place from which he came, so Revelation speaks of the descent of the heavenly world upon earth and the ascension of humanity to glory. In both books the heavenly world, "the world to come," has already begun to invade the earthly world, while the earthly world has begun to have access to the heavenly. The difference is that Revelation is more explicit concerning the substantial reality of the heavenly world. This is a liturgical world, where God, the One who is on the throne, he who was, who is, and "who will come," is saluted and adored as uniquely Holy by the cosmos and all its elements (the four living beings, the twenty-four ancients, the myriads of spirits, etc.). Christ, the Lamb sacrificed and risen—that is, Christ crucified and glorious—causes this earthly world to enter into glory, since those who are with him "follow the Lamb wherever he goes" (14:4; see chaper 7). When he returns glorious at the end, the heavenly Jerusalem will descend upon earth with him who is seated on the throne and with the Lamb (see 21:23).

The Book of Revelation teaches that the world to come is already present in the world now, much as the fourth Gospel showed that the future life is present in this world through union with Christ. It follows that the powers ruling this world, opposed to their creator and in rebellion against him, are in his hands. As Jesus said to Pilate: "You would have no power over me unless it had been given you from above" (Jn 19:11). There is no place in this for those endless struggles between darkness and light that one finds in other religious systems. The victory of the light is assured.

Still, this victory is not without suffering. John proclaims the mystery of the heavenly Jerusalem's building here on earth through the apparent ruin of the people of God and its prophets: the two olive trees planted before the sanctuary must be left for dead before they rise and return to flourish as does the tree of life planted on the shore of the waters (see 11:4–13 and 22:2). Fruitfulness comes from the Word received and accepted with all that entails. The martyrs are testimony that for the grain of wheat to give fruit it must die (see Jn 12:24). The fourth Gospel and Revelation both teach that glory must come through the Cross—the fruit of crucifixion, as it were. The only path leading from this world to the next is the cross, and no one is dispensed.

As it was with Christ, and is now through him and for him, death is life giving, the way to live for God.

Seen like this, Revelation does not tell of a tragedy, despite the drama it describes. It communicates a message of serenity and hope. The Lamb and the Lamb's Spouse have conquered the world. This is confirmed in the promise repeated seven times in the letters at the beginning of the book: "To him who conquers I will give . . ." (2:11, 17). Light and life, key concepts of Johannine thought, run throughout Revelation. Light shines in the midst of darkness, life springs from death. In the fourth Gospel, Christ reveals himself as the Light. In Revelation, the light is seen in the resplendent whiteness of the angels, of the Spouse of the Lamb, of the river running through the holy city, of Jesus himself ("the bright morning star," 22:16). In Christ this light proper to God is communicated to his spouse, the Church. In fact, the city has no other light than the Lamb (see 21:23; 22:5). This light is the divine glory of him who sits on the throne. The elect are co-heirs of Christ himself, through the spouse of the Lamb, the Church, which participates in all his privileges.

The Church, then, is humanity restored in conformity with God's original plan for creation. Moreover, heaven has descended to earth. The Shekinah has been entrusted to us forever, without need for a sanctuary: The whole city merges with the temple because the people are one with their God. Thus, as the fourth Gospel ends with the risen Christ's appearance to Peter and the apostles, Revelation closes with the appearance of the Church—humanity redeemed by his blood and recreated in his image.

Here is that life that Jesus brought of which the fourth Gospel constantly speaks. We have returned to the beginning, to the banks of the river flowing from the throne, in order to eat the fruit of the tree of life (see 22:1–2; 2:7). Life is as characteristic of God as light. God lives for all ages. The Son of Man is the Living One (see 1:18; 2:8). The martyrs "came to life, and reigned with Christ" (20:4). The life of which John speaks in his Gospel is divine life, life in its fullness, communicated to human beings through resurrection from the dead. Everything converges upon the Resurrection, as upon a second and final creation: "Behold, I make all things new" (21:5), to live his life in him forever.

Bibliography

1. General

Aranda, Gonzalo, Florentino García, and Miguel Pérez. *Literatura judía intertestamentaria*. Estella: Verbo Divino, 1996.

Aune, David E. *The New Testament in its Literary Environment*. Cambridge: James Clarke, 1988.

Bauckham, Richard J. *Jesus and the Eyewitness: The Gospel as Eyewitness Testimony*. Grand Rapids: Eerdmans, 2006.

Bouyer, Louis. *La bible et l'Évangile: Le sens de l'Écriture: du Dieu qui parle au Dieu fait homme*. Paris: Du Cerf, 1953.

Brown, Raymond E. *An Introduction to the New Testament*. New York: Doubleday, 1997.

———. *The Death of the Messiah: From Gethsemane to the Grave: A Commentary on the Passion Narratives in the Four Gospels*. 2 vols. New York: Doubleday, 1994.

Chapa, Juan, ed. *Historia de los hombres y acciones de Dios: la historia de la salvación en la Biblia*. Madrid: Rialp, 2000.

Faculty of Theology, University of Navarra. *The Navarre Bible*. Dublin: Four Courts Press; New York: Scepter, 2008.

González Echegaray, Joaquín et al. *La Biblia en su entorno*. 3rd ed. Estella: Verbo Divino, 1996.

Ratzinger, Joseph/Benedict XVI. *Jesus of Nazareth: Part One, From the Baptism in the Jordan to the Transfiguration*. London: Bloomsbury, 2007; *Part Two, Holy Week: From the Entrance into Jerusalem to the Resurrection*. London: Catholic Truth Society; San Francisco, Calif.: Ignatius Press, 2011.

Trevijano, Ramón. *La Biblia en el cristianismo antiguo: Prenicenos, Gnósticos, Apócrifos*. Estella: Verbo Divino, 2001.

2. Johannine Corpus

Boismard, Marie-Émile and Cothenet, Édouard. "La tradition johannique," in Augustin George and Pierre Grelot, eds., *Introduction critique au Nouveau Testament*, 4. Paris: Desclée de Brouwer, 1977.

Brown, Raymond E. *The Community of the Beloved Disciple.* Mahwah, N.J.: Paulist, 1979.

Cullmann, Oscar. *The Johannine Circle,* tr. John Bowden. Philadelphia: Westminster, 1976.

Culpepper, R. Alan. *The Johannine School: An Evaluation of the Johannine School Hypothesis Based on an Investigation of the Nature of Ancient Schools.* Missoula, Mont.: Scholars Press, 1975.

———. Alan, ed. *The Johannine Literature: With an Introduction by R. A. Culpepper.* Sheffield New Testament Guides, Sheffield: Sheffield Academic Press, 2000.

Fernández Ramos, Felipe, ed. *Diccionario del Mundo Joánico.* Burgos: Monte Carmelo, 2004.

Ghiberti, Giuseppe et al. *Opera giovannea.* Leumann/Torino: Elledici, 2003.

Hengel, Martin. *The Johannine Question.* Philadelphia: Trinity, 1989.

Hill, Charles E. *The Johannine Corpus in the Early Church.* Oxford: Oxford University Press, 2004.

Porter, Stanley E., and Craig A. Evans, eds. *The Johannine Writings.* Sheffield: Academic, 1995.

Tuñí, Josep-Oriol, and Xavier Alegre. *Escritos joánicos y cartas católicas.* Estella: Verbo Divino, 1995.

3. Gospel and Letters

Bartolomé, Juan José. *Cuarto Evangelio, Cartas de Juan: Introducción y comentario.* Madrid: CCS, 2000.

Brown, Raymond E. *The Gospel & Epistles of John: A Concise Commentary.* Collegeville, Minn.: Liturgical Press, 1988.

Talbert, Charles H. *Reading John: A Literary and Theological Commentary on the Fourth Gospel and the Johannine Epistles.* New York: Crossroad, 1992.

4. Fourth Gospel

4.1. Commentaries

Aquinas, Saint Thomas. *Commentary on the Gospel of St. John.* Albany, N.Y.: Magi Books, 1980.

Augustine, Saint. *Homilies on the Gospel according to St. John and his first Epistle.* 2 vols. Oxford: John Henry Parker, 1848–1849.

Barrett, Charles K. *The Gospel According to St. John: An Introduction with Commentary and Notes on the Greek Text.* 2nd ed. London: SPCK, 1978.

Beasley-Murray, George R. *John.* WBC 36, Waco, TX: Word, 1987.

Blank, Josef, Paul Visokay, and John J. Huckle. *The Gospel According to St. John*. 3 vols. New York: Crossroad, 1981.
Bouyer, Louis. *The Fourth Gospel*, tr. Patrick Byrne. Athlone: St. Paul, 1964.
Braun, François-Marie. *Jean le Théologian*. 3 vols. Paris: Gabalda, 1959-1966.
Brodie, Thomas L. *The Gospel According to John: A Literary and Theological Commentary*. Oxford: Oxford University Press, 1993.
Brown, Raymond E. *The Gospel According to John*. Garden City, N.Y.: Doubleday, 1966, 1970.
Castro Sánchez, Secundino. *Evangelio de Juan*, Comentarios a la Nueva Biblia de Jerusalén. Bilbao: Desclée de Brouwer, 2008.
Chrysostom, Saint John. *Commentary on Saint John: The Apostle and Evangelist: Homilies [1-88]*. 2 vols. Washington, D.C.: Catholic University of America Press, 1957; reprinted 1959, 1969.
Dodd, Charles H. *The Interpretation of the Fourth Gospel*. Cambridge: Cambridge University Press, 1953.
Elowsky, Joel. *John*. Ancient Christian commentary on Scripture. New Testament 4. Downers Grove, Ill: InterVarsity Press, 2007.
Fabris, Rinaldo. *Giovanni*. Rome: Borla, 1992.
Leon Dufour, Xavier. *Lecture de l'évangile selon Jean*. 4 vols. Paris: Seuil, 1988-1996.
Moloney, Francis J. *The Gospel of John*. Collegeville, Minn.: Glazier – Liturgical Press, 1998.
Quast, Kevin. *Reading the Gospel of John: An Introduction*. New York: Paulist, 1991.
Schnackenburg, Rudolf. *The Gospel According to St. John*. 3 vols., tr. Kevin Smyth, Cecily Hastings. New York: Herder & Herder/Crossroad, 1968, 1980, 1982.

4.2. Studies and Essays

Ashton, John. *The Interpretation of John*. Phildelphia: Fortress, 1986.
———. *Understanding the Fourth Gospel*. Oxford: Clarendon, 1991.
Beasley-Murray, George R. *Gospel of Life: Theology in the Fourth Gospel*. Peabody, Mass.: Hendrickson, 1991.
Brown, Raymond E. *An Introduction to the Gospel of John*, edited, updated, introduced, and concluded by Francis J. Moloney. New York: Doubleday, 2003.
Davies, William D. *Invitation to the New Testament: A Guide to its Main Witnesses*. Garden City, N.Y.: Doubleday, 1966, 373-518.

De la Potterie, Ignace. *The Hour of Jesus: The Passion and the Resurrection of Jesus according to John*, tr. Gregory Murray. New York: Alba House, 1989.

———. *La Vérité dans Saint Jean*. 2 vols. Analecta Biblica, 73–74. 2nd ed., rev. and corr. Rome: Editrice Pontifico Istituto Biblico, 1999.

Dodd, Charles H. *Historical Tradition in the Fourth Gospel*. Cambridge: Cambridge University Press, 1963.

Fabbri, Marco V. "Prologo e scopo del Vangelo secondo Giovanni," in *Annales theologici* 21 (2007), 253–278.

Fortna, Robert T. *The Gospel of Signs: A Reconstruction of the Narrative Source Underlying the Fourth Gospel*. New York and London: Cambridge University Press, 1970.

García-Moreno, Antonio. *El cuarto evangelio: Aspectos teológicos*. Pamplona: Eunate, 1996.

———. *Jesús el Nazareno, el Rey de los judíos: Estudios de cristología joánica*. Pamplona: Eunsa, 2007.

Hoskyns, Edwyn Clement. *The Fourth Gospel*, ed. F. N. Davey. 2nd ed. London: Faber, 1947.

Martin, J. Louis. *History and Theology in the Fourth Gospel*. 3rd ed. Louisville, Ky.: Westminster, 2003.

Moloney, Francis J. *The Johannine Son of Man*. 2nd ed. Rome: Ateneo Salesiano, 1979.

Olsson, Birger. *Structure and Meaning of the Fourth Gospel*. Lund: Gleerup, 1974.

Smith, D. Moody, Jr. *The Composition and Order of the Fourth Gospel: Bultmann's Literary Theory*. New Haven: Yale University Press, 1965.

Tuñí, Josep-Oriol. *El evangelio es Jesús*. Estella: Verbo Divino, 2010.

Wiles, Maurice E. *The Spiritual Gospel. The Interpretation of the Fourth Gospel in the Early Church*. Cambridge: Cambridge University Press, 1960.

5. Letters of John

Bray, Gerald L. *James, 1–2 Peter, 1–3 John, Jude*. Ancient Christian commentary on Scripture. New Testament 11. Downers Grove, Ill.: InterVarsity Press, 2000.

Brown, Raymond E. *The Epistles of John*. Garden City, N.Y.: Doubleday, 1982.

Fabris, Rinaldo. *Lettere di Giovanni*. Rome: Città Nuova, 2007.

Klauck, Hans Josef. *Der Zweite und Dritte Johannesbrief*. Zürich and Braunschweig: Benziger Verlag; Neukirchen-Vluyn: Neukirchener Verlag, 1992.

Morgen, Michèle. *Les Épîtres de Jean*. Paris: Cerf, 2005.

Muñoz León, Domingo. *Cartas de Juan. Comentarios a la Nueva Biblia de Jerusalén*. Bilbao: Desclée de Brouwer, 2010.

Painter, John. *1, 2, and 3 John*. Collegeville, Minn.: Liturgical Press, 2002.

Schnackenburg, Rudolf. *The Johannine Epistles: Introduction and Commentary*, tr. Reginald and Ilse Fuller. New York: Crossroad, 1992.

Strecker, Georg. *The Johannine Letters: A Commentary on 1, 2, and 3 John*, tr. Linda M. Maloney, ed. by Harold W. Attridge. Minneapolis: Fortress Press, 1996.

6. Revelation

Allo, E. Bernard. *Saint Jean. L'Apocalypse*. Paris: Gabalda, 1921.

Bauckham, Richard J. *The Theology of the Book of Revelation*. Cambridge: Cambridge University Press, 1993.

Bianchi, Enzo. *L'Apocalisse di Giovanni*. Monastero di Bose: Edizioni Qiqajon, 2000.

Biguzzi, Giancarlo. *L'Apocalisse e i suoi enigmi*. Brescia: Paideia, 2004.

———. *Apocalisse. Nuova versione, introduzione e commento*. Milan: Paoline, 2005.

Cerfaux, Lucien. *L'Apocalypse de Saint Jean lue aux chrétiens*. Paris: Cerf, 1964.

Contreras Molina, Francisco. "Cristología del Apocalipsis," in Felipe Fernández Ramos, ed., *Diccionario del Mundo Joánico*. Burgos: Monte Carmelo, 2004, 155–170.

Feuillet, André. *L'Apocalypse: État de la question*. Paris: Desclée de Brouwer, 1963.

Hahn, Scott. *The Lamb's Supper: The Mass as Heaven on Earth*. New York: Doubleday, 1999.

Lambrecht, Jean, ed. *L'Apocalypse johannique et l'Apocalyptique dans le Nouveau Testament*. Leuven: Peeters, 1980.

Muñoz León, Domingo. *Apocalipsis. Comentarios a la Nueva Biblia de Jerusalén*. Bilbao: Desclée de Brouwer, 2007.

Prigent, Pierre. *Commentary on the Apocalypse of St. John*, tr. Wendy Pradels. Tübingen: Mohr, 2004.

Vanni, Ugo. *Apocalipsis*. Estella: Verbo Divino, 1982.

———. *La struttura letteraria dell'Apocalisse*. 2nd ed. Brescia: Morcelliana, 1980.

Weinrich, William C. *Revelation*. Ancient Christian commentary on Scripture. New Testament 12. Downers Grove, Ill.: InterVarsity Press, 2005.

Index

A

Abraham, 6, 113, 132, 137–38, 205
Acts of the Apostles, 15–16, 25–27, 32, 199
Adam, 79, 143
Adversus Haereses (St. Irenaeus), 176
Aelia Capitolina, 10
Against the Heretics (Irenaeus), 2
á Lapide, Cornelius, 44
Alexander the Great, 3, 4
Alexandria, 36
Allo, Ernest-Bernard, 74
Anatolia. *See* Asia Minor
Andrew, St., 1, 31, 94, 108, 142
angels, xi, 38, 76, 203, 206, 208, 218–23, 225, 236, 239, 241
Annas, 69, 135, 136
antichrist, 15, 178, 193, 194, 210
Antiochus Epiphanes, 202, 210
Apocalypse. *See* Revelation
apocalyptic literature, xv, 201–5, 205–7, 225
Apollinaris, 42
Apollonius, 2
Apollos, 15
apostles. *See* apostolic preaching
Apostolic Exhortation on the Word of God in the Life and Mission of the Church (Benedict XVI), xv
apostolic preaching: Acts of the Apostles and, 25–27; Gospel of St. John and, xiii; Holy Spirit and, 28; Letters of St. John and, xiii, 27; New Testament and, 27; Revelation and, xiii; Scripture and, 27; Synoptics and, 25
apostolic witness: apostolic preaching and, 25–28; Beloved disciple and, 28–30, 30–35; First Letter of John as, 176; Gospel of St. John as, 25–45; Jesus' appearances and, 26–27, 69; Jesus as Messiah and, 26; Passion and, 26; tradition and, 65
Aquila, 15
Aquinas, St. Thomas, 43
Arab conquest, 4
Aramaic, 5
Arianism, 177
Aristides of Athens, 40
Aristotle, 18
Arius, 41, 42
Armageddon, 211, 222
Asia Minor, 3, 7, 17, 19, 31, 212, 232
Assembly of Yamnia, 9–10, 11, 12
Assyrians, 85
Athanasius, St., 215
Attis, 16
Augustine, St., 41–42, 43, 56, 123, 238

B

Babylon, 212, 222–23, 224

249

250 *Index*

Bailey, John A., 56
baptism, 14, 15–16, 57, 148, 170;
    faith and, 104; Holy Spirit and,
    104, 159, 160; of Jesus, 26,
    49–50, 51, 105, 160, 170; water
    and, 170
Barabbas, 139
bar Kochba, Simon, 10
Barnabas, 171
Barrett, Charles K., 185
Basil, St., 215
Basilides, 40
Bauer, Walter, 195
Baur, Ferdinand C., 44
Bede, St., 42
Beloved disciple, 60, 142, 180,
    186; anonymity of, 32, 34;
    apostolic witness and, 28–30;
    death of, 33; identification
    of, 30–35, 63; tradition and,
    31–32, 34–35, 63
Benedict XVI, Pope, xii, xv, 21, 35,
    58–59, 64, 76, 129, 213, 238
ben Zakkay, Johanan, 9
Bernard, John Henry, 74
Bethany, 29
betrayal, 117, 118, 134, 137
The Bible and the Gospel (Bouyer),
    239
Biguzzi, Giancarlo, 225
Bithynia, 7
Boismard, Marie-Émile, 56, 72
Book of Revelation. *See* Revelation
Bouyer, Louis, 239
Braun, François-Marie, 180
Bread of Life, 58, 68, 71–73, 93, 95,
    103, 109–11, 128, 156, 169
Bretschneider, Karl G., 47

Brown, Raymond, 33, 34, 45, 55,
    56, 70, 179, 185, 195
Bultmann, Rudolf, 15, 44, 45, 56,
    62, 149, 165, 169, 180

C

Caiaphas, 99, 129–30
Cain, 184
Caligula, 236
Calvary, 95
Canaan, 3
Cerinthus, 189, 214
Cerintus, 14
charity. *See* love
Charlesworth, James H., 33
Christiantiy, 36; early expansion of,
    6–8; hostility toward, 17; Jewish
    Revolt and, 9–10; Judaism and,
    3–6, 12–13; persecution of, 10;
    situation of, 3–10
Christian tradition. *See* tradition
Christological controversy, 41, 42
Christology. *See* Jesus Christ
Church, 166–71; baptism and,
    148; beginnings of, xv; cross
    and, 128; Fathers of, xi, 14, 35,
    38, 39, 41, 42, 43, 44, 56, 131,
    168, 177, 191, 275; Gospels and,
    25; growth of, xv; Johannine
    corpus and, 21; Revelation and,
    232–34, 241; sacraments of, xv
The City of God (St. Augustine), 42
Clement of Alexandria, 2, 56, 176
Collins, John J., 202
commandments, 178, 179, 183, 193
Commentary on St. John (St.
    Thomas), 140

Creation, 199
Cross, 32, 68, 73, 78, 79, 100, 101, 105, 112, 116, 122, 126, 128, 189, 231
crucifixion, 69, 112, 116, 126–29, 136, 140–41, 171, 189, 240
Cullmann, Oscar, 169
Culpepper, R. Alan, 18, 34, 74
Cybele, 16
Cyril of Alexandria, St., 41
Cyril of Jerusalem, St., 215

D

Daniel, 157, 201, 203, 221, 231
darkness, 6, 18, 54, 96, 97, 99, 104, 105, 112, 116, 134, 137, 165, 178, 239–41
Dauer, Anton, 56
Dead Sea, 5
DeBoer, Esther, 33
De Carne Christi (Tertullian), 191
Dedication of the Temple, 30, 54, 68, 71, 113
Demetrius, 194
devil, 26, 53, 152, 166, 181, 186, 221, 228, 234, 236, 237
Diatessaron, 40
Didymus the Blind, 29, 38
Dionysius of Alexandria, 214
Diotrephes, 194–95
discourses and dialogues, xiv, 68; about Jesus, judge, good shepherd, one with the Father, 103, 113–14, 129, 130; on authority of Jesus, 102, 107–9; with blind man, 97, 98; Christ, the Light of the world, 103, 111–13; departure of Jesus and, 116–21; farewell, 87, 103; glorification of Christ through his death, 103, 115–16; Jesus as Bread of Life, 73, 103, 109–11; Jesus as resurrection and the life, 103; with Nicodemus, 91, 102, 103–5, 126, 148; with Samaritan woman, 91, 102, 103–5, 105–7, 140
Dobschütz, Ernst von, 180
Docetism, Docetists, 14, 15, 19, 36, 47, 149, 187, 189
Dodd, Charles H., 45, 56, 73
Domitian, Emperor, 17, 212
Dualism, 6, 14, 165–66

E

Egypt, 6, 37, 39, 85
Eleazar, 10
Elijah, 94
Elisha, 94
Enlightenment, 44
Enoch, 202, 203, 206
Ephesus, 3, 7, 15, 16, 31, 36, 212, 214, 217
Epicurus, 18
Epiphanias, 10, 214
Eriugena, John Scotus, 42
eschatology, 161–62, 184, 202, 207, 209
Esdras, 205
Essenes, 5, 9
eternal life, 68, 71, 73, 75, 77–79, 95, 98, 105–6, 108, 110, 114, 117, 119, 125, 141, 143, 150, 162, 162–66, 170, 178–79, 182–83, 190, 239

Eucharist, 52, 58, 89, 93–95, 109–11, 119, 128, 144, 158, 170
Eusebius of Caesarea, 1, 10, 38, 176, 192, 212
Evanson, Edward, 47
evil, 58, 121, 128, 160, 163, 187, 199–200, 204, 205, 207, 213, 218, 220–21, 223, 226, 234–38
Exodus, 86, 110, 131
Ezekiel, xi, 112, 113–14

F

Fabbri, M., 76
Fabris, Rinaldo, 45
faith: baptism and, 104; call to, 27; Gospel of St. John and, xiv; Holy Spirit and, 146; Jesus and, xiv, 6, 12, 55, 74, 83, 104, 163, 190; signs and, 86, 89, 90, 92–93, 97, 99, 163–65
Fathers of the Church, xi, 14, 35, 38, 39, 41, 42, 44, 56, 131, 168, 177, 191, 215, 275
Feast of Tabernacles, 30, 54, 58, 68, 71, 96, 111, 159
Feuillet, André, 226
Fiorenza, Elisabeth Schüssler, 226
First Epistle of St. Peter, 7
First Letter of John. *See also* Letters of St. John: as apostolic testimony, 176; authenticity of, 176–77; authority of, 176; authorship of, 185–86; content of, 177–79; date of composition of, 189, 196; Gospel of St. John and, 181–85; language of, 179; structure of, 179–80; teaching and, 190–91; tradition and, 185; transmission of, 176–77; vocabulary of, 181, 184
Fortna, Robert, 63
Fourth Gospel. *See* Gospel of St. John

G

Gaius, 194–95, 214
Galba, Emperor, 9
Gamaliel II, Rabbi, 12
Gardner-Smith, P., 56
Genesis, 199
Gentiles, 2, 6, 57, 207
Gerizim, 91
Gethsemane, 31, 33, 101, 115, 136–37
Giovanni (Fabris), 45
Girard, Marc, 72
glorification: account of the Passion and, 135–51; apparitions of Jesus and, 141–44; death of Jesus and, 122–33; "giving his life"/"dying for", 128–31; hour of Jesus and, 123–25; "The Lamb of God" and, 131–33; Last Supper and, 133–34; love and, 124; prophetic signs and, 133; "to be raised/exalted", 125–28
Glossa Ordinaria, 42
Gnosticism, Gnostics, 13–14, 39, 44, 47, 165, 187–88
God: glory of, xi, 101; history and, 161; Jesus, exaltation of and, 27; judgment of, 98; kingdom of, 85, 101, 161, 237; knowledge of, 5, 150, 179, 190; Lamb of, 55, 71, 240, 241; love of, 77, 105,

Index 253

190–91; mystery of, 57, 151; power of, 84; Son of, 54–55, 74, 75–76, 98, 153–54, 187; Spouse of, 224, 231, 233, 241; throne of, xi, 229; union with, 177–78, 187, 190; Word of, xi, xii, 14, 39–40, 46, 55, 67, 70, 181–82, 231
Good Shepherd, 68, 97, 98, 99, 103, 113–14, 129, 130, 231
The Gospel According to St. John, 2 vols. (Brown), 45
The Gospel According to St. John, I-III (Schnackenburg), 45
The Gospel of John (Bultmann), 45
The Gospel of John (Moloney), 45
Gospel of St. John: as apostolic testimony, 25–45; audience of, 18; authenticity of, 3, 35, 47; authority of, xiv, 37, 39; authorship of, xii–xiii, 3, 17, 30, 32, 33–34, 47–49; "book of glory" and, xiv, 76, 79, 87, 116–17, 122, 124, 134; "book of signs" and, xiv, 76–77, 116, 120, 122, 125; Christology of, 20, 47–48, 148–58; composition of, 2, 19, 30, 49, 59–64, 186; content of, xiv, 66–69; date of composition of, 35, 36–37; eclesiastical-sacramental meaning of, 147–48; final chapter of, 79–82; First Letter of John and, 181–85; glorification of Jesus and, 122–44; Letters of St. John and, xiv–xv; Old Testament and, 3, 30; place of composition of, 2, 35–36; Prologue of, xii, 5, 20, 42, 60, 67, 70, 79–82, 96; purpose of, xiv; Revelation and, xiii, 17, 20, 215–16, 238–40; signs and, 26, 83–101; structure of, xiv, 51–52, 70–74, 74–77, 78–79; style of, 38, 60; Synoptics and, xii, xiv, 49–57; theology of, xii, 36, 44, 48, 50, 146–72; transmission of, xiv, 37–39, 46
Gospel of St. Luke, 32, 37, 38, 40, 46, 48, 54, 55, 57
Gospel of St. Mark, 50n1, 55
Gospel of St. Matthew, 11, 46, 54, 55–56, 57
Gospel of the Hebrews, 38
Gospels. *See also* Gospel of St. John; Synoptics: Church and, 25; Gospel of St. John and, xiv; Jesus and, 8, 25; Scripture and, xii
Goulder, Michael, 72
grace, 91, 92–93, 95, 106, 171
Gregory the Great, St., xi, 215
Guilding, Aileen, 72

H

Hadrian, 10
Harnack, Adolf, 195
Hellenism, 3–5, 15, 20, 44, 87, 100, 155
Hengel, Martin, 34
Heracleon, 40
Herbrews, 7
heresies, heretics, 14, 42, 43, 149, 187–88, 196, 200
Herod Agrippa I, King, 9
Historia Ecclesiastica (Eusebius), 176, 192

Historical Tradition in the Fourth Gospel (Dodd), 45
history: God and, 161; Johannine corpus and, xiii; meaning of, 217, 218–19, 229; Revelation and, 217, 218–19, 229
Holy Spirit, xv, 2, 21, 27, 39, 64; apostolic preaching and, 28; baptism and, 104, 159, 160; faith and, 146; Gospel of St. John and, 28; grace of, 91; guidance of, xiii; Jesus, baptism of and, 26; Last Supper and, 159; salvation and, 160; truth and, 159–60; water and, 91

I

Ignatius, St., 37
Ignatius of Antioch, St., 39, 189
Interpretation of the Fourth Gospel (Dodd), 45
Irenaeus, St., xi, xiii, 2, 14, 30, 31, 34, 39, 40, 176, 192n2, 201, 212, 214, 235
Isaac, 132, 137–38
Isaiah, 85, 112, 126, 131, 136, 137, 203
Israel, 4, 5, 6–7, 12, 25, 76, 94, 97, 151, 207

J

Jairus, 31
James, St., 28, 31, 171, 192
Jeremiah, Book of, 85
Jeremiah, Joachim, 85, 132
Jerome, St., xi, 13, 31, 191, 212

Jerusalem, 6, 26, 27, 32, 50; destruction of, 9, 10, 11; fall of, 37; familiarity with, 29; feasts and, 30; Jesus' entrance into, 50n1, 52, 68, 100, 115; temple of, 7, 9, 11, 36, 52, 212
Jesus Christ. *See also* signs: apparitions of, 26–27, 50, 69, 141–44; authority of, xiv, 107–9; baptism of, 26, 49–50, 51, 105, 160, 170; birth of, 43; as Bread of Life, 58, 68, 71–73, 93–95, 95, 103, 109–11, 128, 156, 169; death of, xiii, 15, 26, 27, 32, 50, 51, 53, 74, 90, 98–101, 115; discourses and dialogues and, 28, 69, 87; discourses and dialogues of, xiv, 68, 102–21; divinity of, xiv, 14–15, 41–43, 67, 137, 143, 148, 156, 164; entrance into Jerusalem of, 50n1, 52, 68, 100, 115; eternal life and, 77, 79, 93, 98, 114, 150, 163; exaltation of, xiv, 27, 87, 100, 130; faith and, xiv, 6, 12, 55, 74, 83, 104, 163, 190; Father and, 98, 113–14, 148–58; glorification of, xiv, 53, 77, 81, 91, 115–16, 122–44; as Good Shepherd, 68, 97, 98, 99, 103, 113–14, 129, 130, 231; humanity of, 14–15, 41–43, 148, 187; as Lamb of God, 55, 71, 223–24, 226, 227, 229, 230–32, 240; as Messiah, xiv, 6, 12, 25, 26, 50, 54, 55, 74, 75–76, 80, 97, 106, 114, 116, 139, 161, 190, 199, 221; mystery of, xii, xv, 112; as Paraclete,

120, 185; Passion of, xiv, 26, 27, 31–32, 48, 50, 51, 53, 91, 115; as pre-existent one, 154–55; "priestly prayer" of, 69, 79, 120; public ministry of, 67–68, 90; resurrection of, xiii, 26, 27, 50, 53, 74, 90, 93, 98–101, 115; as revealer, 150–52, 158; salvation and, 8, 13, 104, 107, 124, 199; Second Coming of, 8, 117, 162–63, 178, 201, 227, 228, 237; as sent by God, 152–53; as Son of God, 54–55, 74, 75–76, 98, 153–54, 187, 190; as Son of Man, 157–58; suffering of, 53; superiority of, 78; washing of feet and, 117, 134, 170–71; as Word of God, 14, 39–40, 46, 55, 67, 70, 181–82, 231

Jesus of Nazareth (Benedict XVI), 58–59

Jewish Diaspora, 3, 4, 6

Jewish Revolt, 9–10

Jews, 4, 9, 11–12, 26, 93, 96, 112, 127–28

Joachim of Flora, 42–43

Johannine comma, 177

Johannine community, 17–21, 185; Jesus and, 20; Judeo-Christianity and, 19; Letters of St. John and, xv; tradition and, 18

Johannine corpus: authorship and, 1–2, 17; Beloved disciple and, 34; Church and, 21; date of composition of, 11; gnosticism and, 13–15; historical circumstances as framework for, xiii, 10–17; hostile environment and, 16–17; Jesus and, xiii; Johannine community and, 17–21; literary forms of, 17; Old Testament and, 3, 12–13; purpose of, 16; tradition and, 10, 20–21

Johannine question, 47–49

John Chrysostom, St., 41, 43, 215

John Mark, 33

John the Baptist, St., 16, 26, 29n1, 32, 36, 47, 50, 50n1, 67, 73, 75, 105, 108, 131, 147, 154, 165, 170

John the Evangelist, St., 195; authorship and, 1–2; as Beloved disciple, 28–30, 30–35, 60; Christology of, 148–58; death of, 60; dignity of, 195; eagle as symbol of, xi–xii, 46; irony of, 104, 106, 110; selective character of, 57–59; Synoptics and, 47, 48, 55–57; as "the theologian", xii; tradition and, 1–2; writings of, xii

John the Priest, 34, 35

Jordan river, 29, 170

Joseph, 14

Joseph of Arimathea, 69

Judaism, 99, 106, 132, 154, 156, 219; Christiantiy and, 12–13; conflicts with, 11–13; feasts of, 30; final judgment and, 96; Hellenism and, 3–5, 87, 155; historical circumstances as framework for, 3–6; in Israel, 5; Jerusalem, destruction of and, 9; rabbinical, 10, 30; schools of, 5

Judas, 111, 117, 134, 137

Judea, 27, 36
judgment, 97, 98, 112, 113, 116, 162–63, 222
Justin, St., 2, 25, 176, 214
Justine, 40
Justinian, 37

K

Käsemann, Ernst, 195
Klauck, Hans-Josef, 179, 185

L

Lagrange, M. J., 45
Lamb of God, 71, 221, 223–24, 226, 227, 229, 230–32, 233, 240, 241
Lamech, 206
Laodicea, 212, 218
Last Supper, 28, 50, 50n1, 51, 65, 68–69, 79, 94, 117, 124, 133–34, 159, 170
Law, 5, 8, 78, 92, 96, 106
Lazarus, 33, 48, 53, 68, 72, 87, 99, 103, 114
Leben Jesu (Strauss), 44
Letters of St. John. *See also* First Letter of John: apostolic preaching and, xiii, 27; audience of, 18; authenticity of, 3; authorship of, xii–xiii, 17; Christological errors and, 8, 14–15; composition of, 2; date of composition of, 196; as epistolary, 2; formal features of, 2; Gospel of St. John and, xiv–xv; Johannine community and, xv; Judaism, conflicts with and, 13; language and, 3; literary characteristics of, xiii; place of composition of, 2; Revelation and, xiii, 17, 215
Letter to the Hebrews, 57
Letter to the Philippians, 191
Libya, 6
light, 6, 30, 54, 57–58, 73, 78, 96–98, 112, 113, 116–17, 185, 241
Lithostrotos, 29, 140
Loenertz, Raymond, 225
Logos, 5, 18, 39–41, 46, 55, 149, 154, 155, 181–82, 214, 215
Lohmeyer, Ernst, 225
Loisy, Alfred, 33, 45
Lord's Day, 18, 218
love: discourses and dialogues and, 117–20; fraternal, 178–79, 184, 193; of God, 77, 105, 190–91; Jesus and, 34, 79
Luke, St., 32, 37, 38, 40, 48, 54, 55, 57
Luther, Martin, 235

M

Maccabees, 5
Mandeism, 15, 44
Mani, 42
Marcion, 40, 41
Mark, St., 33, 50n1, 55
Martha, 48, 99
martyrdom, 32, 232
martyrdom, martyrs, 240
Mary, the Mother of Jesus, 48, 89, 92, 100, 171–72, 213, 221, 233
Mary Magdalene, 33, 69, 117, 142
Masada, 9

Master of Justice, 5
Matthew, St., 11, 53, 55–56, 57, 192
Matthias, St., 28
Melito of Sardis, 214
Mesopotamia, 6
Messiah, xiv, 6, 12, 19, 25, 26, 50, 54, 55, 74, 75–76, 80, 97, 106, 114, 116, 139, 161, 171, 199, 221
Millenarianism, 214
Miracles. *See* signs
Mollat, Donatien, 71
Moloney, Francis J., 45
Moses, 8, 78, 86, 92, 94, 105, 126, 127, 151, 168, 204, 205
Muratorian canon, 1, 176, 212–13

N

Napoleon, 235
Nathaniel, 29, 32, 76, 78, 108
Nauck, Wolfgang, 180
Nazarenes, 12
Nebuchadnezzar, 85
Neirynck, Frans, 56
Nero, 7, 9, 212
New Covenant, 170, 208
New Jerusalem, 223–24
New Testament, xiii, 6, 132; apostolic preaching and, 27; Christology of, 20; Jesus and, xv; Judaism, conflicts with and, 11; Qumram writings and, 5
Nicholas of Lyra, 43
Nicodemus, 53, 67, 69, 91, 103–5, 112, 141, 143, 148, 164

O

Old Testament, 48, 74, 76, 102, 104, 132, 137, 147, 154, 156; First Letter of John and, 184; Gospel of St. John and, 3, 30; Johannine corpus and, 3, 12–13; Revelation and, 3, 217, 218, 219; signs and, 84–85, 86–87; truth in, 151
O'Neill, John C., 180
On the Trinity (St. Augustine), 42
Origen, 41, 56, 171–72, 176, 214
Otho, Emperor, 9

P

paganism, pagans, 6, 10, 15
Palestine, 2, 3, 4, 5, 9, 10, 29
Papias, 34, 35, 38, 192, 192n2, 214
Parables, 157
Paraclete, 120, 146, 185
Parker, Pierson, 33
Parousia, 184, 238
paschal lamb, 30, 51, 216, 230
Passion, 50, 53, 79, 91, 115, 126; apostolic witness and, 26, 27; arrest, 136–37; burial, 141; crucifixion and death, 140–41; disciples and, 31–32; glorification and, 135–51; Gospel of St. John and, xiv; historical value of, 48; interrogation before Annas, 137–38; last hours of Jesus and, xiv; Peter's denials and, 137–38; Scripture and, 135; Synoptics and, xiv; trial before Pilate, 138–49

Passover, 30, 51, 54, 71, 79, 93, 94, 115, 124
Patmos, 212, 218
Paul, St., 2, 6, 7, 16, 171
Pella, 10
Pentecost, 142–43
Pergamum, 212, 217
Peter, St., 25, 29, 29n1, 31, 32, 81, 142, 169, 171, 192, 241; confession of, 50n1, 59, 95, 111; death of, 37; denials of, 69, 117, 136, 137; First Epistle of, 7; John the Evangelist, St., appearances with of, 32, 33
Phariseeism, Pharisees, 5, 9–10, 11–12, 112
Philadelphia, 212, 218
Philip, Gospel of, 41
Philip, St., 28, 108, 142, 192
Philo of Alexandria, 4–5, 18, 87, 89, 155
Photinus, 42
Phrygia, 16
Plato, 18
Pliny the Younger, 7–8
Polycarp, St., 39, 176, 189, 190–91
Polycrates, 2
Pontius Pilate, 50, 69, 135, 136, 138–49
Pontus, 7
Praxeas, 41
Probabilia de evangelii et epistolarum Joannis Apostoli indole et origine (Bretschneider), 47
prophetic literature, 203
Protestantism, Protestants, 45, 237
Ptolemy, 41

Pythagoras, 18

Q

Qumram, 9
Qumram writings, 5–6, 36–37, 165, 204–5

R

Reitzenstein, Richard A., 44
Resurrection, xiii, 26, 27, 53, 87, 90, 93, 98–101, 142, 147, 231, 238
Revelation, xi, 16; apocalyptic literature and, xv, 201–5, 205–7, 225; apostolic character of, xiii; apostolic preaching and, xiii; audeince of, 212–13; audience of, 1, 18; authenticity of, 3, 224; authorship of, xii–xiii, 214–16, 225; canonicity of, 200–201; Church and, 232–34, 241; composition of, xiii, 2; content of, xv, 217–24; context of, xiii, xv; date of composition of, 212; evil, struggle against and, 234–38; formal features of, 2; God the Father and, 229–30; Gospel of St. John and, xiii, 17, 20, 215–16, 238–40; history and, xiii, 217, 218–19, 229; Jewish roots of, 3; Johannine character of, 238–42; Judaism, conflicts with and, 13; Letters of St. John and, xiii, 17, 215; Old Testament and, 3, 217, 218, 219; place of composition of, 2, 212; prophetic literature and, 203;

purpose of, 213–14, 217; seven seals and, 218–19; structure of, 224–29; style of, 211; tradition and, 238; uniqueness of, 207–10
Rissi, Mathias, 74
Roman Empire, 13, 17, 228, 239
Romans, 9, 11
Rome, 6–7, 10, 212
Rupert of Deutz, 42, 43

S

Sabbath, 7, 30, 50, 54, 68, 71, 93, 97, 107, 134
Sabellianism, 42, 177
Sacred Scripture. *See* Scripture
Sadducees, 9
saints, 209, 210, 219, 223, 232, 236
Salim, 29
salvation, 8, 12, 13, 50, 104, 107, 110, 124, 126, 160, 166, 189, 199
Samaria, Samaritans, 13, 27, 36, 50, 52, 67, 106
Samaritan woman, 53, 91–92, 95, 102, 103–4, 106, 109, 140, 151
Sanders, Joseph N., 33
Sanhedrin, 9, 59, 90, 99, 104, 114, 130, 135
Sardis, 212, 217
Satan, 85, 128, 134, 137, 207, 220, 221, 228, 233, 234, 236–38
schismatics, 14, 15, 190, 194
Schnackenburg, Rudolf, 34, 45, 56, 185
Schniewind, Julius, 56
Scripture: apostolic preaching and, 27; canonicity of, 9; Gospels and, xii; Jesus and, 25; Passion and, 135; value of, 5; as Word of God, xii
Second Book of Kings, 94
Second Coming, 8, 117, 162–63, 178, 201, 227, 228, 237
Second Letter of John. *See also* Letters of St. John: authorship of, 192–93; content of, 193–94; date of composition of, 196; format of, 193
Second Vatican Council, xv
Seven Churches of Asia Minor, 1, 17, 19, 20, 201, 209, 217, 232
signs: anointing at Bethany, 50n1, 52, 68, 100, 115, 133; anointing in Bethany, 50n1, 52, 68; appearance and disappearance of the leprosy, 84; dialogues and discourses and, 102; entrance into Jerusalem, 50n1, 52, 68, 100, 115; faith and, 86, 89, 90, 92–93, 97, 99, 163–65; Gospel of St. John and, 26, 85–88; healing of the man born blind, 53, 68, 72, 87, 96–97, 98, 103, 113; healing of the paralytic, 53, 67, 72, 87, 92–93, 102, 107; healing of the son of a royal official, 53, 67, 72, 87, 92–93; Jesus walks on water, 50n1, 52, 53, 87, 94, 95; miraculous catch of fish, 29, 59, 69, 144; multiplication of the loaves, 50n1, 51, 52, 53, 67–68, 72, 75, 89, 93, 103, 151; of a new order, 88–91; Old Testament and, 84–85, 86–87; purification of the temple, 87, 88, 89, 90,

91, 100, 102, 103, 106, 133; resurrection of Lazarus, 53, 68, 72, 87, 99, 103, 114; turning the staff into a serpent, 84; victory over death, 98–101; wedding feast of Cana, 53, 67, 73, 87, 88–89, 91, 102, 103, 140, 170, 171; of the Word that gives life, 92–93
Simon of Cyrene, 135, 140
Simon Peter. *See* Peter, St.
Smyrna, 212, 217
Sodom and Gomorrah, 206
Solomon, 29
Son of Man, 222
sons of Zebedee, xii, 17, 29, 31, 32, 34
Spouse of God, 224, 233, 241
Strauss, David F., 44
suffering, 53, 126, 136, 214, 220, 230, 232, 239
syncretism, 17
Synoptics, 16, 29, 40, 43, 115, 116; apostolic preaching and, 25; Beloved disciple, identification of and, 31; Christology of, 47; disciples and, 31; Eucharist in, 170; Gospel of St. John and, xii, xiv, 49–57; healing of the son of a royal official, 73; as historical sources, 33; John the Evangelist, St. and, 47, 48, 55–57; language of, 60; literary dependence on, 55–57; narrative content of, 52–53; Passion and, xiv, 126, 135; purification of the temple and, 133; Samaritans and, 13; signs in, 26, 53, 85, 86, 87, 101;
sons of Zebedee, anonymity of and, 32; structure of, 51–52; style of, 60; theology of, 50; vocabulary of, 50; wedding feast of Cana, 73
Syria, 36, 40

T

Tatian, 40
Taylor, Charles, 70
temple of Jerusalem, 7, 9, 11, 36, 52; destruction of, 90, 91, 133, 212; purification of the temple, 88, 89, 90, 91, 100, 102, 103, 106, 133
Teodorus of Mopsuestia, 41
Tertullian, 31, 39, 41, 176, 191, 212, 214
Theodoret, 215
Theodosius, 215
theology: Church and, 167–69; eschatology and, 161–62; faith and signs and, 163–65; of Gospel of St. John, xii, 36, 44, 48, 50, 146–72; Holy Spirit and, 159–61; Jesus and the Father, 148–58; Mary, the Mother of Jesus, 171–72; sacraments and, 169–71; of Synoptics, 50, 165–67
Theophilus of Antioch, 40
Third Letter of John. *See also* Letters of St. John: authorship of, 192–93; content of, 194–95; date of composition of, 196; format of, 193; occasion for, 195

Thomas, St., 28, 29, 32, 33, 69, 76, 80, 83, 92, 98, 140, 142, 143, 149, 192
Thomas Aquinas, St., 43
Thyatira, 212, 217
Titus, 9
Torah, 78, 92, 106, 109, 151
tradition, 8; apostolic witness and, 65; authorship and, 1–2; authorship and, 17, 33; Beloved disciple and, 31–32, 34–35, 63; First Letter of John and, 185; four celestial beings and, xi; Gospel of St. John and, xiii–xiv, 25; Johannine authorship and, xii–xiii; Johannine community and, 18; Johannine corpus and, 10, 20–21; Letters of St. John and, 175; Revelation and, 238
Trajan, 1, 2, 7–8, 10, 36
transfiguration, 33, 52
Transjordan, 10
Treatises on St. John (St. Augustine), 41–42
Trinitarian controversies, 177
Trinitarian controversy, 41, 42
truth, 6, 54, 58, 92–93, 106, 151, 159–60, 179

Tuñí, Josep-Oriol, 179

V

Valentinians, 40
Valentinus, 40, 41
Vanni, Ugo, 226
Verbum Domini (Benedict XVI), xii
Vespasian, 9
Victorinus, 212
Vitellius, Emperor, 9

W

Witherington, Ben, 33
Word of God, xi, xii, 14, 39–40, 46, 55, 67, 70, 181–82, 231

Y

Yabne, 9
Yamnia, 11, 12

Z

Zealots, 9
Zechariah, 112, 126, 203, 206